Revolution and Resistance in Eastern Europe

Challenges to Communist Rule

Edited by
Kevin McDermott and Matthew Stibbe

BERG

**Dedicated to Frances Vera, Alexander Leo
and Nicholas Paul**

First published in 2006 by
Berg
Editorial offices:
1st Floor, Angel Court, 81 St Clements Street, Oxford, OX4 1AW, UK
175 Fifth Avenue, New York, NY 10010, USA

Berg is the imprint of Oxford International Publishers Ltd.

Library of Congress Cataloging in Publication Data
Revolution and resistance in Eastern Europe : challenges to communist rule /
edited by Kevin McDermott and Matthew Stibbe.—1st published in 2006.
    p. cm.
    Includes bibliographical references and index.
    ISBN-13: 978-1-84520-259-0 (pbk.)
    ISBN-10: 1-84520-259-7 (pbk.)
    ISBN-13: 978-1-84520-258-3 (cloth)
    ISBN-10: 1-84520-258-9 (cloth)
    1. Europe, Eastern—History—1945-1989. 2. Communism—Europe,
Eastern. I. McDermott, Kevin, 1957- II. Stibbe, Matthew.

    DJK50.R48 2006
    303.6'4094709045—dc22

                                                                    2006019504

British Library Cataloguing-in-Publication Data
A catalogue record for this book is available from the British Library.

ISBN-13 978 1 84520 258 3 (Cloth)
ISBN-10 1 84520 258 9 (Cloth)

ISBN-13 978 1 84520 259 0 (Paper)
ISBN-10 1 84520 259 7 (Paper)

Typeset by JS Typesetting, Porthcawl, Mid Glamorgan
Printed in the United Kingdom by Biddles Ltd, King's Lynn

www.bergpublishers.com

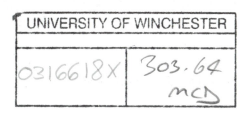

Contents

Acknowledgements

Kevin McDermott would like to thank Susan Reid, whose idea it was to put this volume together and whose expertise in the cultural and material history of post-war Eastern Europe has greatly informed his understanding of events.

Matthew Stibbe would like to express his gratitude to John Davies for sharing his passion for Berlin and its historical treasures, and Sam and Nicholas for putting up with his occasional absences from home.

The editors also gratefully acknowledge the financial support of the Phillips-Price Memorial Trust, which funded the translation of Leonid Gibianskii's essay. Special thanks to John Morison for his excellent translation from the Russian original.

Chapter 4 of this volume, by Johanna Granville, is a shortened and revised version of an article first published in the *Australian Journal of Politics and History*, vol. 48 (2002), pp. 369–95. We are much obliged to the copyright holders, Blackwell Publishing Ltd, for granting us permission to reprint this revised version.

Last, but by no means least, we wish to thank our editor at Berg, Kathleen May, who has supported the project enthusiastically from day one.

Kevin McDermott and Matthew Stibbe
Sheffield, December 2005

List of Abbreviations and Glossary of Terms

ÁVO	State Security Department (Hungary)
CC	Central Committee (of Communist Party)
CIA	Central Intelligence Agency (USA)
Cominform	Communist Information Bureau
CP	Communist Party
CPSU	Communist Party of the Soviet Union
CPY	Communist Party of Yugoslavia
CSCE	Conference on Security and Cooperation in Europe
FDGB	Free German Trade Union Federation (GDR)
FDJ	Free German Youth (GDR)
Fidesz	Federation of Young Democrats (Hungary)
FRG	Federal Republic of Germany
GDR	German Democratic Republic
glasnost	'openness' (in Soviet Union under Gorbachev)
HDZS	Movement for a Democratic Slovakia
HO	State-owned retail organisation (GDR)
K-231	Club of Political Prisoners (Czechoslovakia)
KDNP	Christian Democratic People's Party (Hungary)
KGB	Committee of State Security (USSR)
KKP	Solidarity National Coordinating Committee (Poland)
KOR	Committee of Workers' Defence (Poland)
KOVO	Union of Metalworkers (Czechoslovakia)
KPD	German Communist Party
KPN	Confederation for an Independent Poland
KSS-KOR	Committee of Social Self-Defence of KOR (Poland)
KVP	People's Police in Barracks (GDR)
LPG	State-owned agricultural cooperative (GDR)
MDF	Hungarian Democratic Forum
MKS	Interfactory Strike Committee (Poland)
MNP	Hungarian People's Party
NATO	North Atlantic Treaty Organisation
NKVD	People's Commissariat of Internal Affairs (Stalinist secret police)
nomenklatura	list of key administrative appointments approved by the party
NRT	National Round Table (Hungary)
NVA	National People's Army (GDR)

OF	Civic Forum (Czechoslovakia)
OPC	Office of Political Coordination (of CIA)
ORT	Opposition Round Table (Hungary)
Ostpolitik	policy pursued by successive West German governments from 1966 onwards aimed at 'normalising' relations with Eastern Europe (for instance through closer trade links and recognition of the post-1945 border between Germany and Poland) while stopping short of granting full diplomatic recognition to the GDR as an independent, sovereign state
PDS	Party of Democratic Socialism (Germany)
perestroika	'reconstruction' (of Soviet economy and society under Gorbachev)
Politburo	Political Bureau (of Communist Party)
PZPR	Polish United Workers' Party
RIAS	Radio in the American Sector (of Berlin)
ROPCiO	Movement for the Defence of Human and Civil Rights (Poland)
samizdat	literally means self-publishing; came to refer to the underground publication and circulation of prohibited material
SB	Polish Secret Police
Securitate	Romanian Secret Police
SED	Socialist Unity Party (GDR)
SKS	Students' Solidarity Committee (Poland)
SPD	Social Democratic Party (Germany)
Stasi	Ministry of State Security (GDR)
SZDSZ	Federation of Free Democrats (Hungary)
TKN	Society of Scientific Courses (Poland)
UB	State Security Ministry (Poland)
UN	United Nations
USSR	Union of Soviet Socialist Republics
VPN	Public against Violence (Czechoslovakia)
WRON	Military Council for National Salvation (Poland)

List of Archives and Archival Abbreviations

AAN	Archive of New Documents (Poland)
a. e.	*arkhivna edinitsa* (file)
A FMV ČSFR	Archive of the Federal Ministry of the Interior of Czechoslovakia
AJ	Archive of Yugoslavia
AJBT-KMJ	Josip Broz Tito's Archive: The Marshal of Yugoslavia's Office
APRF	Archive of the President of the Russian Federation
ASSIP-PA	Archive of the Federal Secretariat for Foreign Affairs of Yugoslavia (now Archive of the Foreign Ministry of Serbia and Montenegro), Political Archives
A ÚV KSČ	Archive of the Central Committee of the Communist Party of Czechoslovakia
A ÚV KSS	Archive of the Central Committee of the Communist Party of Slovakia
AVP RF	Foreign Policy Archive of the Russian Federation
d.	*delo* (file)
dob.	*doboz* (box)
dok.	*dokument* (document)
f.	*fond* (collection)
k.	*kötet* (volume)
KVVM	Office for Public Opinion Research (Czechoslovakia)
Landesarchiv Berlin	Berlin provincial archives
l. (ll.)	*list(y)* (folio(s))
MOL	Hungarian National Archive
ő. e.	*őrzési egység* (preservation unit)
old.	*oldal* (page)
op.	*opis'* (inventory)
p.	*papka* (folder)
paczka	box, packet
per.	*perechen'* (list)
PIL	Archive of the Institute of Political History (Hungary)
RGANI	Russian State Archive of Contemporary History
RGASPI	Russian State Archive of Social and Political History
s.	*strona* (page)

SAPMO-BA	Stiftung Archiv der Parteien und Massenorganisationen der DDR im Bundesarchiv (Germany)
SRI	Archive of the Romanian Security Service
SÚA	State Central Archive (Czechoslovakia)
Str. Pov.	*strogo poverljivo* (top secret)
tom	volume
TsDA	Central State Archive (Bulgaria)
ÚVVM	Institute of Public Opinion Research (Czechoslovakia)

Notes on Contributors

Dennis Deletant is Professor of Romanian Studies at the School of Slavonic and East European Studies, University College London. In recognition of his work with the British Government's 'Know-How Fund' in Romania and Moldova he was made an officer of the Order of the British Empire in 1995. He is the author of several studies on Romania, among them *Ceauşescu and the Securitate: Coercion and Dissent in Romania, 1965–89* (1996); *Romania under Communist Rule* (1998); and *Communist Terror in Romania: Gheorghiu-Dej and the Police State, 1948–1965* (1999). His most recent book, *Ion Antonescu. Hitler's Forgotten Ally*, is currently in press.

Leonid Gibianskii is Senior Research Fellow at the Institute of Slavic Studies of the Russian Academy of Sciences in Moscow, specialising in Soviet foreign policy and international relations in Eastern Europe during and after the Second World War, and the history of Yugoslavia. Among his main publications are *The Soviet Union and the New Yugoslavia, 1941–1947* (1987, in Russian); (co-ed.) *The Cominform: Minutes of the Three Conferences 1947/1948/1949* (1994); (co-ed.) *The Establishment of Communist Regimes in Eastern Europe, 1944–1949* (1997).

Johanna Granville was the first American researcher to gain access to Soviet archival documents on the 1956 crises and has worked extensively in Russian and East European archives since June 1992. She is the author of *The First Domino: International Decision Making during the Hungarian Crisis of 1956* (2004), and is currently a postdoctoral Title VIII Scholar in Ekaterinburg, Russia, where she is conducting research for a second book.

Peter Grieder is Lecturer in Twentieth-century History at the University of Hull. His monograph, *The East German Leadership, 1946–1973: Conflict and Crisis*, was published by Manchester University Press in 1999. He is currently writing a second book, entitled *The Writing on the Wall: Totalitarianism in East Germany, 1945–1989*.

Bartosz Kaliski studies at the Institute of Philosophy and Sociology of the Polish Academy of Sciences in Warsaw. He was awarded an MA in Sociology in 2002 and is currently preparing a doctoral thesis on relations between the Catholic Church and the Polish communist state in the period 1945–1980. He is the author of

'Antysocjalistyczne zbiorowisko'? I Krajowy Zjazd Delegatów NSZZ 'Solidarność' (*Anti-socialist Gathering? The First National Congress of Delegates of the NSZZ Solidarity*) (2003).

Tony Kemp-Welch was educated at the LSE, where he took a first degree in International Relations and a doctorate in Government. He has held research posts at the Universities of Oxford, Harvard, Moscow and Cambridge, and is now Senior Lecturer in Politics and International Relations at the University of East Anglia. His *Poland and the Cold War* (two volumes) is forthcoming.

James Krapfl is a Ph.D. candidate in History at the University of California, Berkeley, where he is completing a dissertation on the transformation of popular political culture in Czechoslovakia between 1986 and 1992. He is interested in the comparative history of European revolutions and anthropological approaches to historical interpretation.

Kevin McDermott is Senior Lecturer in Political History at Sheffield Hallam University. He is the author of *Stalin: Revolutionary in an Era of War* (2006); co-author (with Jeremy Agnew) of *The Comintern: A History of International Communism from Lenin to Stalin* (1996); and co-editor (with Barry McLoughlin) of *Stalin's Terror: High Politics and Mass Repression in the Soviet Union* (2003).

Matthew Stibbe is Senior Lecturer in History at Sheffield Hallam University. He is the author of *German Anglophobia and the Great War, 1914–1918* (2001) and *Women in the Third Reich* (2003) as well as several articles in historical journals. He is currently working on a study of civilian internment in Germany during the First World War.

Nigel Swain teaches Twentieth-century Eastern European History at the University of Liverpool. He has published widely in the field, with a particular interest in Hungary, including (with Geoffrey Swain) *Eastern Europe since 1945* (3rd edn, 2003) and *Hungary: the Rise and Fall of Feasible Socialism* (1992).

Kieran Williams is a Research Fellow of University College London's School of Slavonic and East European Studies, and teaches Political Science at Drake University (Des Moines, USA). He is the author of *The Prague Spring and its Aftermath: Czechoslovak Politics, 1968–1970* (1997); co-author (with Dennis Deletant) of *Security Intelligence Services in New Democracies* (2000); and co-author (with Sarah Birch, Frances Millar and Marina Popescu) of *Embodying Democracy: Electoral System Design in Post-Communist Europe* (2002).

Foreword
Pavel Seifter

A distance of sixteen years from the revolutions of 1989 seems to offer sufficient space for serious reflection and recapitulation. Yet although a new generation has grown up in the meantime, it is still memory that dominates the debate over 1989, and also over 1968, 1956 and 1953 – right back to the war. While the cycle of active wartime memory is now closing after sixty years, the battlefield of Cold War memories, the memories of life and resistance under communism, is still alive and noisy.

But memory, by nature contentious and partisan, is a very unreliable and misleading guide to the past. Memory tends to confirm and reinforce itself – and in any case it is impossible to remember how it truly was: not only do people forget, they remember a past that they tend to perpetuate in the present. That is not necessarily a past that happened. Moreover there is no single memory of the past; many of these pasts are competing with, contradicting, fighting and excluding each other, often feverishly following contemporary political and ideological battle lines.

The instrument of true learning about the past can only be history disciplined by rigorous investigation and interrogation. Still relatively soon after 1989 (and the opening of the archives) the real story is emerging only slowly and in pieces. Most historians are busy researching and interpreting fragments in time, nation by nation, and approaching them from the various angles of their profession. Yet the story of what really went on in Eastern Europe in the past sixty years can only be understood in its complexity, as a whole and by keeping in mind that while revolts were attempted on the fringes, their fate was decided by strength or weakness and decline at the core of the system – in Moscow. And, in the end, 1989 will have to be seen not merely from inside communism and explained by its own mechanics. It will be seen as heralding the end of an epoch, first by the implosion of Communist Eastern Europe, followed by change everywhere, in the West, and globally. The world has moved from *samizdat* to virtual communication, and from barbed frontiers to global markets. First attempts to paint a comprehensive new picture of the time that has passed have been made only recently: for such a perspective history needs distance. This volume represents an important contribution to this process.

History can tame memory. It can ask the right questions and answer some. Revolution and resistance under communism will be revisited by every new generation of Poles, Czechs, Slovaks, Hungarians, Romanians, Germans and others. History will assist them as far as it goes. The rest will be told by literature and art: the story of the individual, of utopia and tragedy, of dignity and humiliation, of fear, and of freedom acquired by overcoming fear.

Revolution and Resistance in Eastern Europe:
An Overview
Kevin McDermott and *Matthew Stibbe*

The Cold War spawned a veritable 'Other Europe' – the communist states lying to the east of the Iron Curtain. Ever since the 1950s scholars have been preoccupied with how the diverse peoples of this region reacted to the establishment – many would say imposition – of Soviet-type systems in their lands; how indigenous communist parties interacted with, or challenged, their Soviet overlords; and how local authorities and Moscow dealt with the looming presence of nonconformity, dissent and resistance among relatively broad strata of the population. This volume seeks to explore critically these intriguing questions. It is neither a history of the Cold War in Europe, nor a general survey of post-war developments in the eastern half of the continent.[1] Even less is it a triumphalist reassertion of the innate superiority of capitalist democracy over communist dictatorship. It aims rather to elucidate what can be called the 'flashpoints' in the complex relationship between the USSR and its client states, focusing on such pivotal moments as the Soviet-Yugoslav split of 1948, the East German Uprising of 1953, the Hungarian Revolution of 1956, the Prague Spring of 1968, the rise of Solidarity in Poland and the collapse of communism in the late 1980s. The chapters, written by experts from Britain, the USA, Russia and Eastern Europe, incorporate recently accessible archival material and post-communist historiography, and hence represent the very latest research on their given themes. As a whole, they affirm the diversity of East European responses to perceived Soviet hegemony, both at state and society level. There is no common approach or conclusion among the authors, but all demonstrate the inordinate difficulties experienced by the indigenous communist parties in establishing sustained political legitimacy and social cohesion in their respective domains.

This is not to say that popular 'resistance', 'dissidence' and the threat of revolution everywhere and always outweighed accommodation and conformity – many East European citizens benefited from socialist transformation and broadly supported the regimes, at least at certain times and to varying degrees. Indeed, we do not wish to posit a strict 'us versus them' binary opposition, pitting an isolated, repressive 'state' against a downtrodden, but recalcitrant 'society'. Reality, we believe, was more complicated and subtle. As Lynne Viola has persuasively argued in the context of the USSR in the 1930s: 'Resistance was only one part of a wide continuum of societal responses to Stalinism that also included accommodation, adaptation, acquiescence, apathy, internal emigration, opportunism, and positive support'.[2] What is more, neither was the communist state itself a monolithic entity totally cocooned and divorced from societal strivings and moods. The central authorities could never be sure that their directives and decrees were being fully implemented by regional and local party-state bureaucracies. And, by the 1980s, lower-level communists and functionaries were increasingly influenced by the advent of what many commentators have termed 'civil society' – the emergence of independent and informal groups and trends associated with an embryonic pluralism.[3]

We should begin by briefly defining our terms. Where is 'Eastern Europe'? We have basically adopted a geopolitical definition, equating the region with the countries of the former Soviet bloc, emphatically including East Germany (the GDR), and also Yugoslavia up to the split of 1948, but excluding Albania.[4] What is 'communism'? According to a recent political dictionary, it can be defined as a 'system of government in which a communist party rules, without permitting legal opposition'.[5] In essence, it is a political dictatorship undertaken by the party on behalf of the proletariat. The East European communist systems did allow other parties to exist, but only within a tightly regimented framework in which the Communist Party was guaranteed recognition of its 'leading role' in state and society. The forceful suppression of dissent, both real and imagined, was the fulcrum of communist rule in Eastern Europe between 1948 and 1953, the period of 'High Stalinism'. From the mid-1950s to the early 1960s, Soviet leader Nikita Khrushchev made efforts to curb the worst excesses of the past – the mass purges, arbitrary terror and the all-pervasive 'cult of personality' associated with his predecessor, Josef Stalin. But the brief thaw gave way to the renewed frost of the Brezhnev era, which lasted into the 1980s and came to an end only with the appointment of Mikhail Gorbachev as Secretary General of the Communist Party of the Soviet Union (CPSU) in March 1985.

A whole literature exists on the theory and practice of 'resistance', originating in debates on the nature and extent of popular opposition to the Nazi regime.[6] Of all the competing definitions, we find Viola's the most apt: 'At its core, resistance involves opposition – active, passive, artfully disguised, attributed, and even inferred … [it] may include rebellions, mutinies, and riots; demonstrations and protest meetings; strikes and work stoppages; … arson, assaults, and assassinations … footdragging, negligence, sabotage, theft, and flight … [and] "everyday forms of resistance" [such as] popular discourse(s), ritual, feigned ignorance, dissimulation, and false compliance.'[7] As the following pages show graphically, the history of communism in Eastern Europe is littered with such activities and mentalities. Similarly, 'revolution' is a controversial category. A current definition tells us that it 'seems to mean any major transformation that occurs simultaneously on the social and political level'.[8] However, as Nigel Swain's and James Krapfl's essays clearly demonstrate, fundamental political change does not have to be enforced suddenly through violence. It can be 'negotiated' in a conscious effort to repudiate older traditions of coercion and unfettered voluntarism. Conversely, even when revolutions usher in rapid and uncontrollable changes in social relations, they can still be 'self-limiting' in the political sphere, a phenomenon first highlighted by the sociologist Jadwiga Staniszkis in relation to the events in Poland in 1980–1.[9] We have therefore adopted a flexible approach to the term 'revolution', allowing it to denote sudden/violent or gradual/negotiated transformations that are either predominantly social in nature, or predominantly political, or both.

Communist regimes first emerged in Eastern Europe in the aftermath of fascism's defeat in the Second World War, and were immediately confronted with a series of challenges connected with the Cold War, economic reconstruction, Stalinist purges and the supposed threat from the West. These early experiences, in turn, led to great emphasis on the mobilisation of industrial and cultural resources in order to increase the hold of the state over the lives of its citizens, and do battle with the enemies of socialism, whether internal or external. As in the Soviet Union itself, 'every civilian activity [had] to be examined for the contribution it could make to military preparedness', at least from 1948 onwards.[10] Having said this, it is essential to recognise that communist rule did not rely on political repression alone. Particularly in the post-Stalin era, considerable efforts were made to build a 'socialist consumerism' and leisure industries, which would satisfy the demands of workers for higher living standards and improved quality of goods and services in the shops, albeit combined with continued central control of production and distribution. Admittedly this process went further in some countries than others. In Poland change was evident from the mid-1950s onwards, in the covers of fashion magazines and in the 'modern' appearance of new urban shop fronts,[11] while in Hungary consumerism developed more slowly and thoroughly – 'goulash communism' – helping to uproot 'established patterns of working-class culture' in the decade after the failed 1956 revolution.[12] In more puritanical East Germany, on the other hand, the material and political aspects of de-Stalinisation were given less prominence and were already in abeyance by the late 1950s. Here, the close geographical proximity of the much larger Federal Republic and the GDR's apparent lack of political legitimacy led to a continued insistence that the East Germans were constructing a new socialist state at a higher stage of historical development than their capitalist neighbour to the west. This in turn provided the ideological justification for the construction of the Berlin Wall in August 1961.[13] Czechoslovakia likewise remained hard-line in approach until the mid-1960s, refusing, for instance, to rehabilitate in public the victims of the Stalinist purges and show trials in spite of being encouraged to do so by the examples of Poland and Hungary, and by Khrushchev's own reforms in the Soviet Union.[14]

In respect of resistance, as the essays in this volume suggest, it is also difficult in retrospect to discern any common pattern of development. Rather, challenges to communist rule came from several directions and were met by a diverse range of responses from the rulers themselves. To further this analysis we have identified a four-part typology, as follows:

1. *National communism.* There were two varieties of this: first, regimes which publicly distanced themselves from the Soviet Union in world affairs; and second, those which sought a degree of autonomy in the domestic sphere – or what was sometimes known as a 'national road to communism' – while remaining broadly within the Soviet camp. The foremost representative of the first variant was Tito, as illustrated in Leonid Gibianskii's detailed contribution. But the post-1948 Yugoslav experiment, which involved cautious openings both to the West and to the non-aligned movement, was unusual and found no direct imitators. Other countries that challenged Moscow's claim to speak for the international communist movement, such as Albania and Romania, pursued a policy of partial independence in the diplomatic sphere, 'while remaining grimly Stalinist at home', as David Reynolds puts it.[15] In practice this was little threat either to communist rule or, ultimately, to Soviet hegemony.

The most successful example of the second variant of national communism was Władysław Gomułka, the Polish leader from 1956 to 1970, who, in Raymond Pearson's words, managed to 'negotiat[e] with Khrushchev for major Soviet concessions ... within a more devolved imperial jurisdiction', including a return to private landholding and the granting of considerable freedoms to the Roman Catholic Church in Polish society.[16] Less contained, and therefore less fortunate, were Imre Nagy, the Hungarian Prime Minister in 1956, and Alexander Dubček, the Czechoslovak First Secretary in 1968, both of whom fell victim to Soviet military intervention after allowing domestic reforms to go beyond the limits considered acceptable by the Kremlin (Nagy was executed in June 1958; Dubček was replaced as First Secretary in April 1969 and expelled from the party in 1970).

2. *Intellectual dissent.* The 1950s and 1960s in Eastern Europe produced many admirers of Tito, reformist and dissident Marxists of various kinds, Maoists in Hungarian universities, not to mention a whole range of intellectuals, writers and 'cultural workers', who placed art (form) over life (content) and thereby redefined the boundaries of socialist realism.[17] However, so-called 'revisionism' or 'reform communism' became less of a threat as time went on, especially after the crushing of the Prague Spring in 1968. In Hungary, János Kádár allowed relative freedom to intellectuals, provided they were broadly Marxist in their thinking, while Czechoslovakia and the GDR tended to export their dissidents – in the latter's case in exchange for hard currency. In Romania, open dissent was extremely hard to find, and virtually its only proponent in the 1970s, Paul Goma, was himself a former party member. Otherwise the threat from the Securitate and the regime's own espousal of anti-Russian sentiment from 1968 effectively silenced public intellectual criticism of communist rule, at least until the end of the 1980s.

3. *Armed peasant resistance.* The examples here come mostly from the Balkans which had a long tradition of banditry. For instance, there was a series of rural uprisings in 1949–50 in various parts of Bosnia-Herzegovina, Croatia and Macedonia, some led by outlawed Četnik and Ustaša groups, but others by farmers resisting collectivisation. At Cazin, in north-western Bosnia, over a thousand peasants took part in a rebellion in the spring of 1950, involving widespread looting and attacks on state-owned property. A hard core of a hundred held out for several weeks and were defeated only when the army moved in and executed the ringleaders.[18] In the Romanian case, as Dennis Deletant demonstrates, small groups of anti-communist outlaws took part in acts of sabotage and revenge in the late 1940s and early 1950s, and some evaded capture for remarkably long periods, but their peculiar brand of resistance was never more than a minor or symbolic threat to communist rule and had all but fizzled out by the late 1950s.

4. *Popular protests against communist rule.* These could take various forms, ranging from small-scale strikes and demonstrations to mass uprisings and, in some instances, to what Peter Grieder refers to as 'sudden systemic change' (Hungary in 1956; the whole of the communist bloc in 1989). These collective actions were often sparked by acute, working-class discontent over stagnating living standards, scarce availability of consumer items and especially rapid price rises of staple goods (East Germany in 1953; Poland in 1956, 1970, 1976 and, more famously, 1980; even in the USSR itself in the southern city of Novocherkassk in June 1962). The response of state authorities varied from piecemeal accommodation to outright suppression and persecution of ringleaders. What most concerned the communists was the possibility of a 'united front' of disgruntled workers and sympathetic intellectuals, as occurred in Poland during the Solidarity era.

However, we should be careful here to see differences as well as similarities. For instance, the material factors which caused the strikes in the Czechoslovak town of Plzeň (Pilsen) and in the whole of the GDR in June 1953 were very different to the socio-economic demands of 1989. In the former case, wage cuts or increases in the working day imposed as a result of high production norms were the main factors, along with food shortages and inflated prices for basic goods. In effect, workers were being asked to postpone consumption today in return for a promise of higher living standards in the future, or, as Jonathan Sperber puts it:

> The government of the GDR, with its plans for collectivization, forced industrialization and military mobilization, quite deliberately made consumer goods a low priority – indeed, accepted drastic declines in the popular standard of living. The insurgents' economic demands centred on a reduction of high prices and the need for better and more equitable rationing, rather than for the introduction of a consumer society – which was just barely beginning to come into existence in West Germany.[19]

It might be added that greater democracy in the workplace was also a key demand, both in 1953 in the GDR and in 1956 in Hungary. Adherents of old-style social democracy inside the factories fought for workers' traditional rights and freedoms against the authoritarian tendencies in Stalinism, although admittedly their slogans (free elections, new management structures and the right to strike without fear of state retaliation) had less impact on the younger generation of radicalised workers who had known nothing but the terrible austerity of the war years and the post-1945 period.

In 1989, on the other hand, the main complaint had become the slow deterioration of living standards in comparison with growth rates in the West, combined with the refusal of communist leaders to provide an honest account of the state of indebtedness and stagnation in their respective countries. Consumerism alone was not enough, especially when set against other popular grievances, including environmental damage and lack of basic human rights such as the freedom to travel abroad – issues which, as Sperber notes, were 'inconceivable thirty-six years earlier'.[20]

Political and cultural factors also varied over time and place. Nationalism and religion were important in fostering opposition to communist rule in Hungary and Slovakia and especially in Poland, a point which comes across very vividly in Bartosz Kaliski's piece on the Solidarity movement in this volume. However, they had less of an impact in the Czech lands and the GDR, where industrialisation had taken place prior to the imposition of communism and society was already relatively secularised. In Romania the strong influence of the Orthodox Church (80 per cent of Romanians are members of this faith) acted as a brake on protest and dissent, reinforcing passivity and submission. In the GDR peace was a key factor, reflecting not only the legacy of Nazism, but also the constant shadow of nuclear war. Indeed, it was no accident that East Germany was the only member of the Warsaw Pact that allowed its citizens to perform an alternative to military service in the shape of the so-called *Bausoldaten* (construction soldiers). Even so, the various unofficial peace initiatives of the early to mid-1980s remained the preserve of a small activist minority and failed to inspire mass demonstrations on a par with 1953 or 1989.[21]

The interplay between Moscow and its satellites also impacted on the success or failure of the various challenges to communist rule. The USSR was clearly hegemonic, and its intervention was decisive in saving the regimes in East Germany in 1953 and Hungary in 1956, as Matthew Stibbe and Johanna Granville show in some detail. However, there were also instances where the satellites themselves had an influence on policies formally decided on in Moscow. For example, Granville reconstructs the behind-the-scenes machinations in the 'Polish October' of 1956, which culminated in Khrushchev abandoning any plans for military action in the face of growing anti-Soviet demonstrations. Instead, he agreed to the appointment of the reformist Gomułka as First Secretary of the Communist Party, even though the latter had previously been purged because of his attachment to 'national roads to socialism' and his apparent affinities with Tito. As we have already seen, Gomułka was granted considerable freedom to develop his own domestic policies, provided that he showed complete support for the Soviet Union and the Warsaw Pact in international affairs.[22]

On the other hand, in 1968 the rulers of Poland, East Germany and Bulgaria (Gomułka, Ulbricht and Zhivkov respectively) all played an important role in urging Leonid Brezhnev and other Soviet Politburo members to come down hard on the Czechoslovak leaders of the Prague Spring. Part of their motive, as Mike Dennis notes in relation to the GDR, was their concern at 'the positive reception of the Prague reforms among broad sections of [their own] population', especially among university students and other young people, which threatened the basis of their power. However, it could be that they also hoped, through use of military force, to avoid a recurrence of the terrible civil violence and bloodshed that had characterised the 1956 revolution in Hungary.[23] The 'Brezhnev doctrine', in other words, was not solely a Soviet invention and was supported by communist rulers throughout the region, with the exception of Romania, Yugoslavia and Albania, even if it was opposed by the majority of the people in Eastern Europe.

More generally, the Soviets and their Eastern European comrades proved remarkably resilient in the face of new political challenges, and the lessons of the past were not lost on them. Repression could be brutal, but was usually tempered by concessions in the material and political spheres. After the Warsaw Pact invasion of Czechoslovakia in August 1968, for example, the Soviets chose to negotiate with Dubček rather than install a new hard-line regime immediately, and when Dubček eventually fell in April 1969, he was replaced by another 'centrist' (and fellow Slovak) Gustáv Husák. Under these circumstances, most people appeared resigned to the inevitability of long-term Soviet occupation, while others contented themselves with low-key and largely symbolic acts of opposition to the government's self-styled policy of 'normalisation'. 'Normalisation', as Kieran Williams argues, did not just mean political repression, but also some economic reforms as part of an unwritten 'social contract' between state and society. Even the 1970 purge of the party was undertaken in a limited and controlled way, with the secret police deliberately excluded from the process in order to avoid a return to Stalinist terror (to which Husák himself had fallen victim in the early 1950s).

In Romania, too, timely concessions backed up by selective repression were used to avert open revolt – as in the case of worker and student demonstrations in Bucharest, Cluj, Iaşi and Timişoara in October 1956, and the miners' strike in the Jiu valley in 1977. Intellectuals and workers failed to unite, and dissidents rarely preached outright rejection of the system, even when they operated from a position outside it. Before and during the 1980s the process of liberalisation went furthest in Hungary and Poland, but even in more hard-line Czechoslovakia and East Germany there was a tendency to accept a degree of social criticism and debate, albeit within limits strictly controlled by the party. Over and above this, censorship ensured that dissident authors' works were often better known in the West than in their own countries.[24] The West, in turn, continued to wine and dine communist leaders while simultaneously condemning the lack of human rights in the Soviet bloc.

In fact there was nothing inevitable about the collapse of communism or the rediscovery of a common 'Central European' cultural community in the 1980s. The early to mid-1950s were the least stable time for the Eastern European dictatorships,[25] while the early to mid-1970s were the most stable. Relative economic success (measured in terms of growing car and TV ownership and more private holidays to country retreats) was combined at international level with a growing accommodation with the West. In the GDR the government struck an important deal with Church leaders in 1978, while Honecker's state visit to Bonn in 1987 brought the regime added prestige. The meeting in December 1981 between Helmut Schmidt and Honecker at Werbellinsee, just north of Berlin, which took place on the eve of the declaration of martial law in Poland, seemed to indicate that the two sides could live side by side. Significantly, even former critics of *Ostpolitik* like the Bavarian Prime Minister Franz Josef Strauss were willing to provide the GDR with government-backed loans and credits after the centre-right returned to office in Bonn in 1982.[26] In Slovakia, meanwhile, the ruling communists recognised the Greek Catholic Church for the first time, albeit in a limited fashion. Religion, nationalism and communism no longer appeared completely incompatible, at least to some observers. In Poland the communist leader General Wojciech Jaruzelski even appealed to many non-communists as a national saviour in the face of a threatened Soviet invasion. This was in spite of his decision to impose martial law in December 1981 and to issue a ban on the Solidarity trade union in October 1982.[27]

Ironically, it was the very success of 'normalisation' which contained the seeds of communism's downfall. On the one hand, it gave way to rising expectations in the 1980s which communist regimes were not able to meet – especially as they had to squeeze consumption at home in order to pay off interest on loans raised in the West. Wider TV ownership, for instance, meant that more people could access information about Western lifestyles and attitudes, while eschewing 'conscious-raising' activities like attending trade union branch meetings. Gradual depoliticisation – people turning inwards to the family and consumerism and away from active involvement in political life – was partly offset by increased desire for knowledge and information about the true state of affairs gleaned from non-official, Western or *samizdat* sources. Surprisingly large numbers of Czechs did discuss political issues with family and friends, if the secret opinion polls analysed by Kieran Williams are to be believed. In the GDR party members and ordinary people enthused about Gorbachev and protested when the Soviet magazine *Sputnik* was banned in November 1988. In Poland it was above all the election of Cardinal Karol Wojtyła as Pope John Paul II in October 1978 that symbolised the rebirth of popular nationalism and kept it alive after the collapse of the Solidarity protests, while across the region as a whole 'religious life underwent a considerable revival in the second half of the 1980s', as R.J. Crampton puts it.[28]

At the same time, communist regimes also had to come to terms with small-scale dissidence as the price of their adherence to the Final Act of the Conference on Security and Cooperation in Europe of 1975, also known as the Helsinki Accords. The human rights provisions within these accords, signed by 35 states, including Yugoslavia, the USSR and its Eastern European allies (but not Albania), exposed the governments of the Soviet bloc to unprecedented forms of public criticism and accountability, while also increasing pressure on them to implement domestic reforms. Opposition movements, drawing inspiration from Helsinki, devised new political strategies of their own to fit in with the changing international situation. Thus East German dissidents in the 1980s rejected the violence of 1953 and instead looked to alternative models of peaceful protest – the Prague Spring, the Solidarity movement in Poland and, later still, the student campaigns in Beijing.[29] They now also enjoyed greater protection as the Church–state agreement of March 1978 provided limited 'free spaces' for oppositional activity – contrary to Honecker's intentions.[30] The Poles, who had a 200-year tradition of resisting foreign domination to fall back on, narrowly avoided direct Soviet military intervention in 1981, albeit at a price. By 1987, as Nigel Swain notes, Solidarity was split over its future direction and identity, and significant elements were preparing to compromise with the regime. For Czech and Slovak dissidents, the key lesson from 1968 was how much could be achieved by peaceful protest combined with patience, pragmatism, even 'dialogue' with the authorities. The outcome in the 1970s and 1980s was the human rights movement Charter 77, of which Václav Havel was a leading spokesperson. His seminal tract 'The Power of the Powerless' (1978) arguably did more than any other single document to elucidate the underlying weakness of the supposedly omnipotent 'post-totalitarian' state.[31] In Romania, meanwhile, Paul Goma deftly followed the Czechoslovak example, making several efforts to persuade Ceauşescu to sign a declaration of solidarity with Charter 77, and publishing an open letter condemning communist violations of human rights and other obligations under the Helsinki Final Act.

Patience, indeed, was what was needed. By the mid-1980s the communist regimes faced a major crisis, caused, in part, by developments in the international economy and also by pressures at home. Their increasingly elderly leadership could not keep pace with a burgeoning desire for greater liberalisation on the part of ordinary people, encompassing both economic and political freedoms, including the right to travel abroad. In this situation, groups like Charter 77 and the environmentalist movement in the GDR formed the basis for a revitalised 'civil society' and the eventual legalisation of opposition parties at the end of 1989. Poland and Hungary, however, led the way, ending censorship and releasing political prisoners in the faint hope of eventually obtaining a new political settlement that would favour continued communist rule in some shape or form. The immediate origins of the Hungarian reforms could be traced back to the mid-1980s and were accelerated by the removal of Kádár as party First Secretary in May 1988. Even so, the opening of the border with Austria in May 1989 took many international commentators by surprise, especially when it was followed soon by a renewed agreement between the ruling Hungarian Socialist Workers' Party and the opposition to hold talks aimed at smoothing the path towards democracy and free elections. Thereafter, however, negotiations between the two sides seemed to get stuck in a rut.

In Poland, on the other hand, all partners in the Round Table talks of February to April 1989 expected that the leading role of the communist party would be preserved, along with the country's continued membership of the Warsaw Pact. In the end it was to take a landslide defeat for the communists in the partially free elections in June 1989, and a change of heart on the part of opposition leaders, before General Jaruzelski finally gave way and appointed the first non-communist prime minister, Tadeusz Mazowiecki, in the Soviet bloc for over forty years. However, as Nigel Swain avers, the 'your President, our Prime Minister' formula ensured Jaruzelski's own political survival as the first president of the reformed Polish Republic, a decision carried by the narrowest majority of one in the new parliament and senate. In contrast to 1956 and 1968, Moscow stood by and allowed matters to take their own course (the so-called 'Sinatra doctrine' having now replaced the Brezhnev doctrine). Over two years earlier, during Gorbachev's state visit to Prague in April 1987, a Soviet Foreign Ministry official was invited to explain the difference between *perestroika* and the Prague Spring. 'Nineteen years' was the now famous response.[32]

The reform agenda in Poland and Hungary, and Gorbachev's refusal to intervene, put the rulers of the other communist states in an almost impossible situation. However, only in Romania did events get out of hand, leading to violent clashes between supporters and opponents of the regime and ending in the bloody downfall of Ceaușescu between 21 and 25 December 1989. In East Germany, Czechoslovakia and Bulgaria, by contrast, the ruling parties, which at first strongly resisted the pressure to reform, seemed to give up almost without a fight. In Czechoslovakia, as in GDR, the key slogan of the unarmed demonstrators in November 1989 was no violence – *nenasili / keine Gewalt* – and this strategy paid off. In many ways, as James Krapfl argues, the revolutionaries of 1989 were determined to stage their own 'revolt against a revolutionary tradition which was perceived as violent and unclean'. This then gave rise to the idea of the 'Velvet' or 'Gentle Revolution', a construct used to contrast events in Central Europe (especially in Prague) with previous violent revolutions; or as Richard Vinen puts it:

> The revolutions of 1989 – at least in Hungary, Czechoslovakia, Poland and East Germany – had the advantage of limited expectations. No one talked of 'new men' or the Robespierrian incorruptibility of the true revolutionary. It was understood that politics was not an end but simply a means of earning freedom to do something else.[33]

However, as Krapfl shows, shifts in domestic power relations since the early 1990s meant that not all those involved viewed the events of 1989 in the same romantic light, particularly when the excitement of taking part in world-changing events gave way to the more sober realities and messy compromises of life in a post-communist society. Some even denied that a 'revolution' had taken place at all. In this climate local or national issues were often treated, in retrospect, as more important to understanding what happened in 1989 than the overall demand for freedom from communist tyranny. This can be seen in particular in the case of the Czechs and Slovaks, who negotiated a successful mutual divorce in 1992–3, and in Yugoslavia where the ex-communist Slobodan Milošević used nationalism as a tool for launching his bid for power in Serbia, with appalling consequences for ethnic harmony in the region. Elsewhere, in general, Europe seems to be looking forward to a twenty-first century based on global markets, liberalisation and free trade. However, if the essays in this volume teach us anything, it is that we should be wary of assuming too much about the supposed inevitability of historical processes. The future of post-communist Eastern Europe is still far from certain, even more than fifteen years after the events of 1989.

Notes

1. The term 'Other Europe' was first used, to the best of our knowledge, in the late 1980s. See Jacques Rupnik, *The Other Europe* (London, 1988) and E. Garrison Walters, *The Other Europe: Eastern Europe to 1945* (Syracuse, NY, 1988). Since the collapse of the communist states in this 'Other Europe', there has been an explosion of interest in their history. Among the best English-language sources are: Ivan T. Berend, *Central and Eastern Europe, 1944–1993: Detour from the Periphery to the Periphery* (Cambridge, 1996); Mark Pittaway, *Eastern Europe, 1939–2000* (London, 2004); George Schöpflin, *The Politics of Eastern Europe* (Oxford, 1993); Geoffrey Swain and Nigel Swain, *Eastern Europe since 1945*, 3rd edn (Basingstoke, 2003); and Vladimir Tismaneanu, *Reinventing Politics: Eastern Europe from Stalin to Havel* (New York, 1992). The volume by Grzegorz Ekiert, *The State Against Society: Political Crises and their Aftermath in East Central Europe* (Princeton, NJ, 1996) shares a similar approach as this anthology, but is geographically more limited, focusing almost exclusively on developments in Hungary, Czechoslovakia and Poland. Similarly, Jason Sharman, *Repression and Resistance in Communist Europe* (London, 2003) concentrates on three key events – collectivisation in the USSR, Hungary in 1956 and Solidarity in Poland – and is thus more restricted in its coverage than this volume.

2. Lynne Viola (ed.), *Contending with Stalinism: Soviet Power and Popular Resistance in the 1930s* (Ithaca, NY, 2002), p. 1.

3. On this point, see Moshe Lewin, *The Gorbachev Phenomenon: A Historical Interpretation* (London, 1989), pp. 80–2.

4. Largely for reasons of space, we have not included Bulgaria, a socialist state not noted for its 'resistance' to Soviet dominance.

5. Roger Scruton, *A Dictionary of Political Thought* (London, 1982), p. 81.

6. For example, Ian Kershaw, *Popular Opinion and Political Dissent in the Third Reich. Bavaria 1933–1945* (Oxford, 1983); Detlev Peukert, *Inside Nazi Germany: Conformity, Opposition and Racism in Everyday Life* (London, 1987); and David Clay Large (ed.), *Contending with Hitler. Varieties of German Resistance in the Third Reich* (Cambridge, 1991).

7. Viola (ed.), *Contending with Stalinism*, pp. 18–20.

8. Scruton, *A Dictionary*, p. 406.

9. Jadwiga Staniszkis, *Poland's Self-Limiting Revolution*, ed. Jan T. Gross (Princeton, NJ, 1984).

10. David Holloway, 'War, Militarism and the Soviet State', in E.P. Thompson and Dan Smith (eds), *Protest and Survive* (London, 1980), pp. 136–7.

11. David Crowley, 'Warsaw's Shops, Stalinism and the Thaw', in Susan E. Reid and David Crowley (eds), *Style and Socialism. Modernity and Material Culture in Post-War Eastern Europe* (Oxford, 2000), pp. 25–47.

12. Pittaway, *Eastern Europe, 1939–2000*, p. 73.

13. Erica Carter, 'Culture, History and National Identity in the Two Germanies', in Mary Fulbrook (ed.), *Twentieth-Century Germany. Politics, Culture and Society, 1918–1990* (London, 2000), pp. 247–69. See also Corey Ross, *The East German Dictatorship. Problems and Perspectives in the Interpretation of the GDR* (London, 2002).

14. See, for example, Maria Dowling, *Czechoslovakia* (London, 2002), p. 99. Also Heda Margolius Kovály, *Eine Jüdin in Prag. Unter dem Schatten von Hitler und Stalin* (Berlin, 1992).

15. David Reynolds, 'Europe Divided and Reunited', in T.C.W. Blanning (ed.), *The Oxford Illustrated History of Modern Europe* (Oxford, 1996), p. 290.

16. Raymond Pearson, *The Rise and Fall of the Soviet Empire* (London, 1998), p. 53.

17. See György Péteri (ed.), *Intellectual Life and the First Crisis of State Socialism in East Central Europe, 1953–1956* (Trondheim, 2001); also Anne White, *De-Stalinization and the House of Culture. Declining State Control over Leisure in the USSR, Poland and Hungary, 1953–89* (London, 1990).

18. Misha Glenny, *The Balkans, 1804–1999. Nationalism, War and the Great Powers* (London, 1999), pp. 545–52.

19. Jonathan Sperber, '17 June 1953: Revisiting a Revolution', *German History*, vol. 22 (2004), p. 639.

20. Ibid.

21. Mary Fulbrook, *Anatomy of a Dictatorship. Inside the GDR, 1949–1989* (Oxford, 1995), pp. 201–36. It should be noted, of course, that becoming a 'construction soldier' in East Germany was no easy option; it was longer than the usual period of military service and could also cause considerable damage to the individual's career prospects or chances of gaining a university place (see ibid., p. 203).
22. Cf. R.J. Crampton, *Eastern Europe in the Twentieth Century – and After*, 2nd edn (London, 1997), pp. 286–7.
23. Mike Dennis, *The Rise and Fall of the German Democratic Republic, 1945– 1990* (London, 2000), pp. 128–9.
24. Richard Vinen, *A History in Fragments. Europe in the Twentieth Century* (London, 2000), p. 482.
25. This view is also put forward by Pittaway, *Eastern Europe, 1939–2000*, pp. 7 and 56–61.
26. Timothy Garton Ash, *In Europe's Name. Germany and the Divided Continent* (London, 1993), pp. 31–2.
27. Vinen, *A History in Fragments*, pp. 476–7.
28. Crampton, *Eastern Europe*, p. 414.
29. Sperber, '17 June 1953', p. 640.
30. Fulbrook, *Anatomy of a Dictatorship*, p. 201.
31. Václav Havel et al., *The Power of the Powerless: Citizens against the State in Central-Eastern Europe*, ed. John Keane (London, 1985), pp. 23–96.
32. Garton Ash, *In Europe's Name*, p. 124; Reynolds, 'Europe Divided and Reunited', p. 299; Vinen, *A History in Fragments*, p. 423.
33. Vinen, *A History in Fragments*, p. 487.

Part I

–2–

The Soviet-Yugoslav Split*
Leonid Gibianskii

The clash between the Kremlin and the leadership of the communist regime in Yugoslavia, which ignited in 1948 and lasted until Stalin's death, was the first in a series of internal conflicts which profoundly shook the Soviet bloc. This unprecedented schism immediately attracted the world's attention and has been an object of burning interest among historians and political scientists ever since.[1] For more than four decades after the Tito-Stalin split, documentation on the events was completely inaccessible in the Soviet archives and largely so in the Yugoslav files. Hence, almost no facts were known on the origins of this confrontation and its transformation into an open and savage crisis, except for the information published during the conflict by the respective propaganda machines. While Stalin was still alive, the Soviet side limited itself to fictitious accusations against the Yugoslav leadership of betraying Marxism-Leninism, of anti-Soviet policies and of aiding 'imperialism'.[2] In the post-Stalin period, when the Kremlin was forced to acknowledge the groundlessness of these charges, it generally preferred to conceal the history of the clash. For their part, the Yugoslavs published certain concrete evidence on the origins and behind-the-scenes development of the conflict, but extremely selectively – only that which Belgrade considered politically advantageous.[3] Moreover, the material in some cases was distorted by the addition of clear falsehoods.

As a result, scholars found themselves in a situation where the evidence at their disposal came almost exclusively from the official Yugoslav version. This account portrayed the conflict as a process which had arisen during, and even before, the Second World War, and had continued after its conclusion. The cause of the crisis, so it was asserted, was protracted Soviet dissatisfaction with those policies of the Communist Party of Yugoslavia (CPY) that contradicted Moscow's line. During the war, these comprised the CPY's radical stance on the creation of revolutionary statehood and on the struggle against the Yugoslav émigré government and its pro-Western supporters within Yugoslavia, both of which threatened to complicate the Soviet Union's relations with its Western allies. After the war, Belgrade again claimed that it took an independent position on the Trieste question, the principles of economic collaboration with the USSR and attitudes towards the intensified industrialisation of Yugoslavia. According to this version, the Kremlin's disquiet led to almost constant, though clandestine, tension. This eventually flowed over into sharp Soviet actions against Yugoslavia at the end of 1947 and the beginning of 1948, which in turn occasioned the open clash later in 1948. The official Yugoslav interpretation heavily influenced not only domestic authors, but also much of Western historiography.[4]

Only with the collapse of the USSR and the communist regimes in Eastern Europe did it become possible to study previously secret documents. These new sources, consulted by many scholars, myself included, allow us to peer behind the scenes of the Tito-Stalin split and explain how it happened. As this chapter will show, many aspects of the 'traditional' account are contradicted by this new evidence. Notably, in the early post-war years Yugoslavia emerges not as a renegade, but as an extremely solid link in the formation of the Soviet bloc.

Before the Split: Old Myths and New Evidence on Soviet-Yugoslav Relations

A de facto communist monopoly of power based on the Soviet model had been established in Yugoslavia during its liberation from fascist occupation. In contrast to most other Central and East European countries, this was achieved not through Soviet military presence, but mainly as a result of a mass armed struggle organised and headed by the CPY. By the autumn of 1945 all pretence of a multi-party arrangement had been liquidated and Yugoslavia was, in practice, a one-party state. In 1944–6 virtually all industrial enterprises, banks, transport and wholesale trade were expropriated by the regime, and state-centralised administration of the economy was introduced. This administration was extended into the countryside, where, under the agrarian reform of 1945, only half the land seized from the large landowners was transferred to the poorest peasantry, and the other half became state property on which the first collective farms were created. A brutal system of compulsory delivery of production enveloped both the collectives and all individual peasant holdings. In spring 1947, the Yugoslav leadership announced a direct transition to the 'construction of socialism', the cornerstone of which was the First Five-Year Plan and Stalinist heavy industrialisation.[5]

In foreign policy, too, Yugoslavia steadfastly kept in step with the USSR. The Soviets' increasingly confrontational attitude towards the Western powers, most clearly formulated at the founding conference of the Cominform in September 1947, was endorsed enthusiastically by Belgrade. What is more, close mutual collaboration was not restricted to the international arena, but was evident in bilateral political, military, economic and cultural-ideological relations. Soviet advisers and other specialists worked in Yugoslavia, preparing the country's cadres and functionaries. The USSR was Yugoslavia's main economic partner and played a dominant role in the training and equipping of the Yugoslav army.[6] The closeness of Soviet-Yugoslav relations in these immediate post-war years is epitomised by an episode which never figured in the published Yugoslav material and has only come to light in recently accessible Soviet documents. In mid-1945 the Yugoslav secret services suspected that enemies of the regime might be plotting to assassinate Tito and, under an agreement between Moscow and Belgrade, a large group of Soviet state security personnel were specially seconded to Yugoslavia to protect Tito, one of their number becoming deputy head of his bodyguard.[7] In short, the Yugoslav regime everywhere borrowed Soviet experience and actively collaborated with Moscow.

Given these discoveries, how accurate is the former official Yugoslav version outlined above? The answer depends on the various chronological stages and problems. So far as the war years are concerned, documentary evidence produced earlier by the Yugoslavs, and also the new archival materials, attest to the radicalism of the CPY leaders in their desire for revolutionary statehood and in their struggle against the émigré government and related pro-Western forces in Yugoslavia (the Četnik movement). These policies did not tally fully with Soviet political tactics and provoked a degree of criticism from Moscow.[8] However, recent research has demonstrated that the former Yugoslav account tends to overemphasise these disagreements and tensions. On the contrary, it has been argued convincingly that the mutual ties between the CPY and the Kremlin were firm and both sides shared the same basic political and ideological goals. Furthermore, the CPY leadership on the whole corrected its line in accordance with Moscow's directives.[9] Most importantly, hitherto top-secret Soviet archival sources, the so-called papers (*spravki*) and memoranda (*zapiski*) compiled by the Central Committee (CC) apparatus of the Soviet party after the end of the war, indicate that up to 1948 there were no critical comments on the CPY's wartime policies. Far from it – they were, in effect, praised to the skies, even in a document written as late as August–September 1947.[10] This means that on the eve of the Soviet-Yugoslav split, no special significance was attached in Moscow to the partial tactical divergences that occurred in the war.

When it comes to mutual relations in the immediate post-war years, it is noteworthy that Soviet leaders invariably mentioned Yugoslavia first among the East European People's Democracies in their public pronouncements.[11] Neither was this a purely superficial gesture; it expressed the genuine attitude of the Kremlin as disclosed in the secret Central Committee *spravki* drawn up before 1948, which singled out Yugoslavia as the country that had gone furthest along the path of 'democratic development', a euphemism for the creation of a communist system. It was stressed that the prerequisites for the transition to socialism had already been set out in Yugoslavia. All these materials show that in its foreign policy Yugoslavia stood resolutely behind the USSR and was the bulwark of Moscow's line in the Balkans and in its opposition to the West.[12] At the founding conference of the Cominform, where the Kremlin openly proclaimed the doctrine of its 'democratic camp' (subsequently 'socialist camp') in opposition to the 'imperialist camp', the Soviet and Yugoslav representatives collaborated extremely closely. Andrei Zhdanov, the CPSU ideological chief, and Georgii Malenkov, one of Stalin's top associates, evaluated the position of the Yugoslav delegates very highly in their daily reports on the conference to the Soviet leader.[13] Yugoslav domestic and foreign policy was fulsomely praised, both in a series of policy articles published at the end of 1947 in the leading Soviet theoretical journal *Bol'shevik*[14] and in the CC secret memorandum on the influence of the Cominform meeting on Yugoslavia, composed in late January 1948.[15] Thus, just months before the clash of 1948 the Soviet assessment of Belgrade's post-war line was fundamentally very positive.

Nevertheless, it cannot be denied that Soviet-Yugoslav relations at this time were not without certain complications. But how 'real' were they and what were they linked to? It can be concluded from the newly accessible documents that almost no aspect of Yugoslav domestic policy drew the Kremlin's wrath before 1948. Belgrade's drive for industrialisation, its policies towards the countryside and its practical organisation of the power system aroused no dissatisfaction in Moscow. It is true that the CC materials prepared prior to the conflict stated that, although power belonged fully to the CPY, the party did not appear overtly as the ruling force. The 'People's Front', entirely controlled by the party, figured in that role. But even this practice was regarded as a specific tactical ploy and no adverse comment was voiced.[16] Criticism arose only later in the course of the conflict, when such tactics began to be treated as politically criminal – 'the dissolving of the CPY into the People's Front'.[17]

It is also the case that secret Soviet memoranda occasionally hinted displeasure at the failure of the CPY to hold a party congress after the war and at the irregularity of its Central Committee meetings, which resulted in all the most important decisions being taken exclusively by the ruling foursome – Tito and his closest collaborators, Edvard Kardelj, Alexander Ranković and Milovan Djilas. But even here no firm conclusions were reached and it is therefore difficult to say how concerned Moscow was by this situation.[18] Perhaps the only time the Soviets reacted sharply to one of the Yugoslav moves was in March 1945, when the temporary coalition government was established in Belgrade. The cabinet was to include, alongside the majority CPY and its adherents, several émigré politicians, as agreed by the USSR and its Western allies, notably Britain. But as the new body was in the final stages of formation, Tito, for tactical reasons, replaced one of the candidates for vice-premier with a person more desirable to the Western allies. However, he did not seek Soviet sanction for this manoeuvre and, as a consequence, he received a secret and very severe reprimand from the Kremlin, in response to which the Yugoslav leaders were compelled to repent for their 'mistake' to their Moscow patron.[19] But, judging from the archival sources, the Soviets did not thereafter refer to this episode.

Economic Disputes and Foreign Policy Complications

There were also frictions in the economic relations between the two countries, most evident in the creation of the mutual Soviet-Yugoslav share companies in various branches of the Yugoslav economy. After the split, the official Belgrade version maintained that the idea of founding these companies came from the Soviet side, with the intention of exploiting Yugoslav mineral resources in an almost colonial manner. This interpretation then became widespread in Western historiography.[20] But it has now come to light that the formation of joint share companies was first proposed to Moscow by Kardelj, on behalf of the Yugoslav government at the end of 1944.[21] In 1945–6, the Yugoslavs initiated further contacts on this issue between the two governments.[22] Consequently, an agreement on Soviet-Yugoslav economic collaboration was signed on 8 June 1946, providing for the creation of a series of joint share companies.[23] However, difficulties soon arose. Belgrade insisted that the value of the raw materials underground should be included in the calculation of the value of its investment, but the Soviets rejected this claim.[24] Dissatisfaction with the Soviet position was expressed at a CPY Politburo meeting in September 1946, some participants even equating this with the policy of the 'capitalist countries' which had exploited Yugoslavia's natural resources before the war. The Soviet Ambassador in Belgrade learnt of this dissent and in turn informed his Ministry of Foreign Affairs.[25] But Stalin, in the end, preferred not to exacerbate the problems. At a meeting on 19 April 1947 with Kardelj, who ranked next to Tito in the Yugoslav leadership, he proposed to abandon the creation of joint companies and render Soviet assistance to the industrialisation of Yugoslavia through the supply of equipment and materials on credit and the provision of specialists in the construction of enterprises.[26] The corresponding agreement was initialled on 25 July 1947.[27]

All in all, it is hard to assess the impact on Soviet-Yugoslav relations of these economic tangles and wrangles. Suffice to say that the problem of joint share companies was not mentioned in the Soviet evaluations of Yugoslav policy made on the eve of the crisis. What the new documents do show is that some of Belgrade's steps in the international arena caused more than a measure of consternation in Moscow, but even here we see a few surprises. Thus, contrary to existing historiography, Soviet dissatisfaction was linked neither to Yugoslav support for the communists in the Greek civil war, nor to the attempts to launch a similar partisan movement in Spain, nor to the differing positions taken by Soviet and Yugoslav delegates at the UNO in autumn 1947 over the Palestine question. As far as Greece and Spain are concerned, recent archival research has uncovered extremely close Soviet-Yugoslav cooperation up to the beginning of 1948 on the illegal transference of arms, military hardware and communist cadres from Yugoslavia to these countries.[28] As for the Palestine question, it is well known that the Yugoslavs voted for the creation of an Arab-Jewish federation in the UN General Assembly in November 1947. Although the USSR initially favoured this variant, for tactical reasons it finally voted for the formation of two separate states, Jewish and Arab. Yugoslav historians and memoirists have often asserted that Soviet representatives expressed their distinct displeasure to the Yugoslav delegates in the lobbies of the UN.[29] But from materials in the Russian archives it is apparent that the Yugoslav conduct elicited no special negative reaction in the Kremlin. Indeed, when the Soviet UN delegation informed

Moscow of the Yugoslav position on Palestine, Molotov reckoned there was no need to change this stance; and what is more Stalin endorsed Molotov's decision.[30]

Archival sources have also shown the groundlessness of the Serbian historian Djoko Tripković's version of the Yugoslav reaction to the Marshall Plan. In the 1990s he alleged that Belgrade initially vacillated in favour of the plan, contrary to the Soviet position. Tripković referred in his argument to the Yugoslav note sent to the British, French and Soviet governments and published on 27 June 1947 which expressed interest in the Marshall Plan. According to Tripković, it was only after pressure from the USSR that the Yugoslav leadership altered its stance in early July, and announced its refusal to participate in the plan.[31] What Tripković did not know was that the Yugoslav memorandum of 27 June was itself the consequence of a previous Soviet instruction dispatched to Belgrade on 22 June, ordering the Yugoslavs to participate in preparatory talks for the plan.[32] What was going on is explained by documents in the Russian and other East European archives. At the end of June and beginning of July 1947, the Kremlin itself was vacillating in its attitude to the plan as it elaborated and re-elaborated its tactics. Therefore, in the space of little more than two weeks it changed its directives to the East European communist leaders three times.[33] Hence there was absolutely no anti-Soviet wavering in the Yugoslav attitude to the plan, as Tripković has intimated. Belgrade was simply following, in a disciplined manner, all the twists and turns of Moscow's changing line. In reality, there was no Soviet dissatisfaction with Yugoslav conduct over the Marshall Plan. Equally illusory is the notion that the Kremlin decided henceforth to curb any further independent activity by Tito, and that his 'dissent' was the most pressing problem to be resolved if order was to be restored to the Soviet bloc.[34]

The real source of Soviet anxiety over Yugoslav foreign policy emanated from such important international issues as the Trieste question and relations with the other Balkan People's Democracies, above all Albania and Bulgaria. Here, Moscow believed that Tito's regime was taking immoderate actions without prior agreement with its Soviet patron. Soviet-Yugoslav tensions over the Trieste question have long featured in the historiography. Moscow's sharp démarche to the Yugoslav leadership in early June 1945 became well known from the correspondence published by Belgrade in August 1948. It was provoked by Tito's public speech in Ljubljana on 26 May 1945, at the height of the Trieste crisis, when the Yugoslavs attempted to resist the demand of the British and Americans that Yugoslav troops be evacuated from Trieste and the adjoining part of the Julian region, which they had previously occupied. Furthermore, the Western allies insisted that these territories should be transferred to the control of the Anglo-American forces.[35] In view of this, Tito stated in his speech that Yugoslavia did not wish to be 'small change', an object of 'the policy of spheres of interest'. Moscow reasoned that these words could be interpreted as a grievance directed not just at the Western allies, but also at the USSR. Hence it secretly but pointedly warned the Yugoslav leadership that such statements were inadmissible. Belgrade agreed with the criticism of its 'mistake' and submitted its apologies.[36]

However, the Yugoslavs rejected the accusation that Tito's speech was directed at Moscow. They did so in June 1945 at the start of the contretemps, and again in 1948 when the conflict was already under way and the Soviet side recalled the incident.[37] But soon after, when it was asserted that the confrontation with the USSR had already begun during the Second World War, Yugoslav propaganda and its attendant historiography maintained that, on the contrary, the speech was indeed aimed at the Kremlin, in view of its lack of support for Yugoslavia over the Trieste issue. This new assertion was borrowed unquestioningly by Western historians.[38] But, as before, this claim was not based on documentary evidence and therefore it remained unclear which of the two Yugoslav versions corresponded to the truth.[39] Whatever the case, the main point is that Moscow evaluated Tito's speech very negatively.

These complex post-war imbroglios impacted on Soviet-Yugoslav relations in differing ways. In his private contacts with Stalin, Tito expressed deep gratitude when the USSR firmly supported Yugoslav demands to the Western allies, but also discontent when the Kremlin favoured one or other compromise concession, which in Belgrade's opinion should have been avoided. One response could follow the other in short order, depending on changes in the ongoing situation. For example, at the end of May 1946, during Tito's visit to Moscow, he warmly thanked Stalin and Molotov for Soviet backing at the meeting of the Council of Foreign Ministers in Paris, which had taken place between 25 April and 16 May.[40] But already by July, Stalin received a telegram from Tito reproaching the Soviet representatives in Paris for displaying insufficient regard for Yugoslav interests and inclining towards a compromise in the form of a 'Free Territory of Trieste', and the drawing of the Yugoslav-Italian border on the line proposed by France. In reply, Stalin decisively rejected such reproaches and Tito, faced with this tough response, then tried to smooth over the incident.[41]

Moscow, however, did not forget Belgrade's 'incorrect position' on the Trieste question. In the memorandum drawn up by the Soviet Central Committee apparatus in August–September 1947 in preparation for the founding conference of the Cominform, the Yugoslav government was accused of ignoring 'the general interests of the democratic forces', and the Yugoslav press rebuked for the 'unacceptably sharp' criticism of the Italian Communist Party, and its leader Palmiro Togliatti, for its line on the Trieste issue, a line which did not satisfy Belgrade.[42] It was even mooted that Zhdanov, in his report to the forthcoming Cominform meeting, should criticise the CPY for its '"leftist" errors', as they were described in one of the preliminary variants of the speech. However, the Soviet leadership finally decided to refrain from such a harsh step, and this fragment was omitted from the report.[43]

The Soviet memorandum of August–September 1947 claimed that 'some leading figures of the Yugoslav Communist Party occasionally manifest national narrow-mindedness, not taking into account the interests of other countries and sister communist parties', as characterised by the Yugoslavs' 'incorrect position' on the Trieste question. In a similar vein, it spoke of the existence among CPY leaders of 'certain tendencies ... to over-rate their achievements', and of their 'aspiration to turn the Communist Party of Yugoslavia into a type of "leading" party in the Balkans'.[44] Examples of this arrogance were, first, public criticism of the Bulgarian party at the end of 1946 for failing to define the Macedonians as a national minority in the published draft of the Bulgarian constitution;[45] second, Belgrade's ambitions in Albania were broached: the Yugoslav leaders were 'very jaundiced towards Albania's efforts to forge direct links with the Soviet Union. In their opinion, Albania should have ties with the Soviet Union only via the Yugoslav government'.[46]

Yugoslav patronage of the Albanians had emerged during the war, and at that time the Soviets had reacted positively.[47] Immediately after the war, links between Moscow and Tirana, particularly arms supplies, had operated through the Yugoslavs,[48] and Stalin favoured this state of affairs in his meeting with Tito in May 1946. Moreover, he did not raise any objection – at least, not verbally – to Yugoslav aspirations to include Albania in the Yugoslav federation, but he did warn that such a step would be premature before the resolution of the Trieste question. Stalin proposed that for the time being Belgrade should limit itself to agreements on the further development of mutual links with Albania, and Tito agreed.[49] However, once direct Soviet-Albanian contacts, including the dispatch to Tirana of Soviet economic and military specialists, began to be established from the summer of 1947, the Yugoslavs viewed this as a breach of their dominant position in Albania.[50] This attitude contradicted the hierarchy of the Soviet bloc and the undisputed hegemony of the Kremlin. There is no doubt that at this time Moscow regarded Belgrade's intentions vis-à-vis Albania with suspicion.

Though the Soviets were aware of these encroachments by Belgrade and regarded them negatively, Moscow's general assessment of Yugoslav policy was still rather positive. Criticism was partial and moderate. This is especially apparent if we compare Soviet attitudes towards the communist parties of Poland, Czechoslovakia and Hungary, contained in the same secret analytical memoranda. These parties and their leaders were accused of far more serious nationalist and even opportunist vacillations for underestimating the experiences and role of the USSR.[51] It was their policies, not Tito's, that were the Kremlin's chief concern in Eastern Europe immediately prior to the foundation of the Cominform,[52] and hence there are no grounds for the former Yugoslav version that the Cominform was created by Moscow with the express purpose of punishing the Yugoslav party.[53]

New archival studies also undermine the claim that the establishment of the Cominform was the result of a joint 'factional' action by Zhdanov and Tito, and that the Kremlin's subsequent campaign of criticism of Yugoslavia was due to Stalin's or Malenkov's punishment of Zhdanov, who allegedly acted as the ally of the Yugoslavs.[54] The documents demonstrate, on the one hand, that the Yugoslav leadership, like the leaders of the other parties who attended the meeting at Szklarska Poręba in Poland, had not been informed in advance about the Soviet intention to found the Cominform.[55] On the other hand, there is no proof (on the contrary, it is rather disproved) that the idea of creating the Cominform and the doctrine of 'two camps' belonged to Zhdanov and that he had maintained special contact with Belgrade.[56] Recently accessible materials suggest that more realistic were those Western authors who argued that the Soviet-Yugoslav conflict originated in many respects from the problems in Yugoslavia's relations with Bulgaria and Albania, and from the plans to set up a federation in the Balkans. It is now possible in large measure to reconstruct a picture of the events that transpired.

Towards the Split

The Kremlin's deep discontent served as a point of departure, when in early August 1947 Yugoslavia and Bulgaria concluded a treaty of friendship, cooperation and mutual assistance. They did this contrary to Stalin's directive. Indeed, he found it necessary to postpone this agreement until the peace treaty with Bulgaria took effect (in September 1947), which made invalid the British and American veto on the conclusion of a treaty between Bulgaria, as a former enemy state, and Yugoslavia.[57] On 12 August Stalin, in a secret telegram to Georgi Dimitrov and Tito, sharply condemned their action. In response, they admitted their mistake and later initialled the Bulgarian-Yugoslav treaty only after they had received Soviet sanction.[58] The episode, which was kept secret by the three sides, appeared to have been settled.

However, two further incidents were triggered by Tito's and Dimitrov's independent foreign policy initiatives. The first was connected with Belgrade's desire to strengthen its patronage over Tirana. In late 1947, fearing that Albania might be transferred to immediate Soviet control, Tito sought to obtain Stalin's approval for a reduction of the Soviet presence in Albania and for a consolidation of the Yugoslav priority position there.[59] At the talks with Djilas, held in Moscow in mid-January 1948, Stalin expressed his seemingly positive view of Yugoslav wishes, although it is still unclear whether this was serious or just a tactical ploy.[60] Whatever the case, the Soviets' negative reaction followed in a matter of days after Tito, without seeking Kremlin approval or even notifying it, wrung Enver Hoxha's consent for the introduction of a Yugoslav army division into Albania on the pretext of protecting the country from Greek invasion.[61] Simultaneously, another incident occurred eliciting the same sharp Soviet response. This was Dimitrov's public statement, also made without having informed the Kremlin, on the prospects of establishing a federation of East European 'people's democracies', including Greece.[62]

Following Moscow's reprimand, supplemented on the latter occasion by criticism in *Pravda*, Tito and Dimitrov once again obediently acknowledged their 'mistakes': on Tito's orders the division was not sent to Albania, and Dimitrov openly repudiated his statement about the federation.[63] However, the Soviet leadership, seriously concerned by Sofia's and Belgrade's continuing willful actions, summoned

Bulgarian and Yugoslav representatives to Moscow, where, at a secret meeting on 10 February 1948, Stalin severely chastised them for the two incidents and for their earlier headstrong conduct with respect to the Bulgarian-Yugoslav treaty. In order to strengthen Soviet control, bilateral Soviet-Bulgarian and Soviet-Yugoslav protocols were signed on 11 February, obliging mutual consultations on international issues. At the gathering on 10 February, Stalin placed a ban on the deployment of Yugoslav troops in Albania. Having condemned Dimitrov's idea of an East European federation, however, Stalin spoke in support of a Bulgarian-Yugoslav federation, to be established in the near future and to be joined later by Albania. Consequently, instead of Albania's actual incorporation into Yugoslavia – an intention favoured by Belgrade – Yugoslavia would have found itself in a position as just one of three members of the federation proposed by Stalin.[64]

While the Bulgarian leadership consented to the early formation of a federation with Yugoslavia,[65] the CPY Politburo rejected the idea at its session convened on 19 February to hear the report of the Yugoslav delegation on its return from Moscow. This decision was confirmed at an extended Politburo meeting on 1 March, where it was concluded that, owing to Soviet influence in Bulgaria, a federation with the latter could be turned into a lever of undesirable control over Yugoslavia. The Politburo also set the course for the reconsolidation of Yugoslavia's position in Albania.[66] In late February and early March, under renewed pressure from Belgrade, the Albanian leadership, as yet unaware of the Moscow meeting of 10 February, raised again before the USSR the question of introducing Yugoslav troops into Albania due to the Greek threat, and the Yugoslavs started prevailing on Tirana to propose Albania's merger with Yugoslavia.[67] Furthermore, in opposition to Stalin's view that guerrilla warfare in Greece should be ended, the Yugoslav and Greek communist leaders, meeting on 21 February, agreed to promote the partisan movement and to render Yugoslav assistance to it.[68]

The importance of these steps cannot be overestimated. Belgrade, which until then had conducted itself, as a rule, in compliance with the hierarchical relations in the Soviet bloc, had begun to act contrary to Moscow's instructions. This line of action was combined with the more general conclusion, reached at the meeting of the CPY Politburo on 1 March, that the USSR flouted the interests of both Yugoslavia and the other 'people's democracies' by exerting undue pressure and imposing its will on them. Consequently, the Yugoslavs decided to rely on their own resources for the development of the economy and the strengthening of the army. The Kremlin was almost immediately made aware of these resolutions via Politburo member, Sreten Žujović, who secretly alerted the Soviet Ambassador to Yugoslavia, Anatolii Lavrent'ev. He, in turn, dispatched a damning dossier to the Soviet leaders who, unsurprisingly, regarded the Yugoslav stance as hostile.[69] There is some new archival evidence that, until this time, Moscow was not intent on spearheading a conflict with Belgrade;[70] but Žujović's inside information, obtained from Lavrent'ev, abruptly changed this situation.

On 9 March 1948, Lavrent'ev reported to Moscow that, contrary to accepted practice, the Economic Council of Yugoslavia had refused to supply confidential data of the country's economy to the Soviet trade representative. The Yugoslav explanation – that the trade representative had not exactly been rebuffed, but referred to superior authorities, namely the Central Committee of the CPY and the government – was not mentioned in the Ambassador's report, and the conclusion was drawn that the refusal 'reflects changes' in the Yugoslav leaders' attitude to the USSR.[71] There are no data in the archival materials which allow us to judge the relative trustworthiness or biased nature of the information supplied by Lavrent'ev. It has been revealed, however, that between autumn 1947 and early 1948 the reports by Lavrent'ev and General Georgii Sidorovich, the Soviet military attaché in Belgrade, became increasingly more alarming, with accusations that a number of Yugoslav leaders, even Tito himself, were guilty of 'national narrow-mindedness', manifested in their underestimation of Soviet military experience and of the USSR's role in the liberation of Yugoslavia. The absence of a clear-cut ideological and political orientation was also noted, as were Tito's over-exaggerated ambitions as a leader ('chieftainship'), in contrast to Stalin's 'justified' charisma, as the authors of these memoranda put it.[72] The question is: what gave rise to such harsh reports, and were they the result of the writers' own initiatives or had they been encouraged, even directly inspired, by someone in Moscow? Archival documents, as yet, provide no real clue for the actions taken by Lavrent'ev and Sidorovich, although some of the former's assertions were described as tendentious by the head of the Balkans Department of the Soviet Foreign Ministry in his note to Molotov on 8 October 1947.[73] What is more, before March 1948, Lavrent'ev's accusations were not reflected in the relevant assessment materials on Yugoslavia drawn up at the CPSU Central Committee.

However, the Ambassador's memorandum of 9 March, together with Žujović's information, eventually produced a mighty shift. Lavrent'ev was immediately summoned to Moscow, where, on 12 March, he reported on the situation at a meeting chaired by Stalin and attended by almost all Soviet Politburo members.[74] So far, no documents on the discussions and decisions of this session have been located. The hitherto unknown telegram, sent by Molotov to Tito on 13 March, gave no hint of Soviet concern and expressed a readiness, so it seemed, to continue talks to solve the problem of Soviet economic and military assistance to Yugoslavia. This suggests that for the moment, for some reason, the Kremlin preferred to postpone sharp measures.[75] This brief pause came to an abrupt end on 18 March, when Molotov despatched a second telegram to Tito, accusing him of unfriendliness to the USSR and informing him that all Soviet civil specialists and military advisers were being recalled from Yugoslavia.[76] Instead of repentance, Tito defiantly rejected the indictments, which precipitated the notorious letter of 27 March, signed by Stalin and Molotov, charging the Yugoslav leadership with pursuing an anti-Soviet course, opportunist mistakes and revision of the most important Marxist-Leninist theses.[77]

This pattern of political and ideological accusation by the Kremlin, and rejection by a Yugoslav leadership which was confronted with the alternative of either surrendering to Stalin's punishment or resolutely maintaining its position, was continued in subsequent secret correspondence between Moscow and Belgrade. The Soviet leaders compared the Yugoslavs' stance to that of Eduard Bernstein, the Russian Mensheviks, Bukharin and the ultimate Soviet bogey, Trotsky.[78] The charges of opportunism and departure from Marxism-Leninism had no basis in Yugoslav foreign or domestic policy. The only truth to the Soviets' claims was their criticism of the anti-democratic procedures in the CPY and the semi-secret nature of its activity. But the Kremlin had little concern for democracy in the Yugoslav party, and merely threw in this arraignment to reinforce its general onslaught against the Yugoslav leadership.

New Evidence on the Split

Most of the Soviet accusations have long been common knowledge and have been analysed many times. To avoid repetition, I shall concentrate here on several important, but hitherto unknown, aspects which have come to light with the discovery of new documents. For example, it has transpired that the memorandum cumbersomely entitled 'On the Anti-Marxist Positions of the Leaders of the Communist Party of Yugoslavia on Questions of Foreign and Domestic Policy', prepared on orders from above by the Central Committee Foreign Policy Department, served as a basis for Stalin and Molotov's letter of 27 March.[79] It was presented to CC Secretary Mikhail Suslov on 18 March, the day Molotov initially telegrammed Tito. The memorandum included parts of Lavrent'ev's and Sidorovich's reports of autumn 1947 and early 1948, and certain critical remarks from previous secret assessment materials on Yugoslavia, albeit now transmuted into extremely harsh and exaggerated criticisms. Among the latter was the thesis that the Yugoslavs had laid 'claim to a leading role in the Balkan and Danubian countries'.[80] However, neither this assertion, nor the accusations regarding Albania, were mentioned in the Soviet missives to the Yugoslav leadership.

Also omitted was Belgrade's radical reaction to political developments in Austria and Italy, although it was this radicalism that in February to March 1948 provoked the Soviet leadership's dire discontent, apparently adding to the Kremlin's tough stance. In mid-February, Zhdanov and Suslov learned from the Austrian communist leaders that the Yugoslavs had advised them to push for the division of the country, with a separate state governed by the CP of Austria to be set up in the Soviet zone of occupation. In reply, Zhdanov informed the Austrians of Moscow's belligerent opposition to the Yugoslav recommendations.[81] The Kremlin responded in the same way when, at the close of March, the Hungarian and Italian communist leaders, Mátyás Rákosi and Palmiro Togliatti, reported that the Yugoslav and Hungarian parties supported armed action in the event of US intervention to thwart the forth-coming parliamentary elections in Italy, in which the bloc of communists and socialists expected to win 50 per cent or more of the vote. Molotov notified Togliatti, via the Soviet embassy, of the Kremlin's negative attitude and specifically warned that the advice of the Yugoslavs and Hungarians had nothing in common with the Soviet leadership's position.[82]

These practical concerns were not referred to in the correspondence with Belgrade, but by transferring the charges against the Yugoslavs exclusively to the sphere of anti-Sovietism and ideological deviation from Marxism-Leninism, Moscow resorted to its traditional stance, this time in order to bring Tito and his close circle to heel by threatening to proclaim them traitors to the communist cause. In this way, a canonic ideological foundation had been laid for the fight against the Yugoslavs should they persist in their obstinacy. The same politico-ideological justifications were used by the Kremlin in late March to obtain censure of Belgrade from the leaders of the other Cominform parties. Notable, however, is the discovery that the communist leaders of Poland, Czechoslovakia, Romania and Bulgaria were initially in no hurry to condemn their Yugoslav colleagues, and it was only after they had been goaded by the Soviets, with the help of the Hungarians, that they joined the campaign of pressure on Belgrade in the second half of April.[83]

New archival research has also revealed that in late March and early April 1948 the CPSU's Foreign Policy Department prepared memoranda, on orders from above, in which the communist parties of Czechoslovakia, Poland and, to a lesser extent, Hungary were accused of pursuing similar policies to those of Yugoslavia, policies which had already been characterised very negatively by the Soviets.[84] Hence some Russian historians have argued that in late 1947 or early 1948 the Kremlin decided to suspend the concept of 'national roads to socialism' and impose Soviet-style uniformity on the countries of Central and Eastern Europe. Moscow planned to replace the leaders of the three communist parties, and those of the Yugoslav Party, because they had displayed undue independence. Allegedly, the Soviet-Yugoslav conflict originated as part of this plan.[85] The problem with this interpretation is that, first, there is no evidence, either in the March–April memoranda or in other archival documents, that such a plan existed. The authors of this version have merely surmised the intentions of the Soviet leadership and have overlooked the real causes, brought to light by new sources. Second, the Yugoslav leaders, unlike several of their Czechoslovak and Polish colleagues, acted not as advocates, but as opponents of the policy of 'national roads to socialism' and faithfully followed the Soviet model. Third, a comparison of all four memoranda, both in terms of their actual content and the time each was written, shows that there was no single plan whatsoever. The report on the Yugoslav party was most likely required by the incipient conflict with Belgrade, while the remaining three memoranda were composed some time later, probably in connection with the evolving situation in Yugoslavia.[86] It may be that the three memoranda were prepared as 'spare' accusations to be used if the

Czechoslovak, Polish and Hungarian leaders refused to participate in the attack against Belgrade. Since they did join in, these reserves proved superfluous.

Finally, new documents have offered an unprecedented opportunity to recreate in detail the preparations for, and holding of, the second Cominform conference in June 1948.[87] In particular, it has transpired that the Kremlin carefully prearranged the decisions of the conference in the belief that the Yugoslavs would not attend, and so the open registration of the split would be inevitable. In the lobbies the Soviet delegation spread rumours that the Yugoslav leadership was infiltrated by agents of Western intelligence services, although there was no mention of this in the speeches at the conference or in its resolutions. The documents demonstrate that Traicho Kostov, a leading Bulgarian communist, and Togliatti were especially zealous in taking up this idea.[88] The conference resolutions, entirely prompted by the Soviets and dutifully supported by the delegates of all attending communist parties, underlay the key tendencies which had determined the origins and nature of the conflict. As a result, the Soviet bloc was torn asunder, with a communist regime for the first time finding itself in open rebellion with the Kremlin.

Conclusion

What do the recently declassified archives tell us about the Soviet-Yugoslav rift? First, they demonstrate conclusively that relations between the two countries, and between Stalin and Tito, were generally sound before late 1947 and early 1948. The roots of the crisis are, therefore, less deep than the former Yugoslav version would have us believe. Tensions no doubt existed, but in the immediate post-war years Yugoslavia was, in essence, a steadfast ideological and political ally of the USSR. Second, there were many twists and turns in the Soviet reaction to Yugoslav policies; at times, Stalin and Molotov adopted a conciliatory stance and at others were more reproachful and severe. There does not appear to be a long-standing Stalinist 'plan' to excommunicate the Yugoslavs. The Soviet leaders, in a sense, stumbled into the clash. Third, the concrete causes of the split were Belgrade's own interests in south-eastern Europe, especially its designs on Albania, which contradicted decisions taken by Moscow as the Soviet bloc's directive centre. Fourth, what really alarmed the Soviets was Tito's inclination to take decisive steps without prior sanction from the Kremlin. For Stalin, this was a major breach of Marxist-Leninist 'proletarian internationalism': the leading role of the USSR, and by definition of its great 'Leader', was absolutely binding on all communist parties and could not be flouted. Ultimately, Belgrade was prepared to break this unwritten law of the emerging Soviet bloc. In this lay the Yugoslavs' 'national communism' – a stance that was unacceptable to Stalin and his model of the 'socialist camp'.

Notes

*This article was translated from the Russian by John Morison. The Phillips-Price Memorial Trust kindly funded the translation.

1. See Leonid Gibianskii, 'The 1948 Soviet-Yugoslav Clash: Historiographic Versions and New Archival Sources', in Jasna Fischer et al. (eds), *Jugoslavija v hladni vojni – Yugoslavia in the Cold War* (Ljubljana, 2004), pp. 49–70.
2. For an English translation (and the Russian originals) of these accusations, see Giuliano Procacci et al. (eds), *The Cominform: Minutes of the Three Conferences 1947/1948/1949* (Milan, 1994), pp. 610–21, 962–9.
3. Among the most important sources are *Pisma CK KPJ i pisma CK SKP(b)* (Belgrade, 1948); Vladimir Dedijer, *Josip Broz Tito: Prilozi za biografiju* (Belgrade, 1953); for English translations of some of this material, see Royal Institute of International Affairs, *The Soviet-Yugoslav Dispute* (London, 1948); Stephen Clissold (ed.), *Yugoslavia and the Soviet Union, 1939–1973: A Documentary Survey* (London, 1975). See also, Vladimir Dedijer, *Dokumenti 1948*, vols 1– 3 (Belgrade, 1979); Vladimir Dedijer, *Novi prilozi za biografiju Josipa Broza Tita*, vol. 2 (Rijeka, 1981) and vol. 3 (Belgrade, 1984); Edvard Kardelj, *Borba za priznanje i nezavisnost nove Jugoslavije 1944–1957: Sećanja* (Ljubljana-Belgrade, 1980), [in English as *Reminiscences: The Struggle for Recognition and Independence of the New Yugoslavia, 1944–1957* (London, 1982)]; Aleš Bebler, *Kako sam hitao: Sećanja* (Belgrade, 1982). Only Milovan Djilas, *Conversations with Stalin* (London, 1962) exceeded the limits of Yugoslav propaganda.
4. See, especially, Clissold (ed.), *Yugoslavia and the Soviet Union*; and, to some extent, Adam Ulam, *Titoism and the Cominform* (Cambridge, MA, 1952).
5. See Vojislav Koštunica and Kosta Čavoški, *Stranački pluralizam ili monizam: Društveni pokreti i politički sistem u Jugoslaviji 1944–1949* (Belgrade, 1983); and Branko Petranović, *Politička i ekonomska osnova narodne vlasti u Jugoslaviji za vreme obnove* (Belgrade, 1969).
6. See L. Ia. Gibianskii, *Sovetskii Soiuz i novaia Iugoslaviia, 1947–1948 gg.* (Moscow, 1987), pp. 140–92; and Branko Petranović, *Istorija Jugoslavije 1918–1988*, vol. 3 (Belgrade, 1988), pp. 162–96, 199–200.
7. See L. Ia. Gibianskii, 'Ot pervogo ko vtoromu soveshchaniiu Kominforma', in G.M. Adibekov et al. (eds), *Soveshchaniia Kominforma, 1947, 1948, 1949: Dokumenty i materialy* (Moscow, 1998), p. 352; and T.V. Volokitina et al. (eds.), *Sovetskii faktor v Vostochnoi Evrope, 1944–1953: Dokumenty*, vol. 1 (Moscow, 1999), docs 60, 66.
8. For details, see Clissold (ed.), *Yugoslavia and the Soviet Union*, docs 62–73; and *Otnosheniia Rossii (SSSR) s Iugoslaviei, 1941–1945 gg.: Dokumenty i materialy* (Moscow, 1998), docs 98, 100, 126.

9. Gibianskii, *Sovetskii Soiuz i novaia Iugoslaviia*; Nikola Popović, *Jugoslovensko-sovjetski odnosi u drugom svetskom ratu (1941–1945)* (Belgrade, 1988).

10. See the Russian State Archive of Social and Political History (RGASPI), f. 575, op. 1, d. 41, ll. 2–24.

11. See, for example, Zhdanov's report in *Pravda*, 7 November 1946; and Molotov's report a year later in *Pravda*, 7 November 1947.

12. See the memorandum on Yugoslavia cited in note 10, and also the summary report comparing the characteristics of all the People's Democracies in RGASPI, f. 575, op. 1, d. 3, ll. 103–16.

13. Adibekov et al. (eds), *Soveshchaniia Kominforma*, pp. 322–3, 326. The assertion that the Yugoslavs opposed the Soviet plan to create the Cominform, made by Kardelj, *Borba za priznanje*, pp. 110–11, is a complete fiction.

14. Ia. Mirov, 'Kompartii Evropy v bor'be za mir, demokratiiu i nezavisimost' narodov', *Bol'shevik*, no. 21 (1947), pp. 53, 55; and V. Moshetov and V. Lesakov, 'O demokraticheskikh preobrazovaniiakh v stranakh novoi demokratii', *Bol'shevik*, no. 22 (1947), pp. 38–44, 46–7.

15. G.P. Murashko et al. (eds), *Vostochnaia Evropa v dokumentakh rossiiskikh arkhivov, 1944–1953*, vol. 1 (Moscow and Novosibirsk, 1997), doc. 254.

16. Ibid., doc. 240, p. 705.

17. Clissold (ed.), *Yugoslavia and the Soviet Union*, docs 118, 120. The Russian originals of these Soviet accusations were first published in L. Ia. Gibianskii, 'Sekretnaia sovetsko-iugoslavskaia perepiska 1948 goda', *Voprosy istorii*, nos 4–5 (1992), p. 128, and no. 10 (1992), pp. 147–8.

18. Murashko et al. (eds), *Vostochnaia Evropa*, vol. 1, doc. 240, pp. 706–7.

19. *Otnosheniia Rossii (SSSR) s Iugoslaviei*, docs 553, 555, 556; RGASPI, f. 575, op. 1, d. 413, ll. 11, 68.

20. See Clissold (ed.), *Yugoslavia and the Soviet Union*, p. 43.

21. *Otnosheniia Rossii (SSSR) s Iugoslaviei*, doc. 497, pp. 379–80.

22. Josip Broz Tito's Archives: The Marshal of Yugoslavia's Office (AJBT-KMJ), I-3–b/616; Foreign Policy Archive of the Russian Federation (AVP RF), f. 0144, op. 30, pap. 118, d. 10, l. 6; d. 15, l. 26.

23. See Leonid Gibianskii, 'The Soviet Bloc and the Initial Stage of the Cold War: Archival Documents on Stalin's Meetings with the Communist Leaders of Yugoslavia and Bulgaria, 1946–1948', *Cold War International History Project Bulletin*, no. 10 (1998), pp. 112–20, 124.

24. AVP RF, f. 0144, op. 30, pap. 118, d. 16, ll. 75, 109–10.

25. Branko Petranović (ed.), *Zapisnici sa sednica Politbiroa Centralnog komiteta KPJ (11 jun 1945 – 7 jul 1948)* (Belgrade, 1995), p. 176; AVP RF, f. 0144, op. 30, pap. 118, d. 16, ll. 75–6; f. 06, op. 9, pap. 81, d. 1284, l. 7.

26. Former Archive of the Federal Secretariat for Foreign Affairs of Yugoslavia (now the Archive of the Foreign Ministry of Serbia and Montenegro), Political Archives (ASSIP-PA) (1947), f. IV, Str. Pov. 1234; AJBT-KMJ, I-3–b/639, ll. 2–3.

27. *Izvestiia*, 29 July 1947 and *Borba*, 30 July 1947.
28. See, for example, the Archive of Yugoslavia (AJ), f. 507, CK SKJ, IX, 119/I-12; 119/I-15; 119/I-27.
29. Bebler, *Kako sam hitao*, pp. 233–4; Dedijer, *Novi prilozi*, vol. 3, pp. 260–2; and Djoko Tripković, 'Početak i eskalacija sukoba Tito-Staljin prvih meseci 1948 godine', in *1948 – Jugoslavija i Kominform: pedeset godina kasnije* (Belgrade, 1998), p. 53.
30. RGASPI, f. 558, op. 11, d. 108, l. 15.
31. Djoko Tripković, 'Jugoslavija i Maršalov plan', *Istorija 20. veka*, nos 1–2 (1990), pp. 63–70. The same argument was repeated in his 'Početak i eskalacija', pp. 85–94.
32. The document was published in G. Takhnenko, 'Anatomiia odnogo politicheskogo resheniia', *Mezhdunarodnaia zhizn'*, no. 5 (1992), p. 125, and is reproduced in English in Scott Parrish, 'The Marshall Plan, Soviet-American Relations, and the Division of Europe', in Norman Naimark and Leonid Gibianskii (eds), *The Establishment of Communist Regimes in Eastern Europe, 1944–1949* (Boulder, CO, 1997), p. 279.
33. Takhnenko, 'Anatomiia', pp. 113–27. For more details, see Mikhail Narinsky and Scott Parrish, *New Evidence on the Soviet Rejection of the Marshall Plan, 1947: Two Reports*, Cold War International History Project, Working Paper, no. 9 (Washington DC, 1994).
34. Tripković, 'Početak i eskalacija', p. 53.
35. For details on the confrontation between the Western allies and Yugoslavia over the Trieste crisis, see Bogdan C. Novak, *Trieste, 1941–1954: The Ethnic, Political, and Ideological Struggle* (Chicago and London, 1970); and Roberto G. Rabel, *Between East and West: Trieste, the United States, and the Cold War, 1941–1954* (Durham and London, 1988).
36. *Pisma CK KPJ i pisma CK SKP(b)*, pp. 40–2; in English, Clissold (ed.), *Yugoslavia and the Soviet Union*, docs 110–12. See also AVP RF, f. 0144, op. 29, pap. 116, d. 16, ll. 7–8; AJ, f. 507, CK SKJ, IX, 1–I/22, ll.18, 52.
37. AVP RF, f. 0144, op. 29, pap. 116, d. 16, l. 7; AJ, f. 507, CK SKJ, IX, 1–I/22, l. 52; *Pisma CK KPJ i pisma CK SKP(b)*, p. 5.
38. See the works of Novak and Rabel in note 35.
39. Tito had hardly any cause to address the USSR in this manner, especially in public, regardless of his dissatisfaction with Moscow's occasionally conciliatory approach to its Western allies. See L. Ia. Gibianskii, 'Triestskii vopros v kontse Vtoroi mirovoi voiny (1944–1945)', *Slavianovedenie*, no. 4 (2001), pp. 8–24.
40. Gibianskii, 'The Soviet Bloc', pp. 119, 121.
41. AJBT-KMJ, I-3–b/634; AVP RF, f. 0144, op. 30, pap. 118, d. 16, ll. 28–9.
42. Murashko et al. (eds), *Vostochnaia Evropa*, vol. 1, doc. 240, p. 708.
43. Procacci et al. (eds), *The Cominform*, p. 461, note 10.
44. Murashko et al. (eds), *Vostochnaia Evropa*, vol. 1, doc. 240, p. 708.

45. Ibid.
46. Ibid., pp. 708–9.
47. RGASPI, f. 495, op. 74, d. 599, ll. 54, 57; d. 178, l. 1; d. 31, l. 5.
48. See, for example, 'Novye dokumenty o Velikoi Otechestvennoi voine', *Kommunist*, no. 7 (1975), p. 52.
49. Gibianskii, 'The Soviet Bloc', pp. 120–2.
50. AJBT-KMJ, I-3-b/651, ll. 1–5; ASSIP-PA, 1947, f. IV, Str. Pov. 1765; RGASPI, f. 77, op. 3, d. 99, l. 2.
51. RGASPI, f. 575, op. 1, d. 14, l. 42; d. 32, ll. 26–8; d. 39, ll. 21–7.
52. For more details, see Leonid Gibianskii, 'The Soviet-Yugoslav Conflict and the Soviet Bloc', in Francesca Gori and Silvio Pons (eds), *The Soviet Union and Europe in the Cold War, 1943–1953* (Basingstoke, 1996), pp. 227–9.
53. The assertion in Yugoslav historiography that a punitive Stalin chose Belgrade as headquarters of the Cominform is groundless. Archival materials testify that he wanted the Cominform to be located in Warsaw, but the Polish communists objected at the conference in Szklarska Poręba, while Kardelj and Djilas, on the spot, offered Belgrade as an alternative site for the Cominform. See Adibekov et al. (eds), *Soveshchaniia Kominforma*, pp. 325–7, 333.
54. The Soviet Politburo's resolution of 10 July 1948, 'On the Reorganisation of the CC CPSU (B) Apparatus', sharply narrowed Zhdanov's functions.
55. AJBT-KMJ, I-3-b/643, l. 3; RGASPI, f. 77, op. 4, Zhdanov's materials, Zhdanov to Stalin, 17 September 1947.
56. See L. Ia. Gibianskii, 'Dolgii put' k tainam: istoriografiia Kominforma', in Adibekov et al. (eds), *Soveshchaniia Kominforma*, pp. xxxvi–xxxviii.
57. Central State Archive, Sofia (TsDA), f. 146b, op. 4, a. e. 539, l. 9; and Gibianskii, 'The Soviet Bloc', p. 128.
58. Ivo Banac (ed.), *The Diary of Georgi Dimitrov, 1933–1949* (New Haven, CT and London, 2003), pp. 421–3, 425; AJBT-KMJ, I-2/17, ll. 69–70; AJ, f. 507, CK SKJ, IX, 1–II/79, l. 1; ASSIP-PA, 1947, f. IV, Str. Pov. 1685.
59. AJBT-KMJ, I-3–b/651, ll. 1–5; ASSIP-PA, 1947, f. IV, Str. Pov. 1765; RGASPI, f. 77, op. 3, d. 99, l. 8.
60. AJBT-KMJ, I-3–b/651, ll. 6, 10–11; also Djilas, *Conversations with Stalin*, pp. 143–6.
61. AJ, f. 507, CK SKJ, IX, 1/I-154, ll. 1–2; AJBT-KMJ, I-3-b/34, and I-3-b/651, ll. 9, 24; and 'Konflikt, kotorogo ne dolzhno bylo byt' (iz istorii sovetsko-iugoslavskikh otnoshenii)', *Vestnik Ministerstva inostrannykh del SSSR*, no. 6 (1990), pp. 57, 59.
62. Dimitrov's statement is in *Rabotnichesko delo*, 20 January 1948; Stalin's secret telegram to Dimitrov in response is in Banac (ed.), *The Diary*, p. 435; and public criticism in *Pravda*, 28 January 1948.
63. 'Konflikt', p. 59; *Rabotnichesko delo*, 29 January and 3 February 1948.

64. Archival documents dealing with this meeting have been published in Gibianskii, 'The Soviet Bloc', pp. 128–34; and Banac (ed.), *The Diary*, pp. 436–44.

65. Banac (ed.), *The Diary*, p. 444; TsDA, f. 147b, op. 2, a.e. 62, ll. 42–9; AJ, f. 507, CK SKJ, IX, 15/I-102; 15/I-104.

66. Petranović (ed.), *Zapisnici*, pp. 234, 238–40, 242–4.

67. AJ, f. 507, CK SKJ, IX, 1/I-135, 1/I-163, 1/I-164, 1/I-166, 1/I-169; RGASPI, f. 17, op. 128, d. 472, ll. 78–9, 84–6; AJBT-KMJ, I-3–b/35, ll. 1, 3.

68. AJBT-KMJ, I-2/35.

69. See Gibianskii, 'Sekretnaia', *Voprosy istorii*, nos 4–5 (1992), p. 135, note 25; TsDA, f. 147b, op. 2, a.e. 1083, ll. 1–3.

70. See L. Ia. Gibianskii and V.K. Volkov, 'Na poroge pervogo raskola v "sotsialisticheskom lagere": Peregovory rukovodiashchikh deiatelei SSSR, Bolgarii i Iugoslavii, 1948 g.', *Istoricheskii arkhiv*, no. 4 (1997), docs 4, 6, 7; and AVP RF, f. 0144, op. 32, pap. 128, d. 8, l. 107; pap. 129, d. 18, ll. 7–8.

71. 'Konflikt', p. 60; AVP RF, f. 06, op. 10, pap. 1, d. 2, ll. 102–3.

72. The reports by Lavrent'ev and Sidorovich are analysed in I.V. Bukharkin and L. Ia. Gibianskii, 'Pervye shagi konflikta', *Rabochii klass i sovremennyi mir*, no. 5 (1990), pp. 159–63.

73. AVP RF, f. 0144, op. 31, pap. 124, d. 29, ll. 7–9.

74. 'Posetiteli kremlevskogo kabineta I. V. Stalina: Zhurnaly (tetradi) zapisi lits, priniatykh pervym gensekom 1924–1953 gg.', *Istoricheskii arkhiv*, nos 5–6 (1996), p. 29.

75. Gibianskii, 'Sekretnaia', doc. 1.

76. Ibid., doc. 3; AVP RF, f. 06, op. 10, pap. 1, d. 2, l. 102.

77. See these documents in English in Clissold (ed.), *Yugoslavia and the Soviet Union*, docs 117, 118.

78. This part of the correspondence is in ibid., docs 119–23.

79. Murashko et al. (eds), *Vostochnaia Evropa*, vol. 1, doc. 267.

80. RGASPI, f. 17, op. 128, d. 1163, l. 9; see also l. 16.

81. RGASPI, f. 77, op. 3, d. 100, ll. 6, 14.

82. RGASPI, f. 17, op. 128, d. 1165, l. 79; and several documents from the Archive of the President of the Russian Federation (APRF, f. 3, op. 3, d. 198, ll. 55–9) quoted in Michail Narinskij, 'Stalin, Togliatti e Thorez (1944–1948)', in Francesca Gori and Silvio Pons (eds), *Dagli Archivi di Mosca: L'URSS, il Cominform e il PCI (1943–1951)* (Rome, 1998), pp. 82–3.

83. For more details, see Gibianskii, 'The Soviet-Yugoslav Conflict', pp. 239–40.

84. Murashko et al. (eds), *Vostochnaia Evropa*, vol. 1, docs 269, 272, 274.

85. S. Lel'chuk and E.I. Pivovar (eds), *SSSR i kholodnaia voina* (Moscow, 1995), pp. 89–97; and T.V. Volokitina, *'Kholodnaia voina' i sotsial-demokratiia Vostochnoi Evropy, 1944–1948 gg. (Ocherki istorii)* (Moscow, 1998), pp. 69–72.

86. For more details, see L. Ia. Gibianskii, 'Forsirovanie sovetskoi blokovoi politiki', in N.I. Egorova and A.O. Chubar'ian (eds), *Kholodnaia voina. 1945–1963 gg. Istoricheskaia retrospektiva: Sbornik statei* (Moscow, 2003), pp. 171–4.

87. The preparations for the conference are analysed in Silvio Pons, 'The Twilight of the Cominform', in Procacci et al. (eds), *The Cominform*, pp. 483–503. Archival documents dealing with the conference proper are published in ibid., pp. 506–641; and Adibekov et al. (eds), *Soveshchaniia Kominforma*, pp. 399–505.

88. See Adibekov et al. (eds), *Soveshchaniia Kominforma*, pp. 483, 485, 488.

The SED, German Communism and the June 1953 Uprising: New Trends and New Research*

Matthew Stibbe

All kinds of details to report. First of all a thought. What jubilation there was that day at the Party Congress, when the PEOPLE'S Police marched into the hall. No longer *against* the workers – your brothers and sons, *your* protectors!! And now? They are more hated than the Russians, who maintain discipline and don't shoot to kill…

Victor Klemperer, diary entry, 2 July 1953[1]

On 16 June 1953 construction workers on the prestigious Stalinallee building site in East Berlin downed tools and marched on the House of Ministries, the headquarters of government, to demonstrate their opposition to the new work norms announced by the ruling Socialist Unity Party (SED) in the previous month. This event proved to be the starting point for a wave of strikes and protests that engulfed virtually the whole of East Germany by 17 June and led to the first full-scale uprising against communist rule in the post-1945 Soviet bloc. Party officials, union leaders and supporters of the East German regime were taken very much by surprise by these events. Only three months earlier Stalin had died; now it seemed as if the German Democratic Republic (GDR), the first experiment in socialism on German soil, might die with him. Even after the uprising had been crushed by Soviet tanks, thus forestalling any moves towards the dismantling of socialism in East Germany, many GDR loyalists felt disoriented and let down by the party. How had it come to this? How could the workers revolt against the 'Workers' and Peasants' State'?

Similar questions may well have been on the lips of many communist veterans in the summer and autumn of 1989, when the GDR was again faced with a mass movement demanding political reforms and the end of the SED power monopoly. On 31 August 1989, for instance, the long-serving head of the Stasi or East German secret police, Erich Mielke, wondered aloud at a meeting with his regional commanders whether there would be another 17 June. This time, however, there was no Soviet military intervention to quell the unrest and prevent the collapse of communist rule.[2] More recently, 1953 has been at the forefront of discussions about the origins and nature of the East German dictatorship, and in particular about the relationship between the SED/state hierarchy and the ordinary people who had to accommodate themselves to living under communism.[3] One German author even claimed, in a book published on the fiftieth anniversary of the uprising, that 17 June was a 'milestone' in the post-war history of Germany and of Eastern Europe as a whole: '[It] is proof that the most dangerous moment for autocratic regimes is not the point of greatest repression, but the point where they are forced to release the pressure – a situation which the Soviet system experienced on several occasions and which ultimately led to its downfall.'[4]

The purpose of this essay is to examine changing trends in historical writing on 17 June 1953 since the collapse of the GDR in 1989 and the opening up of East German (and, to a more limited extent, Soviet) archives. In particular, two main themes can be identified. First, the uprising is no longer regarded simply as a 'workers' revolt', rooted in opposition to the new work norms, but rather as the product of a much broader level of popular dissatisfaction with the SED regime and its attempts to impose socialism by force on the German people.[5] Many farmers, for instance, were already voting with their feet against the collectivisation of agriculture by fleeing to West Germany via the escape hatch of West Berlin. The sealing of the inner-German border in May 1952, and the compulsory 'evacuation' of tens of thousands of local residents from the new five-kilometre frontier zone with West Germany, also caused mass resentment. Strikes and go-slows were commonplace in factories in 1952 and 1953, particularly after what was perceived to be an unfair distribution of Christmas bonuses in December 1952. Above all, protestors in all parts of East Germany on 17 June were united in their demand for free elections and the resignation of the government. There were also calls for the abolition of the pro-communist people's police (*Volkspolizei*) and its paramilitary wing, the so-called *Kasernierte Volkspolizei* (KVP or people's police in barracks), and police stations were indeed frequently targeted by the demonstrators.[6]

Second, from the summer of 1952 to the summer of 1953 it now seems that the SED leadership was pursuing its own hard-line agenda, not simply following Moscow's orders, and indeed actually ignoring advice from the Kremlin on several occasions, both before and after Stalin's death in March 1953. Indeed, the whole crisis may have been caused by the GDR's increasingly independent course from July 1952, combined with a series of internal power struggles within the East German Politburo itself, which led, ultimately, to an open bid to depose Walter Ulbricht as de facto leader of the SED in late June and early July 1953. However, Ulbricht was perhaps cleverer than his opponents. His aims were to thwart any Soviet moves towards abandoning the GDR in favour of a deal with the West on German reunification, a possibility which was still very much on the cards in the early 1950s, and at the same time to strengthen his own position inside the SED, which was threatened by the emergence of potential rivals. In both these aims he had been successful by the end of 1953, although arguably his status as leader of the party was not entirely secure until 1958, or even 1961.[7]

In what follows I will review the latest literature on June 1953 in light of the two propositions above: namely that 1953 was a popular uprising led by workers, but involving broader sections of East German society; and that it was caused by the uncompromising attitude not of Moscow, but of the SED and its ruling elite. I will also consider how veteran communists and senior figures within the SED later tried to come to terms with the idea that the people had revolted against the system. Were they privately as cynical as Bertolt Brecht, who argued in his famous poem that if the people did not like the government, the simplest thing would be for the government to dissolve the people and elect a new one? Or did they genuinely believe their own propaganda, which suggested that June 1953 had been a 'fascist provocation' caused by imperialist agents and class traitors acting under orders from Washington and Bonn, and not by any particular faults in the system?

The Origins of the Crisis

While there had already been many serious rifts between the East German people and their communist rulers before 1952, especially over reparations policy and relations with the USSR, a new low point was reached with the 'accelerated construction of socialism', announced by Ulbricht at the second party conference of the SED on 9–12 July 1952. This proclamation set in train a series of measures which were intended to transform the GDR into a socialist society along Soviet lines, while rooting out real and suspected enemies of the state and the party. In the economic sphere, this meant a ruthless campaign against independent farmers and small businessmen, who were forced to join new agricultural cooperatives (*Landwirtschaftliche Produktio nsgenossenschaften*, or LPGs), causing many to leave for the West. It also meant concentrating on investment in heavy industry, and improving productivity rates in this sector, while reducing the output of consumer goods. In the short term at least, workers and their families would feel the pinch, as shortages of food and other basic household products were almost certain to occur. Indeed, a key demand in June 1953 was for the reduction of the prices charged to ordinary consumers in the state-owned retail chain, the *Handelsorganisation* (HO).[8]

In the ideological sphere, the 'accelerated construction of socialism' led to increased pressure on artists and intellectuals to fall into line with the requirements of 'socialist realism'. The leading role of the party would have to be accepted in the arts, the universities and in the field of scientific research. Persecution of the churches was also stepped up: for instance, religious education was banned from secondary schools, several leading church officials were arrested and members of the evangelical youth group, *Junge Gemeinde*, were blacklisted and expelled from universities. Again, those whose careers or livelihoods were threatened by these measures were forced to consider moving to the West.[9]

Any prospects of unity with West Germany were now curtailed, not only by the sealing of the inner-German border in May 1952, but also by the decision to abolish the traditional German *Länder* at the end of July and replace them with fourteen new *Bezirke*, or regional administrative districts, which had no basis in Germany's past, but were entirely arbitrary creations. Each *Bezirk* was ruled by a *Bezirksrat* (regional council), and the office of *Bezirkssekretär* (regional chief secretary) was placed in the hands of an SED member, thus ensuring full party control over regional and local government.[10]

Finally, the 'accelerated construction of socialism' was cemented by an increased emphasis on internal security and an intensification of the battle against crime, with policing and justice now identified as crucial instruments in the ongoing class struggle. 'Criminal' and 'subversive' elements were arrested in their thousands for petty offences against state property, and the prison population itself rose from around 45,000 at the end of 1952 to 66,317 in May 1953.[11] Other 'enemies of the people' were placed before the courts, charged with tax evasion or illegal currency and black market trading. A series of raids on private hotels and guest houses on the Baltic coast in early February 1953, for example, led to dozens of convictions and the confiscation of holiday properties which were then handed over to the FDGB (the SED-controlled trade union federation) to use as workers' convalescent homes.[12]

According to Peter Grieder, 'the imposition of this crash course in Sovietization united East Germans against the SED, unleashed dangerous social tensions and deepened divisions with the West'.[13] More than this, it caused problems in the SED's relationship with the 'friends' in Moscow, who took the unusual step of staying away from the second party conference in July 1952, in order to make clear their doubts about the applicability of Soviet-style methods to the GDR. By late 1952 evidence was growing that the 'accelerated construction of socialism' was not working, that it was unpopular and that it was causing a split between the SED and the workers it was supposed to represent. This, in turn, undermined the viability of the GDR as a separate state in the eyes of the Soviet leadership. Indeed, even Stalin himself seems to have had reservations about Ulbricht, noting in a conversation in October 1952 that the East German leader was a good communist but a poor theoretician: 'when he laid his fist on the table it was sometimes bigger than his head'.[14]

Nonetheless, the new measures do seem to have been popular with many senior SED functionaries, at least until the end of 1952. The intensification of the 'class struggle' against landowners, capitalists, priests and other 'enemies of the people' was almost bound to be popular with veteran communists, especially those who had been victims of Nazi persecution and had seen how the churches, the aristocracy and the property-owning middle classes had helped von Papen and then Hitler into power. It is thus not surprising that Ulbricht enjoyed genuine support among the party faithful in the summer of 1952. Indeed, as Catherine Epstein has argued convincingly, many veterans of the communist movement remained stuck in the world of the early 1930s, when they battled for control of the streets against the Nazis and the police, and for control of the labour movement against the 'class traitors' in the SPD and the free trade unions.[15] Attachment to the principles of Marxism-Leninism and faith in the absolute goodness of the Soviet cause gave them confidence that the course of history would prove them right, even though they knew how little support they had among the East German people and that they had to rely on the Soviet occupiers and the KVP to remain in power. The mentality of the KPD/SED in this period was summed up by Arthur Koestler, himself a party member between 1932 and 1938, in an essay published in 1950:

> What is the difference between a gun in the hands of a policeman and a gun in the hands of a member of the revolutionary working class? The difference ... is that the policeman is a lackey of the ruling class and his gun an instrument of oppression, whereas the same gun in the hands of a member of the revolutionary working class is an instrument of the liberation of the oppressed masses.[16]

Against such 'iron logic', it was, of course, very difficult to admit that the party could ever make mistakes or do harm to the workers' interests.

The Tension Mounts

During 1952 Ulbricht was clearly the driving force behind SED policy and possessed an authority above that of his comrades in the Politburo, especially in respect of decisions involving internal security and relations with the Soviet Union and West Germany. Nonetheless, by the end of 1952 some senior East German communists were beginning to voice concerns about certain aspects of Ulbricht's 'personal rule'. At various Politburo meetings, for instance, Fred Oelßner, Anton Ackermann, Friedrich Ebert and Prime Minister Otto Grotewohl all appeared to advocate a more moderate course in particular areas, although none of these figures openly challenged the concept of party hegemony or opposed the more general leftward shift in policy from July 1952. Tensions within the upper echelons of the SED increased following Stalin's death in March 1953, but were, of course, kept largely hidden from public view. One of the more persistent advocates of change was Rudolf Herrnstadt, editor of the party newspaper *Neues Deutschland*, who had spent the Nazi era in the Soviet Union and still had contacts in Moscow. His attempts, from the early 1950s onwards, to rescue the party from what he saw as Ulbricht's sectarian tendencies, were backed by Wilhelm Zaisser, the Minister of State Security and Spanish Civil War hero, who had also spent much time in the USSR before 1945 and had acquired Soviet citizenship.[17]

In the lower ranks of the party, too, discontent was mounting. Party activists were finding it increasingly difficult to sell government policy to discontented workers and housewives, many of whom were suffering materially as a result of the 'accelerated construction of socialism'. According to Volker Koop, living standards had fallen below the levels of 1947 by the end of 1952, and things only got worse after the Soviets refused to bail the GDR out of its economic difficulties in January 1953.[18] The final blow came on 9 April 1953, when the East German Council of Ministers announced a series of price rises and the withdrawal of food subsidies for two million 'non-essential' workers, followed on 28 May by a new government decree raising work norms in industry by 10 per cent. These measures were designed to stem the economic crisis caused by the fall in agricultural output and the subsequent problems in the food supply since 1952, and to improve living standards for ordinary workers in the long run. But they were introduced without any discussion in the broader ranks of the party or mass organisations like the FDGB, thus further fanning the flames of popular discontent.[19]

Matters came to a head in early June 1953, when the SED leaders Ulbricht, Grotewohl and Oelßner were called to Moscow. The new-found willingness of the USSR to negotiate with the Americans over Korea, coupled with British Prime Minister Churchill's proposal for an international conference to solve the 'German question' on 11 May 1953, had caused some consternation to the rulers in East Berlin, and they in turn sought assurances from the Kremlin about the Soviet leadership's continued commitment to the GDR. Such assurances, it became clear, would only be forthcoming if the SED agreed to adopt a New Course, especially with respect to economic policy. Or, as Vladimir Semyonov, the new Soviet High Commissioner, subsequently put it after the return of the SED leaders to East Berlin on 6 June: 'Do away with the *old* measures and replace them with *new* ones!'[20]

At its meeting on 9 June 1953, which Semyonov attended in person, the East German Politburo formally approved the New Course, thus signalling a major personal defeat for Ulbricht. An official communiqué, which was drafted by Herrnstadt and endorsed by the Council of Ministers on 11 June, admitted that the SED and the government had committed a 'series of errors' which they now intended to rectify. In particular, measures would be undertaken to raise 'the standards of living of the workers, intellectuals, peasants, artisans and other sections of the middle class'. Furthermore, farmers and hotel owners who had fled to the West were to be encouraged to return by the promise that their lands and property would be restored; and persecution of the *Junge Gemeinde* and other Christian groups would cease. Middle-class children would no longer be discriminated against when applying for university places, and travel restrictions between East and West Germany, and between the different sectors of Berlin, would be eased. Finally, the price increases and the withdrawal of food subsidies to two million people, announced in April, would also be reversed. Significantly, however, the communiqué made no mention of the 10 per cent increase in work norms which were due to come into effect on 30 June, so that workers still faced an effective cut in their wages.[21]

Once again, this abrupt reversal of policy did not go down well with the party rank and file, or with the broader East German population. Police and internal party reports from the Berlin area, for instance, suggest that the latest measures were widely interpreted as an admission of failure rather than as a positive sign that the party was willing to listen to the people. Few anticipated improvements in their standard of living. Workers in some factories suspected that the New Course would increase pressure on housing and other public services, and demanded assurances that 'asocial' and 'criminal' elements who had fled across the border would not be allowed to return to the GDR. Likewise, many housewives voiced their concern that the redistribution of ration cards would allow thousands of West Berliners to come to East Berlin in search of cheap food, leading to renewed shortages and longer queues outside shops.[22] In Wedding, West Berlin, a woman was reported to have spread a story she had heard on the U-Bahn that Ulbricht had shot himself 'because of the new measures'. And in Weißensee, East Berlin, a pensioner expressed her bitterness at the apparent imminent return of private landlords, seeing this as a slap in the face for loyal communists and GDR citizens like herself.[23]

As the above examples demonstrate, the increased work norms were not the only issue on people's minds in the run-up to 17 June, although they certainly remained a key concern for those engaged in the building trade and other forms of heavy manual labour.[24] On 14 June *Neues Deutschland*, then still under the editorship of Herrnstadt, published an article hinting that the government was about to make concessions here too. On 16 June, however, the official trade union paper, *Tribüne*, brought out a piece which defended the new work norms in no uncertain terms: 'The work quotas are not being raised in order to force down wages but in order to produce more, better, cheaper goods for the same amount of work but with more effective working methods'.[25] This was reportedly the spark that led the construction workers on the Stalinallee to stop work and march to the headquarters of the FDGB to demonstrate. From there they proceeded to the House of Ministries, where they issued a call for a general strike the following day unless immediate changes in government policy were implemented, including the cancellation of the new work norms, the granting of free elections and a guarantee against reprisals. They also sent representatives to the offices of RIAS, the American public radio station in West Berlin, which agreed to broadcast news of their demands – without openly endorsing the strike call – in the late afternoon of 16 June.[26] Thus began the first mass uprising against a communist state in post-1945 Europe.

The Uprising

The exact course of events in East Berlin and elsewhere in the GDR on 17 June 1953 has now been reconstructed in the minutest detail and does not need to be repeated here at any great length. The figures speak for themselves. In East Berlin an estimated 90,000 people poured on to the streets, and throughout East Germany the number of demonstrators swelled to around 418,000. Strikes were called in 593 factories, with just under half a million workers, or 5 per cent of the workforce, taking part.[27] Outside Berlin, the areas most seriously affected were the industrial regions of Halle, Magdeburg and Leipzig, traditionally strongholds of the German left and the workers' movement; but there were also disturbances in many smaller towns as well.[28] In some places angry crowds targeted buildings belonging to the SED or affiliated organisations, such as the FDGB and the FDJ (East German Youth), looting them and burning them to the ground. In other places they attempted to take over prisons and free political prisoners. The SED-controlled media, for instance, made much of the fact that in Halle, 'fascist provocateurs' had succeeded in storming the local jail and releasing a woman prisoner, Erna Dorn, who was alleged to be a former officer at the Ravensbrück concentration camp and was serving a fifteen-year prison sentence for various crimes against humanity.[29] Rumours were also spread that the town of Görlitz had been taken over temporarily by former Nazis.[30]

Meanwhile, although the larger demonstrations were crushed by Soviet tanks in the latter half of 17 June, isolated disturbances continued for up to a week afterwards. In total, figures from GDR sources suggest that 373 towns and villages were in a state of unrest between 17 and 23 June, including 113 out of 181 district towns and 14 out of 15 regional capitals.[31] Only the northern *Bezirke*, those concentrated in the former state of Mecklenburg, were relatively unaffected, as were *Bezirk* Suhl in Thuringia and *Bezirk* Karl-Marx-Stadt in Saxony.[32] Elsewhere there was evidence of support for the aims of the rebels, even in areas at some distance from the main centres of the uprising. In Neustrelitz, for example, a 15-year-old schoolboy was arrested on 20 June 1953 for distributing flysheets calling for strikes and work stoppages.[33] In other places, including Zossen, Jessen and Mühlhausen, rural communities reacted to the news from Berlin by organising their own spontaneous demonstrations, which, in the latter two instances, had to be dispersed forcibly by Soviet troops. The response of farmers to the uprising was quite mixed, however, and most reacted passively, preferring to await the outcome of further events. Intimidation and fear of violence also stopped the rebellion from spreading; indeed an SED report of July 1953 noted that, in some areas, workers on collective farms had formed their own defence organisations against the 'provocation' in the countryside and had even threatened to kill returning private landowners rather than give them back their land and property. Nonetheless, 58 collective farms and been dissolved and another 112 were on the verge of collapse by 30 June.[34]

The number of civilians who lost their lives during and immediately following the events of June 1953 is still unclear, even after the opening of the relevant state and party archives. At least 51 demonstrators are estimated to have been killed by Soviet forces and the *Volkspolizei* on 17 and 18 June – some shot and some crushed to death by tanks.[35] Members of the *Volkspolizei* were themselves attacked by angry crowds, and a handful died or were seriously assaulted.[36] By 22 June, up to twenty people had been summarily executed after appearing before Soviet military tribunals.[37] Among them were at least three policemen, who were found guilty of disobeying orders, as well as two 17-year-olds and one 15-year-old, who had supposedly taken part as ringleaders in demonstrations.[38] However, Soviet tank commanders were apparently under orders to avoid civilian casualties wherever possible and it is now accepted that the number of deaths was much lower than the several hundred reported by some Western sources during the Cold War era.[39]

Even so, in the aftermath of the uprising about 6,000 people were taken into police custody, a figure which rose to between 8,000 and 10,000 by 1 July 1953, and to 13,000 by 1 August 1953.[40] In addition, several hundred anti-communist 'suspects' were arrested by Soviet enforcement agencies and deported to Siberia; they were released along with the last remaining POWs from the Second World War only after Adenauer's visit to Moscow in 1955.[41] Significantly, internal GDR reports suggest that at least 70 per cent of those detained for questioning by the *Volkspolizei* were ordinary East German workers, including some SED members. Less than 5 per cent were citizens of West Berlin or the Federal Republic.[42] Most of the detainees were released without charge, but East German courts imposed two death sentences and 1,524 prison sentences, ranging from up to a year (in 546 cases) and up to five years (in 824 cases), to ten years and over (in 13 cases) and life (in 3 cases). Only 76 of the people who stood trial in the GDR for offences allegedly committed in association with the June uprising were acquitted by the courts.[43] The purpose of these trials was to intimidate potential opponents of the regime as well as to punish the individuals concerned. East German justice now had an even more overtly political ring to it, as the death sentence passed on Erna Dorn, the alleged 'Kommandeuse'of Ravensbrück, on 22 June, clearly shows.[44]

The Aftermath

After 22 June, unrest seemed to move from the streets into the factories. Stoppages, go-slows and absenteeism continued for several weeks, with the people's police apparently powerless to intervene.[45] On 23 June, for instance, Ulbricht, Grotewohl, Herrnstadt and Ebert were all heckled as they addressed groups of disgruntled workers in factories in different parts of East Berlin. Ulbricht was accompanied by dozens of bodyguards and police as he tried to talk to employees at the state-owned machine tool factory '7 October' in Berlin-Weißensee, but he was still greeted with shouts, boos and cat calls. An SED member who was present complained about the lack of freedom of speech: 'We have always upheld the right to ... criticise. But now things have got so bad that we no longer dare to open our mouths'. Another worker posed the following question to Ulbricht: 'If I don't do my job properly, then I get the sack. You have publicly admitted that you have failed in your political work, but you are still here. So what will you do now?'[46] None of this appeared in the official party press, of course, which was at pains to deny any further evidence of unrest once the Soviets had succeeded in crushing the 'attempted fascist putsch'. *Neues Deutschland*, for example, commented on 24 June 1953:

The workers, employees and members of the intelligentsia in these factories greeted the representatives of the Socialist Unity Party with a hearty applause... All four meetings ended with thousands of workers declaring their unanimous and categorical rejection of the ... Putsch as an attempt by fascists and their West Berlin backers to prevent the implementation of the latest decrees issued by the government of the German Democratic Republic, and to start a new war.[47]

Prominent academics like Ernst Engelberg were also mobilised to provide 'scientific proof' of the 'fascist' character of the June uprising and to ensure a uniform approach among East German scholars. As early as 26 June 1953, Engelberg told the SED historians group in Leipzig:

We must show that there is method in their madness, that the parallels between *Kristallnacht* in November 1938 and the 17 June [uprising] are more than superficial... Who can forget the columns of SA thugs and murderers from the period before 1933?... The same rabid mindless infatuation, the same violent rowdiness, the same raucous mendacity. No one shall come along and claim any connection between the 16 and 17 June and the real workers' movement.[48]

While the SED seemed determined to deny any responsibility for the uprising, an important question mark still hung over Ulbricht and his position as party General Secretary. The events of 17–18 June, when the top SED leaders were forced to take refuge in the Soviet military headquarters at Karlshorst in the eastern outskirts of Berlin, had seriously damaged Ulbricht's standing in the eyes of his comrades and among the population as a whole. For a time it looked as if his days in office were numbered and that a majority in the Politburo was now against him.[49] However, he survived, partly because of the ineptitude of his rivals, who failed to seize the right moment on 8 July 1953 to push Herrnstadt forward as their candidate, and partly because at some point shortly after this Moscow switched sides, deciding to ditch any plans they may have had to force a leadership change in East Berlin. Thenceforth it was relatively plain sailing for Ulbricht. On 18 July 1953 Zaisser, who had already been forced to undergo self-criticism for his alleged lack of vigilance in the run-up to the June uprising, was formerly relieved of his post as Minister of State Security. Five days later Zaisser, Herrnstadt, Elli Schmidt, Hans Jendretzky and Anton Ackermann were removed from the Politburo for 'factionalism' and undermining party unity, and in January 1954 Zaisser and Herrnstadt were also expelled from the SED, never to be readmitted.[50]

The arrest of the Soviet Minister of Interior, Lavrentii Beria, in Moscow on 26 June 1953, and the subsequent 'revelation' that he had plotted, among other things, to dismantle socialism in the GDR, may also have helped Ulbricht's cause. At a Central Committee meeting on 24 July 1953, for instance, Ulbricht deliberately implied that Zaisser and Herrnstadt had been secretly colluding with Beria in pursuit of a 'capitulatory policy which would have ended in the restoration of capitalism', and cited alleged findings of the Central Committee of the CPSU to this effect.[51] However, there is no hard evidence that Beria was in direct contact with the anti-Ulbricht faction in East Berlin, and even if he had been, Herrnstadt and Zaisser denied this to the end. Neither did the Soviets ever make such allegations, sticking to the line that Beria had acted alone.[52]

Once confirmed back in power, Ulbricht's main priority was to increase the strength of the state's internal security organs. Particular attention was paid to the Stasi, which was deemed to have failed badly under Zaisser. If major 'provocations' were to be avoided in the future, this would have to be, first and foremost, the task of the secret police, using its intelligence arms inside and outside the GDR. The KVP was also built up even further, becoming the nucleus of the NVA, the National People's Army, in 1956. At the same time, the party was purged of those suspected of having social democratic or 'defeatist' tendencies. Max Fechner, ex-SPD member and Minister of Justice, was not only sacked but actually imprisoned for two articles he published in *Neues Deutschland* on 30 June and 2 July, defending the right to strike and advocating a milder treatment of demonstrators. The SED leadership now lived in constant fear of another 'Day X', so much so that on the first two anniversaries of the uprising, all police units, including the KVP and the special 'combat groups of the working class' (*Kampfgruppen der Arbeiterklasse*), were ordered to remain on a 'state of heightened readiness'.[53] Meanwhile, in 1960 Ulbricht, Grotewohl and other SED leaders moved from their original residences in the Berlin suburb of Pankow to a new, highly secluded and well-guarded estate at Wandlitz in Brandenburg, where they would be more effectively protected in the event of further public disturbances. Ernst Wollweber, Zaisser's replacement as Minister of State Security, who was himself purged in 1957, later recalled that the 'fright of June 17, 1953 still haunted' Ulbricht, years after the event.[54]

The building of the Berlin Wall in August 1961 was undoubtedly another symptom of Ulbricht's fears. But communist rule after 1953 did not depend on political repression alone. Rather, the SED was also forced into making a number of important concessions to workers and peasants in the aftermath of the June uprising. For instance, workers benefited from the new tendency to 'manage' disputes over pay and conditions of service within individual state-owned companies, giving them considerable, if largely hidden, negotiating power at the plant or factory level, including an informal right to consultation over company social policy.[55] Independent farmers were also able to wage a hidden campaign against state interference in village life, and were aided in this by party functionaries at the grass roots, who decided not to push through collectivisation in areas where it was unpopular with local people. Even after a renewed collectivisation campaign in 1959–60, many LPGs 'existed in little more than name', according to Corey Ross.[56] Finally, a series of price reductions in state-owned shops, and wage increases for the lowest paid, meant that by September 1954 an estimated 3.7 billion East German marks had been redistributed to the general population.[57]

The Soviets also loosened their economic grip on the GDR to some extent, keeping their promise to end reparations payments by 1 January 1954, and providing financial aid to help improve living standards for ordinary workers.[58] Why did they save Ulbricht instead of replacing him with Herrnstadt? According to Peter Grieder, on 8 July 1953 Ulbricht 'came within a hair's breadth of losing the SED leadership'.[59] We will probably never know for sure why he survived, but one contributory factor may have been Moscow's concern that unseating him would be perceived both in Germany and internationally as a concession to 'fascist' rebels, and therefore as a sign of impotence in the face of continued 'provocations' from the West. There were also fears – not altogether unfounded – that unrest could spill over into neighbouring communist states if the June uprising was seen to succeed. The Kremlin's longer-term plans for the GDR still remained unclear, however, and Ulbricht was obliged to pay lip service to the New Course at least until June 1955, even if he was able to resume many of his more hard-line polices before then.[60]

Conclusion: Consequences

The period June–July 1953 was a remarkable one in the history of post-war East Germany. For a few short weeks 'the grip of Stalinism was loosened', as Gareth Pritchard puts it.[61] The evidence emerging from police and party records also justifies the thesis that what took place was a 'people's uprising' against communism and not simply a 'workers' uprising' in reaction to the raised work norms. The strikes and demonstrations were led by workers in most cases, but also involved farmers, youths, housewives, schoolchildren and members of the middle class. Having said this, the extent of popular support for the uprising should not be exaggerated, and nor should its revolutionary potential. Only half a million people (in a population of just over 17 million) participated directly in the protests, and most of these were workers. Political self-determination was high on their agenda, but so too was economic hardship and hostility towards the privileges granted to the *Vopos* or people's police. It seems likely that it was these material resentments that caused the uprising to become political, rather than vice versa, a point which was not entirely lost on the SED and its Soviet masters. The repression which followed, while fierce, was also tempered by compromise on the economic front.[62]

There were of course other reasons why the 17 June uprising failed to develop into a full-blown revolution against communist rule on a par with 1989. The most important factor was the readiness and ability of Soviet tanks to intervene to save the GDR from collapse, and the decision by the Western powers in Berlin – and by the Adenauer government in Bonn – to restrict their reactions to verbal protests.[63] On top of this, the uprising found little support among East German students, intellectuals and church leaders, most of whom adopted a passive stance which stopped short of endorsing the strikers' demands. The main explanation for this seems to lie in anxieties about the possibility of a third world war, or a desire not to endanger the concessions announced by the party under the New Course.[64] Furthermore, at least a part of the intelligentsia had an intrinsic distrust of the masses and a respect for political realities. For instance, the historian Joachim Petzold, who was a student in East Berlin in 1953, later remembered: 'I wanted reform, took on board the [government's] assurance that it would come, and opposed the revolutionary unrest, because I believed nothing good would come of it and because it was pointless anyway in view of the intervention of Soviet troops'.[65]

As we have seen, many 'ordinary' East Germans also stood aloof from the events of 17 June, preferring to adopt a 'wait and see' policy. Some feared that political change would only lead to greater economic chaos, especially if the borders with West Germany and West Berlin were opened too wide. Others were put off by the violence of some of the demonstrators, or by the absence of clear leadership in the opposition camp. In particular, it is worth remembering that the original leaders of the old SPD and the bourgeois parties had already fled west or been driven underground through a series of arrests and denunciations in the late 1940s, leaving nobody of any standing who could negotiate with the SED on behalf of the rebels in June 1953.[66]

Last, but by no means least, the East German regime could still rely on hundreds of thousands of loyal supporters in 1953. For veteran communists, even those who had become disillusioned with SED rule, the idea of unification with Adenauer's West Germany, an unreformed capitalist state in which Nazism and militarism were allegedly still rampant, was too much to stomach. In the words of Victor Klemperer, a university professor and Holocaust survivor from an impeccable bourgeois-liberal background, who had converted to communism after 1945, the GDR was the 'lesser evil' and therefore had to be supported.[67] Bertolt Brecht, the playwright and theatre director, was even clearer in his condemnation of the uprising, in spite of harbouring private doubts. In an open letter to Ulbricht, published in *Neues Deutschland* on 23 June 1953, he wrote:

> On the morning of 17 June, when it became clear that the workers' demonstrations were being exploited for war-like purposes, I declared my solidarity with the Socialist Unity Party. I now hope that the provocateurs will be isolated and their communication networks destroyed. But I also hope that the workers who have demonstrated because of just grievances will not be tarred with the same brush, so that the urgent exchange of views regarding the mistakes made by all sides will not be prevented from the outset.[68]

Even so, there is no doubt that June 1953 did lasting damage to the unity and purpose of the party. As Brecht's words show, few veteran communists really believed the official line that this was simply a 'fascist provocation', with no real basis among the East German people themselves. Indeed, even as loyal a party functionary as Fritz Selbmann, who as GDR Minister of Industry played a leading role in the suppression of the uprising, showed signs of dissatisfaction with the way the party had dealt with the growing evidence of worker unrest in 1953. That part of his memoirs dealing with the early history of the GDR, although written shortly before his death in 1975, could not be published until after 1989, among other things because of a passage which revealed the extent of his (and others') misgivings over the price rises of April 1953 and the sudden reversal of that policy a few weeks later:

> In discussions about these issues I repeatedly expressed my opposition to the decisions [adopted by the party and approved by the Council of Ministers]. Of course I was aware that the extraordinarily high costs of investment in heavy industry placed considerable demands on the state budget and that these demands would have to be met by new tax measures and to some extent by price increases in state-owned retail outlets. Nonetheless I did not agree with all the decisions taken in March [and April] 1953.[69]

Likewise, Klemperer became increasingly frustrated by the apparent failure of the SED leadership to learn from its past mistakes or to reassess its policies in the wake of June 1953. In one his diary entries in August 1957, which has been published only recently, he noted: 'Everywhere it is power that is at stake, between states, between parties, within parties... At the moment things are evidently more brutal, Asiatic here than in the Adenauer state. But over there is the most blatant return to Nazism – here to Bolshevism. De profundissimis.'[70]

Open criticism of the party's role in June 1953 was rare, however. Only after 1990 did the post-communist PDS, the successor party to the SED, come to a different interpretation of the events of 1953. In 2003, for instance, the Executive Committee of the PDS issued a statement marking the fiftieth anniversary of the uprising, in which it declared:

> The SED's claim to be realising 'objective social interests' and to be leading society towards an association of equals, was neither realistic nor truly emancipatory against the background of its dictatorial abuse of power. Its policies helped to create political and social structures which prevented socialism from developing into a persistent movement for human rights. These structures both inhibited and stifled initiatives, innovations and attempts at democratic renewal. Above all, 17 June 1953 shows that the construction of a socialist society cannot be achieved by means of a dictatorship.[71]

In the end, though, this was too little too late. The failure to come to terms with the mistakes of 1953, like the failure to come to terms with the mistakes of 1932–3, damaged the cause of German communism long before the events of the summer and autumn of 1989 finally overthrew the SED regime, and with it the first experiment in socialism on German soil. A year later the GDR itself disappeared, swallowed up by its much larger neighbour, the capitalist *Bundesrepublik*. Today the uprising is remembered first and foremost as a landmark in recent German history. However, it was also the first chink in the armour of Soviet hegemony in Eastern Europe as a whole.

Notes

*I would like to thank Peter Grieder for his helpful comments on an earlier draft of this chapter.

1. Victor Klemperer, *The Lesser Evil. The Diaries of Victor Klemperer, 1945–1959*, translated by Martin Chalmers (London, 2003), p. 420.
2. Charles S. Maier, *Das Verschwinden der DDR und der Untergang des Kommunismus* (Frankfurt/Main, 2000), p. 252.
3. For an excellent account which looks at the view from the bottom up, see Corey Ross, *Constructing Socialism at the Grass-Roots. The Transformation of East Germany, 1945–65* (Basingstoke, 2000). Still very useful is Mary Fulbrook, *Anatomy of a Dictatorship. Inside the GDR* (Oxford, 1995).
4. Hubertus Knabe, *17. Juni 1953. Ein deutscher Aufstand* (Munich, 2003), pp. 431–2.
5. The most influential study putting across this new view is Ilko-Sascha Kowalczuk, Armin Mitter and Stefan Wolle (eds), *Der Tag X – 17. Juni 1953. Die 'Innere Staatsgründung' der DDR als Ergebnis der Krise 1952/54* (Berlin, 1995). This interpretation is nonetheless contested by some historians, who emphasise the proletarian and class-specific roots of the uprising. See, in particular, Torsten Diedrich, *Der 17. Juni 1953 in der DDR. Bewaffnete Gewalt gegen das Volk* (Berlin, 1991), pp. 148–50. Even Diedrich has accepted the 'people's uprising' thesis in his latest book – see Diedrich, *Waffen gegen das Volk. Der 17. Juni 1953 in der DDR* (Munich, 2003), pp. 155–65. For a useful overview of the most recent publications, see also Jonathan Sperber, '17 June 1953: Revisiting a German Revolution', *German History*, vol. 22 (2004), pp. 619–43.
6. 'Bericht der Hauptverwaltung Deutsche Volkspolizei über die Unruhen in der Zeit vom 16.6 bis 22.6.1953' (no date), reproduced in Dierk Hoffmann, Karl-Heinz Schmidt and Peter Skyba (eds), *Die DDR vor dem Mauerbau. Dokumente zur Geschichte des anderen deutschen Staates, 1949–1961* (Munich, 1996), pp. 163–71.
7. Peter Grieder, *The East German Leadership, 1946–1973. Conflict and Crisis* (Manchester, 1999), esp. pp. 53–107.
8. 'Bericht der Hauptverwaltung Deutsche Volkspolizei', p. 169.

9. Udo Baron, 'Die fünfte Kolonne? Die evangelische Kirche in der DDR und der Aufbau des Sozialismus', in Kowalczuk et al. (eds), *Der Tag X*, pp. 311–33.

10. Hermann Weber, *Geschichte der DDR*, new edn. (Munich, 2000), p. 155.

11. Falco Werkentin, *Politische Strafjustiz in der Ära Ulbricht. Vom bekennenden Terror zur verdeckten Repression*, 2nd edn (Berlin, 1997), pp. 339–40 and 375–9.

12. Ibid., pp. 56–64.

13. Grieder, *The East German Leadership*, pp. 58–9.

14. Ibid., p. 59.

15. Catherine Epstein, *The Last Revolutionaries. German Communists and their Century* (Cambridge, MA, 2003).

16. Richard Crossman (ed.), *The God that Failed. Six Studies in Communism* (London, 1950), pp. 55–6.

17. Grieder, *The East German Leadership*, pp. 53–4.

18. Volker Koop, *Der 17. Juni 1953. Legende und Wirklichkeit* (Berlin, 2003), p. 41.

19. Fulbrook, *Anatomy of a Dictatorship*, pp. 180–1.

20. Grieder, *The East German Leadership*, p. 69.

21. 'Kommuniqué der Sitzung des SED-Politbüros, 9.6.1953', reproduced in Koop, *Der 17. Juni 1953*, pp. 361–4.

22. 'Stimmungsbericht aus der Bevölkerung über das Kommuniqué des Politbüros vom 9.6.1953', 12 June 1953, in Landesarchiv Berlin, C Rep. 303–26, No. 094, Bl. 40–6.

23. 'Stellungnahme zum Kommuniqué des Politbüros der SED vom 9.6.53', 12 June 1953, in Stiftung Archiv der Parteien und Massenorganisationen der DDR im Bundesarchiv (henceforth SAPMO-BA), DY6/4626/514.

24. See the evidence in 'Stimmungsbericht aus der Bevölkerung', Bl. 40.

25. The article is reproduced in Arnulf Baring, *Der 17. Juni 1953*, 2nd edn (Stuttgart, 1983), pp. 170–4.

26. Diedrich, *Der 17. Juni 1953*, pp. 62 and 219–20.

27. Figures in ibid., p. 288.

28. Hans-Peter Löhn, '*Spitzbart, Bauch und Brille sind nicht des Volkes Wille!*'. *Der Volksaufstand am 17. Juni 1953 in Halle an der Saale* (Bremen, 1994), esp. pp. 9–10.

29. See the reports on Dorn in *Neues Deutschland*, 23, 24 and 26 June 1953. Also the draft statement written by Rudolf Herrnstadt and presented to the Central Committee of the SED at its fourteenth plenum on 21 June 1953. Reproduced in Koop, *Der 17. Juni 1953*, pp. 381–3. On 22 June 1953, one day after the Central Committee meeting, Dorn was sentenced to death by a court in Halle, and the sentence was carried out on 1 October 1953 in Dresden. After 1989 it transpired that Dorn was a mentally ill woman who had been tricked into confessing to various crimes by the Stasi. In all probability, she had not been at

Ravensbrück during the war at all, although she had confessed to this several times in interviews with her captors. Her conviction was finally overturned in 1994. See Löhn, *'Spitzbart, Bauch und Brille'*, pp. 96–103; Werkentin, *Politische Strafjustiz*, pp. 183–99; and Jens Ebert and Insa Eschebach, *'Die Kommandeuse'. Erna Dorn – zwischen Nationalsozialismus und Kaltem Krieg* (Berlin, 1994).

30. Klemperer, *The Lesser Evil*, p. 418 (diary entry for 19 June 1953). In fact, it was the SPD that had been refounded in Görlitz – see Diedrich, *Der 17. Juni 1953*, pp. 129–30.

31. Diedrich, *Der 17. Juni 1953*, pp. 132 and 289–93.

32. 'Bericht der Hauptverwaltung Deutsche Volkspolizei', p. 165.

33. 'Bericht der BDVP Neubrandenburg', 21 June 1953, in SAPMO-BA, DO1-11/1226, Bl. 100.

34. 'Analyse über die Vorbereitung, den Ausbruch und die Niederschlagung des faschistischen Abenteuers vom 16.-22.6.1953', 20 July 1953, in SAPMO-BA, DY30/IV/3688, Bl. 111–12.

35. For a discussion of numbers killed, see Knabe, *17. Juni 1953*, pp. 343–4; and Koop, *Der 17. Juni 1953*, pp. 310–11.

36. 'Gesamtbericht der Hauptverwaltung Deutsche Volkspolizei über die Ereignisse am 17.6.1953', 18 June 1953, in SAPMO-BA, DO1-11/45, Bl. 11–16.

37. Knabe, *17. Juni 1953*, p. 348, states that nineteen death sentences were passed by the Soviets, and eighteen were carried out. Richard J. Evans, *Rituals of Retribution. Capital Punishment in Germany, 1600–1987* (London, 1996), p. 831, gives the slightly lower figure of sixteen. Weber, *Geschichte der DDR*, p. 166, suggests at least twenty, possibly forty, but the latter figure is probably too high.

38. Knabe, *17. Juni 1953*, pp. 349–50; Evans, *Rituals of Retribution*, pp. 831–2, suggests that as many as five East German policemen were executed for disobeying orders, two in Erfurt and three in East Berlin.

39. Cf. Koop, *Der 17. Juni 1953*, p. 311.

40. Evans, *Rituals of Retribution*, p. 831; Weber, *Geschichte der DDR*, p. 166; Knabe, *17. Juni 1953*, p. 357.

41. Knabe, *17. Juni 1953*, p. 354.

42. 'Bericht der Hauptverwaltung Deutsche Volkspolizei', p. 171. Of the 6,057 persons in police custody by 22 June 1953, 5,777 were citizens of the GDR, compared to 42 citizens of West Germany and 238 citizens of West Berlin.

43. Werkentin, *Politische Strafjustiz*, p. 150.

44. Ibid., pp. 194–9. See also note 29 above.

45. Gareth Pritchard, 'Workers and the Socialist Unity Party of Germany in the summer of 1953', in Patrick Major and Jonathan Osmond (eds), *The Workers' and Peasants' State. Communism and Society in East Germany under Ulbricht, 1945–71* (Manchester, 2002), pp. 112–29.

46. Knabe, *17. Juni 1953*, p. 274.

47. *Neues Deutschland*, 24 June 1953.

48. Cited in Ilko-Sascha Kowalczuk, 'Die Historiker der DDR und der 17. Juni 1953', *Geschichte in Wissenschaft und Unterricht*, vol. 44 (1993), p. 721.

49. At the Politburo meeting on 8 July only two of the thirteen comrades present spoke in favour of Ulbricht's continued stay in office – Hermann Matern and Erich Honecker. Two others, Erich Mückenberger and Fred Oelßner, declined to express a clear view, while the remaining comrades concluded that Ulbricht would have to go. See 'Diskussion im Politbüro am 8.7.1953: handschriftliche Aufzeichnungen Otto Grotewohls', reproduced in Hoffmann et al. (eds), *Die DDR vor dem Mauerbau*, pp. 174–6. Also Nadja Stulz-Herrnstadt (ed.), *Das Herrnstadt-Dokument. Das Politbüro der SED und die Geschichte des 17. Juni 1953* (Reinbek bei Hamburg, 1991), pp. 126–7.

50. For a more detailed discussion, see Grieder, *The East German Leadership*, pp. 74–85.

51. Stulz-Herrnstadt (ed.), *Das Herrnstadt-Dokument*, pp. 160–1.

52. In 1961, and again in 1963, the Central Committee of the CPSU added the former Soviet Prime Minister Georgii Malenkov as a co-conspirator with Beria, but there was still no mention of any East German involvement in the alleged plot to abandon the GDR to the West. See François Fejtö, *A History of the People's Democracies. Eastern Europe since Stalin* (London, 1974), p. 37.

53. Richard Bessel, 'The People's Police and the People in Ulbricht's Germany', in Major and Osmond (eds), *The Workers' and Peasants' State*, p. 71.

54. Epstein, *The Last Revolutionaries*, p. 160.

55. Peter Hübner, *Konsens, Konflikt und Kompromiß. Soziale Arbeiterinteressen und Sozialpolitik in der SBZ/DDR, 1945–1970* (Berlin, 1995), esp. pp. 178–210; Stefan Berger, *Social Democracy and the Working Class in Nineteenth and Twentieth Century Germany* (London, 2000), pp. 163–6.

56. Corey Ross, 'East Germans and the Berlin Wall. Popular Opinion and Social Change Before and After the Border Closure of August 1961', *Journal of Contemporary History*, vol. 39 (2004), p. 28.

57. Knabe, *17. Juni 1953*, p. 421.

58. Weber, *Geschichte der DDR*, p. 171.

59. Grieder, *The East German Leadership*, pp. 79–80.

60. Ibid., p. 89; Mario Frank, *Walter Ulbricht. Eine deutsche Biografie* (Berlin, 2001), pp. 258–60. Interestingly, Frank places the events of June–July 1953 at the beginning of his biography of Ulbricht, seeing them as the decisive event in his career. Like Grieder, he concludes that the general secretary survived by the skin of his teeth, and only because the Soviets were anxious about making the GDR look weak in the aftermath of the uprising (see ibid., p. 26).

61. Pritchard, 'Workers and the Socialist Unity Party', p. 113.

62. Diedrich, *Waffen gegen das Volk*, pp. 29–30 and 215–16. For a contrasting view, which stresses the idea that 17 June was not simply an uprising, but a genuine 'people's revolution', rooted in long-term popular and political resistance to socialism, see Gary Bruce, *Resistance with the People. Repression and Resistance in Eastern Germany, 1945–1955* (Lanham, MD, 2003).

63. Of the three Western powers in Berlin, only the USA seriously considered supplying arms to the East German rebels in June 1953. However, even President Eisenhower very wisely insisted, at a meeting of the National Security Council on 18 June, that the revolt would have to become more serious and more widespread before America could risk intervening in such a direct manner, and in the end the plan came to nothing. For a further discussion, see Knabe, *17. Juni 1953*, pp. 400–16.

64. Ibid., p. 246. See also Ilko-Sascha Kowalczuk, 'Volkserhebung ohne "Geistesarbeiter"? Die Intelligenz in der DDR', in Kowalczuk et al. (eds), *Der Tag X*, pp. 129–69.

65. Joachim Petzold (with Waltraud Petzold), *Parteinahme wofür? DDR-Historiker im Spannungsfeld von Politik und Wissenschaft*, ed. Martin Sabrow (Potsdam, 2000), p. 60.

66. Bruce, *Resistance with the People*, esp. pp. 65–118.

67. Klemperer, *The Lesser Evil*, passim.

68. *Neues Deutschland*, 23 June 1953.

69. Fritz Selbmann, *Acht Jahre und ein Tag. Bilder aus den Gründerjahren der DDR* (Berlin, 1999), p. 265.

70. Klemperer, *The Lesser Evil*, p. 495 (diary entry for 10 August 1957).

71. 'Erklärung des Parteivorstandes der PDS zum 50. Jahrestag des 17. Juni 1953', Berlin, 26 May 2003 (online version at http://www.pds-online.de/partei/geschichte/index.htm.) On the PDS and post-communist historiography, see also Ilko-Sascha Kowalczuk, '"Faschistischer Putsch" – "Konterrevolution" – "Arbeitererhebung": Der 17. Juni 1953 im Urteil von SED und PDS', in Rainer Eckert and Bernd Faulenbach (eds), *Halbherziger Revisionismus. Zum postkommunistischen Geschichtsbild* (Munich, 1996), pp. 69–82; and the more sympathetic account offered by Stefan Berger, 'Former GDR Historians in the Reunified Germany. An Alternative Historical Culture and its Attempts to Come to Terms with the GDR Past', *Journal of Contemporary History*, vol. 38 (2003), pp. 63–83.

–4–

Poland and Hungary, 1956: A Comparative Essay Based on New Archival Findings*
Johanna Granville

The American naval historian Alfred Thayer Mahan once wrote: 'Force is never more operative than when it is known to exist but is not brandished'.[1] This essay examines the different courses of events in Poland and Hungary in October 1956 and attempts to answer a question that has long intrigued scholars. Why did the Soviet Union intervene in Hungary, but not in Poland? Historians have developed three theses over the past four decades. First, the 'historical thesis' emphasises the two countries' divergent historical experiences. Advocates of this interpretation posit that, for the Russians, dealing with the Hungarians was a novel experience, since no part of Hungary had ever been under Russian rule until after the Second World War. Furthermore, the Second World War was less traumatic for Hungarians than for Poles, and therefore the former were perhaps more willing to fight the Russians in 1956.[2] A second explanation for Soviet actions focuses on the role of individuals. Adherents of this 'personality thesis' argue that the outgoing heads of the Stalin-era leadership, Edward Ochab in Poland and Ernő Gerő in Hungary, shaped events the most.[3] Moreover, Władysław Gomułka and Cardinal Stefan Wyszyński were wiser bolder leaders, better able to deter Soviet aggression than were Imre Nagy and Cardinal József Mindszenty.[4] The third line of argument – the 'neutrality thesis' – maintains that, in contrast to the Poles, the Hungarians alarmed the Soviet Union by going too far, especially by declaring neutrality, withdrawing from the Warsaw Pact and establishing a multi-party system.[5]

Well over a decade has passed since communist bloc archives began to open, and it is now appropriate to ask: do the new documents significantly alter these older explanations? This essay will compare the events of 1956, drawing on recently declassified materials from Hungarian, Polish and Russian archives. I conclude that, while the documents do not change previous interpretations fundamentally, they do yield a more nuanced view of Gomułka and Nagy, and the ways in which they interacted with their colleagues and constituencies.

Historical and Personality Theses

Scholars can challenge the first 'historical' explanation by pointing to three examples: the Tsarist invasion in 1849, which helped the Austrians suppress the Hungarian revolution; the communist regime under Béla Kun (March–July 1919); and the experience of the thousands of Hungarian POWs in the USSR, many of whom were not permitted to return to Hungary until well into the 1950s. Moreover, one could easily reach a different conclusion: the Russians' alleged inexperience in dealing with the Hungarians might very well have discouraged them from intervening twice. Likewise, extensive experience with the Poles might very well have prompted the Soviet leadership to order a full-scale invasion.

As for the second interpretation, it is true that particular personalities shaped events to a great extent. This and the next few sections will compare the personalities of several leading figures, notably Gomułka and Nagy, and also provide the necessary historical context of the events of 1956.

Just two weeks after Nikita Khrushchev delivered his famous 'Secret Speech' to the Twentieth Party Congress of the Communist Party of the Soviet Union (CPSU) on 25 February 1956, Ochab replaced Bolesław Bierut, who had died of a heart attack during the congress. In Poland, as in the other 'satellite' countries, a rift existed between the so-called Stalinist 'Muscovites', those communist leaders who had stayed in the USSR during the Second World War, and the 'home communists', those who had languished in Nazi and Stalinist prisons at home. In Poland, however, the Muscovites (Bierut, Ochab, Hilary Minc and others) never quite established dominance in the Polish United Workers' Party (*Polska Zjednoczona Partia Robotnicza*, or PZPR) in the early post-war years. Gomułka and the indigenous communist underground had too much authority.[6] While Ochab had lived in the USSR during the war and developed strong loyalty to Moscow, he was nevertheless a middle-of-the-roader, who eventually relinquished power peacefully to Gomułka. He even ultimately admitted that Gomułka should not have been arrested as a 'rightist deviationist', and agreed to nominate him and his closest political allies for Politburo membership at the eighth plenum of the CP, which took place on 19 October 1956.

Poznań, June 1956

Before turning to the Hungarian case, it is necessary to examine the Poznań revolt of 28–29 June 1956, which further contributed to the difference in the October events in the two countries. Many scholars mention this revolt only in passing,[7] while others omit it from their historical narrative altogether.[8] Still others have described the uprising more extensively, but due to the lack of archival sources say very little or nothing about the Polish political and military decision-making process during the crisis.[9] Also sorely lacking in secondary literature is a detailed comparison of Polish and Hungarian crisis management styles in the Poznań revolt and the 23 October Hungarian student demonstration, respectively.

On Saturday 23 June 1956, workers of the 'Stalin Works' locomotive plant in Poznań met and decided to send a delegation to Warsaw to persuade the central authorities to meet five key demands, including a 20 per cent wage increase. By 28 June the delegation still had not received an answer from the authorities, and rumours were spreading that the delegation had been arrested.[10] Thus, early that Thursday morning (later known as 'Black Thursday'), the workers on the night and day shifts of the plant, which employed a total of 12,000 people, decided to stage a demonstration. Assuming the original delegation had been arrested, the crowd first stormed the city jail, freed the prisoners and seized weapons from the guards. Then the workers attacked the radio station engaged in jamming Western broadcasts. Still looking for allegedly arrested delegates, the demonstrators next raided the headquarters of the District Office of Security. This is where the first shots were fired, at about eleven o'clock.[11] The demonstration escalated into major anti-government riots in Poznań and other Polish cities.

The Poznań revolt differs from the Hungarian student demonstration on 23–24 October 1956 in a number of ways. First, the Poznań crisis was mainly a workers' revolt, caused by acute economic distress. Polish archives are full of top-secret, unpublished letters sent to the Central Committee of the party which illustrate this distress.[12] Due in part to the limited nature of the crisis, the Polish authorities were eventually able to contain it. Second, Ochab and his colleagues were physically present in Poland on 28 June and hence could take action, albeit after initial delay. Furthermore, the Politburo decided to send a governmental delegation to Poznań, led by Prime Minister Józef Cyrankiewicz.[13] Third, Ochab wisely did not berate the local workers over the radio during the crisis. Indeed, at the plenary session of the Central Committee in late July, a resolution was passed which contritely acknowledged the 'bureaucratic distortions' and the 'numerous manifestations of callousness toward the grievances and needs of the workers', all of which played an important role in the Poznań events.[14] Surprisingly, new archival documents reveal that not all party members – even the more liberal ones – agreed that what happened was a spontaneous expression of workers' grievances. For instance, Edward Gierek, who was considered a progressive Politburo member, thought the demonstration had been planned well in advance.[15]

Fourth, the Polish leaders managed the Poznań crisis on their own, without calling in Soviet troops. This possibility was apparently never even mentioned.[16] Rather, as Central Committee secretary Jerzy Morawski later claimed in a television interview, the Polish authorities 'reacted fiercely' to the Poznań events in order to reassure the Russians that their 'military assistance' would not be needed.[17] Some analysts say that the Polish authorities even overreacted and the riots could have been contained with little or no military force whatsoever.[18] Finally, the Polish army and security forces did follow orders more or less. Although a few officers reportedly tried to resist firing on the crowds, most members of the armed forces, especially the Internal Security Corps, were willing to carry out their orders. (It should be remembered that the Polish military establishment was dominated by many Soviet commanders and pro-Soviet Polish officers.)

The Poznań revolt was thus an important learning experience, both for the Polish communist leadership and the armed forces. Despite their initial hesitation when faced with this emergency, Ochab and his colleagues discovered that they could address the workers' grievances and still maintain the party's political monopoly, while conforming to Soviet foreign policy and security interests. The Poznań experience made the Polish authorities more cautious and eager to avoid bloodshed in further rebellions in Poland itself, as well as in a conflict with the Soviet Union several months later in October.[19] Reflecting on the recent events, Gomułka told an audience in Katowice on 4 December: 'In my opinion [Poznań and] the Eighth Plenum came in time to show us a new way. It is important to understand new ideas and content'.[20] The Khrushchev leadership also learned valuable lessons from Poznań. Initially it blamed the crisis on 'imperialists', who were 'fomenting disunity' in the Soviet bloc.[21] Later, the Soviet leaders admitted that their alarm was unfounded and that Ochab and Gomułka were reliable.[22] Thus, in all likelihood, the Poznań experience indirectly helped to convince the Khrushchev leadership that the Poles could deal with the 'Polish October' themselves.

The Hungarian Leadership and 23 October Student Demonstration in Budapest

In comparison to the Polish leadership after Khrushchev's 'Secret Speech', the Hungarian 'Stalinist' leader Mátyás Rákosi clung to power until July 1956 – longer than any other Stalinist leader, with the exception of Gheorghe Gheorghiu-Dej in Romania and Walter Ulbricht in the German Democratic Republic (GDR). Like Ochab, Rákosi spent the Second World War in the Soviet Union and developed strong loyalties to Moscow, but he guarded his power jealously. Using the 1948 conflict between Stalin and Tito as a pretext, Rákosi (nicknamed the 'Bald Murderer') authorised a particularly cruel wave of purges in the Hungarian party, beginning with his rival, László Rajk, who was innocent of the 'crimes' for which he was executed in 1949. After the uprising in East Germany in 1953, the Soviet leaders curtailed Rákosi's monopoly of power by forcing him to relinquish one of his posts, the prime ministership, and to share power with the new Prime Minister, Imre Nagy. As someone who stood outside Rákosi's inner circle and who was not Jewish, Nagy, so the Soviet leaders thought, could perhaps remedy some of the mistakes of the overzealous Stalinists by advocating 'New Course' policies (increased production of consumer goods, relaxation of terror and concessions to the peasantry).[23] As long as Rákosi remained First Secretary, however, the New Course was doomed to fail, as he sabotaged Nagy's efforts from behind the scenes. This dual leadership caused extreme tension among both political elites and the general population.

When Soviet Prime Minister Georgii Malenkov was removed in February 1955, the New Course policies quickly lost favour. Nagy, too, was ousted as Prime Minister the following April for 'rightist deviation', and expelled from the party altogether in November. Rákosi prevailed as head of the party, but Hungarian workers and intellectuals did not forget Nagy, whom they saw as an alternative to Rákosi. In February 1956 the Polish and Hungarian parties took their cues from Khrushchev's 'Secret Speech' denouncing Stalin's crimes and 'cult of personality'. Purge victims were rehabilitated. Communist writers who had supported the Stalinist regime now heard the grisly details of the prisoners' experiences, and many became demoralised. The question of responsibility surfaced and led to sharp intra-party debates. As in Poland, the rift deepened in Hungary between the Stalinist 'Muscovites', led by Rákosi and Gerő, and the 'home communists' around János Kádár and Géza Losoncsy, with the latter group gaining popularity. As their criticism grew more radical, their audiences rapidly multiplied, especially at debates held in the so-called Petöfi Circle (*Petőfi Kör*), a discussion group of young party members. On 29 March, Rákosi reluctantly admitted that Rajk had been an innocent victim of 'provocation', the police having 'misled' the government.

Finally, in July 1956 Rákosi was forced to retire as party First Secretary. In contrast to Ochab who assisted the reformer Gomułka, Rákosi had promoted Gerő, a like-minded hardliner, to succeed him. Indeed, it can be plausibly argued that, had Rákosi been replaced much earlier with a more liberal reformer like Nagy or Kádár, the entire Hungarian Revolution could have been avoided. But this did not happen, fostering a groundswell of hatred for the so-called 'Rákosi-Gerő clique' and the 'personality cult', an antipathy which was absent in Poland.

This intense anger exploded in autumn 1956. On 23 October, about ten thousand students participated in a silent demonstration in Budapest. Gomułka's rise in Poland provided these Hungarian students and intellectuals with an opportunity to express their grievances against the Stalinist leaders and Soviet domination. The demand for Nagy's return was intended to parallel Gomułka's return to power. Chanting slogans such as, 'Independence based on freedom and equality! Poland shows us the way, let's follow the Hungarian way!', they hung up Polish and Hungarian flags with the coat-of-arms symbol representing the communist regime cut out of the middle.[24] In contrast to the disgruntled workers in Poznań, the students' demands were more political and harder for a conservative regime to meet. In their 'Sixteen Points', the students tested the limits of the authorities by boldly calling *inter alia* for the dismissal of Rákosi's successor, Gerő, and the reinstatement of the reformer Nagy; the total withdrawal of Soviet troops from Hungary; and true independence and equality with regard to the Soviet Union.

Whereas in Poland the overwhelming majority of soldiers obeyed orders, the regular Hungarian army units wavered and some deserted to the side of the so-called freedom fighters. Troops were forbidden to shoot unless fired upon. Only the State Security Department (ÁVO) units could shoot unhesitatingly at the Hungarian demonstrators. Unlike the Polish leaders during the Poznań crisis, the top Hungarian party figures were absent in these crucial days. They were in Yugoslavia from 14 to 23 October to patch up their differences with Tito. The delegation returned from Belgrade to Budapest on the day of the student demonstration. Although Gerő did not know about the march before his departure, he suspected that the political situation in Hungary was grave and expressed his anxiety to Soviet Ambassador, Iurii Andropov.[25] According to new archival documents, a secret emergency meeting of the CPSU Presidium and invited East European communist leaders was held in Moscow on 24 October, at which Khrushchev wondered aloud why Gerő, Prime Minister András Hegedüs and others would dare to 'spend time by the sea' when there were 'signs that the situation in Hungary is extremely serious'.[26] Thus, the situation in Budapest rapidly escalated, partly because the remaining leaders could not make key decisions until Gerő's delegation returned. By the time they arrived in Budapest in the afternoon of 23 October, their options had narrowed. The Hungarian security forces and army had basically failed to contain the violence.

In contrast to Ochab's conciliatory approach to the Poznań protesters, Gerő delivered a scathing radio speech at eight o'clock that evening, denouncing the Hungarian demonstrators as counter-revolutionaries, further enraging his audience. The Hungarian decision-makers had almost by reflex assumed that they would have to call in Soviet troops. Gathered in Gerő's room between nine and half-past nine that evening, they went through the motions of debating the pros and cons of calling in Soviet troops, but in reality they were merely aiding Gerő in his phone conversation with Khrushchev, during which he asked for Soviet military assistance.[27] They feared Hungarian troops were neither sufficiently conditioned nor trustworthy, and the Minister of Defence said nothing to dispel their fears. Even Soviet Presidium members, Anastas Mikoian and Mikhail Suslov, who were dispatched from Moscow to Budapest and remained there from 24 October, thought the Hungarian communists were 'exaggerating the strength of the enemy and underestimating their own strength'.[28] According to Nagy's later testimony, none of the members of the party's central leadership said a word when Gerő announced that he had requested Soviet troops to march towards Budapest.[29] Thus, unlike the Polish communists, the Hungarian leaders did not seriously consider refraining from calling for Soviet aid, seemingly associating anti-Sovietism automatically with anti-socialism.

Hence, the first Soviet intervention in Hungary, on 23–24 October, was actually an invasion by invitation. Although Nagy was later blamed for inviting the troops, and Hegedüs actually signed the official written invitation *ex post facto*, it was Gerő who verbally requested them. The circumstances behind the request are rather puzzling. It is now known that Gerő summoned the Soviet military attaché and petitioned him for armed assistance. Soviet ambassador Andropov then attempted to call into action the Special Corps in Hungary, headed by Piotr Lashchenko, who replied that he needed a direct command from Moscow.[30] The Soviet Presidium could not take action, however, until it received a formal request from the Hungarian leadership. When Khrushchev later phoned Gerő to invite him to the emergency meeting on 24 October in Moscow, the latter declined, insisting that the Hungarian situation was too serious, but strangely he did not say a word about his earlier call for military aid. Only after Andropov informed Khrushchev did the Soviet leader then call Gerő again to tell him the request would be fulfilled, but only if submitted in writing. Gerő refused, saying he did not have time to summon a meeting.[31]

The Hungarians' initial request on 23 October for Soviet military assistance appears to have led the CPSU leaders to conclude that the Hungarian communists, unlike the Polish, could not by themselves maintain order in their country. Recall again Khrushchev's exasperation expressed at the 24 October meeting. Furthermore, 'one of the most serious mistakes of the Hungarian comrades', Mikoian and Suslov cabled from Moscow that same day, 'was the fact that, before midnight last night, they did not permit anyone to shoot at the participants in the riots'.[32] The initial crackdown, when it occurred, only sparked further anti-Soviet rage among the population and caused more problems, including disorganisation within Nagy's new government and lynchings of ÁVO personnel. The Soviet leaders ultimately decided to invade massively a second time on 4 November. Had there been a 'Hungarian Poznań', perhaps the Hungarian leadership might have been able to close ranks.

Gomułka and Nagy – Similarities and Differences

Advocates of the 'personality thesis' focus on Gomułka and Nagy to explain the different outcomes in Poland and Hungary. In this section, I will compare these two leaders and their behaviour in the October–November events.

Historians have described Gomułka as more Machiavellian than Nagy.[33] Much of Gomułka's attraction was his closeness to the workers, an image bolstered by his pre-war history of organising strikes. His admittance into the clandestine Communist Party of Poland in 1926, and election as national secretary of the Chemical Workers' Union in 1930, brought him into repeated clashes with the police. Soon after the war, Gomułka was elected a member of the Politburo and Secretary General of the Central Committee, but was expelled from the party in 1949 accused of 'nationalist deviationism', including his opposition to the Cominform in September 1947. He was then arrested in July 1951, but following the Poznań riot was rehabilitated and readmitted into the party in August 1956. On 19 October he was again elected First Secretary. Gomułka was also keenly aware of the new territory Poland had acquired from Germany on the basis of the Potsdam agreement in July 1945. Thus, he fully appreciated the presence of Soviet troops in Poland to help defend the country's western border and was not about to submit to popular demand for their withdrawal. He grasped the fact that, ultimately, only the USSR could guarantee Poland's new western frontiers.

The Hungarian leader had much in common with Gomułka. Both men were devoted to Marxist ideology and received their ideological training in Moscow. Both had once held top positions in their respective communist parties. Both were ostracised in the party due to their stubborn adherence to nationalist convictions and disapproval of fast-paced collectivisation, as well as their refusal to recant. The popularity of both 'reformist' leaders wronged by Stalinists rose sharply in the era of de-Stalinisation. Nagy, first appointed Prime Minister in 1953, but demoted in 1955 and then expelled from the Communist Party as a whole, was readmitted into its ranks on 13 October 1956, just ten days before the student demonstration.

There the similarity ends. Although nine years older than Gomułka, Nagy has been described by most scholars as less experienced and pragmatic; an idealistic scholarly individual, who innocently fell victim to the Kremlin's political intrigues. However, recent archival findings suggest that there were more facets to Nagy's personality than were readily apparent. His loyalty to the Soviet Union may have outweighed his idealist tendencies. As we now know, Nagy served as an NKVD informer in the 1930s and was probably protected by the NKVD/MVD, thus escaping the fate of Gomułka in the anti-Titoist purges. Of the total number of people on whom Nagy is reported to have informed, fifteen were 'liquidated' (shot) or died in prison.[34] In contrast to Gomułka, who studied in Moscow for only one year, Nagy spent fourteen years in Moscow, from 1930 to 1944. Due to this long tenure, Nagy was one of the so-called 'Muscovite' communists, although a minor one, and this heritage may have weakened his ability to appeal to nationality to the same extent as Gomułka. In December 1944, Nagy served as Minister of Agriculture in the first Hungarian coalition government. He was briefly appointed Minister of the Interior after the free elections of 1945, but resigned after six months as it required a pitiless personality so antithetical to his own.[35]

Most revealingly, new archival documents from Nagy's interrogations in 1957 prove that he originally opposed both the student demonstration of 23 October and the declaration of Hungary's neutrality.[36] He even opposed the general workers' strikes taking place in Hungary after the Soviet intervention of 4 November.[37] To be sure, he made these statements under duress, and one must balance these documents with eyewitness reports and scholarly analyses. Nevertheless, Nagy's statements in the last two years of his life remained remarkably consistent and courageous. While Gomułka concentrated on political positions, Nagy tended to focus on cogent arguments. He seemed to believe that if he could logically prove the correctness of his position, according to Marxist-Leninist principles, then others would change their behaviour. Even in captivity in Romania, he wrote letters to the Central Committee of the re-formed communist party calling for 'a thorough and profound Marxist scientific and political analysis of the October–November events.' Seemingly oblivious to the possibility that he might soon be hanged, Nagy assumed an almost pedantic 'I told you so' attitude towards his future executioners: '[I]n July 1956 ... I told comrade Mikoian that Rákosi's anti-national, humiliating policies had caused more damage to Soviet-Hungarian relations ... than had Dulles and American propaganda. Comrade Mikoian listened to it all. But if today ... he recalls this discussion, he will definitely admit that many problems could have been prevented if he had taken my words into account'.[38]

The Eighth Plenum and Gomułka's Behaviour in the 'Polish October'

Let us now return to Gomułka and examine his actions before, during and after the eighth plenum of the Polish party, which also helps to explain why the Soviet leadership decided to intervene in Hungary rather than Poland. We will then compare Gomułka's activities to Nagy's in the days leading up to the second Soviet intervention on 4 November.

First, Gomułka and other Polish communist officials were more aware of the long-term problems brewing in Poland and were better able to define them. According to the recently declassified protocol of the Politburo meeting on 8–10 October, the leaders articulated four specific reasons for the crisis in the party: (1) a lack of unity in the Politburo; (2) lack of connections between the leadership and the party activists; (3) a lack of authority among the leadership; and (4) an 'unfair situation in the relations between the PRL [Polish People's Republic] and the Soviet Union'.[39] The latter item refers to the Polish coal sold to the USSR at very low prices, and to the large number of senior officers in the Polish army who neither spoke Polish nor held Polish citizenship. The problem of non-Polish officers in high military ranks was easily identified and solved. Knowing the importance of positions, Gomułka insisted that all Soviet officers and advisers from the Polish Armed Forces and security apparatus be removed, especially Marshal Konstantin Rokossovskii from the party Politburo. This process began after Gomułka came to power.

Much controversy has centred on the Soviet leaders' trip to Warsaw on 19 October. This visitation was not completely unexpected, as some writers have claimed.[40] On 18 October, the eve of the eighth plenum of the Polish party, the Soviet Ambassador to Poland, Pantaleimon Ponomarenko, told Ochab that the CPSU Presidium had decided to send a delegation to Warsaw in order to discuss the situation in the party and the country. Gomułka later told the plenum that the Poles had informed the Soviets that: 'it would be better if you arrived on the second day of the plenum or maybe in two days, but not before the plenum. And that must have made them even more nervous. Well, maybe not nervous, but it must have appeared suspicious. They decided to come immediately.'[41]

The Soviet delegation, which arrived at seven o'clock on the morning of 19 October, was high-powered, including Khrushchev, Mikoian, Lazar Kaganovich, Viacheslav Molotov and Marshal Georgii Zhukov. After an initial two-hour meeting, the two sides agreed that the eighth plenum would begin at ten that morning to allow

Gomułka and others to be elected to the Central Committee, but that no further decisions would be taken until the meeting with the Soviets had ended. Ochab opened the eighth plenum, proposing the 'election of Comrade Władysław Gomułka to the post of First Secretary' and suggesting that the 'number of Politburo members be limited to nine in order to secure unity and greater efficiency.' He then asked the plenum to adjourn so that talks could be held with the Soviet leaders who had arrived unexpectedly. As Gomułka later said: 'We opened the plenum, we broke it, and we started talking to them'.[42]

The Soviet delegation returned to Moscow early the next morning. That day Gomułka delivered a long speech to the eighth plenum, explaining the gist of his talks with the Russians. This speech was not published in the USSR, because Soviet leaders thought it would have to be accompanied by extensive commentary and would spark too much debate.[43] Gomułka received tumultuous applause from a relieved crowd of about 500,000 citizens when, on 24 October in front of the Palace of Culture and Science, he announced that Khrushchev had just promised to stop the advance of Soviet troops towards Warsaw within two days.[44]

Polish Deterrence of a Soviet Intervention

Khrushchev and his colleagues did not suddenly fly to Warsaw on 19 October expressly to prevent Gomułka's election as First Secretary of the Polish party, as some accounts of the crisis imply. As Khrushchev pointed out in his memoirs, Gomułka held 'a position that was most advantageous for us. Here was a man who had come to power on the crest of an anti-Soviet wave, yet who could now speak forcefully about the need to preserve Poland's friendly relations with the Soviet Union and the Soviet Communist Party'.[45] What worried him, however, was the impression that the populist demonstrations which had formed the background to Gomułka's meteoric rise were anti-Soviet in nature. In a handwritten account of the Polish-Soviet confrontation of 19 October, Gomułka shows that he too understood why Moscow was concerned about the imminent new appointments in the Polish leadership: 'I am returning to work under an anti-Soviet slogan... [For the Soviets] the question is not about people, but [about] what kind of politics is lurking [behind the proposed] personnel changes. The atmosphere in Poland is anti-Soviet and the organisational decisions are anti-Soviet.'[46]

Scholars have also claimed that Gomułka's tough self-confident stance helped to convince Khrushchev that the Pole had things under control in his own country. However, one gets the impression from an interview with Ochab that Gomułka's posturing may actually have worked against him. As Ochab said: 'Presumably they thought Gomulka [sic] would put the country in order and was the one to stake their bets on... But Gomulka ... displayed considerable toughness of character during those difficult talks.'[47] The secondary literature, moreover, implies that Gomułka's behaviour during Khrushchev's sudden visit is what convinced the Soviet leader that military intervention was not necessary. However, according to the declassified notes composed by Vladimir Malin, head of the General Department of the Soviet Central Committee, on the secret Presidium session on 20 October, the Kremlin leaders had not completely ruled out a military intervention.[48] On the day they returned to Moscow, they said: 'There's only one way out – put an end to what is happening in Poland.' Apparently, the need to order 'manoeuvres', 'prepare a document' and 'form a committee' was mentioned.[49] This suggests that Gomułka's bold stance during the Soviet leaders' visit to Warsaw had not convinced them completely that an intervention was not necessary. Indeed, new documents reveal that the Khrushchev leadership was still extremely worried about the Polish situation as late as 24 October, as illustrated by the convening of the emergency meeting of all communist party leaders in Moscow on that day to discuss the Polish situation.[50]

Focusing still on Gomułka's role to explain the Soviet decision not to intervene, one should thus bear in mind the significance of his statements and leadership *after* the eighth plenum. This aspect has been relatively neglected in the secondary literature, which tends to view the 'showdown' between the two delegations on 19–20 October as the main turning point of the Polish crisis. Indeed, Gomułka's political position was perhaps less secure than commonly thought. The situation in Poland was still volatile in late October and November 1956. Strikes and demonstrations continued to erupt in Polish cities – in Gdańsk, Szczecin and Wrocław – well after the eighth plenum. In Bydgoszcz people called for the 'overthrow of the Stalinist regime in Poland' (i.e. Gomułka's) and protested against Soviet coercion of Poland.[51] Had Gomułka displayed weak leadership or approved too strongly of the Hungarian uprising, the Soviet leaders could easily have decided to send tanks rolling back into Poland.

Another aspect of Gomułka's behaviour that helped to reassure Khrushchev that a military intervention was not necessary was the measured pace and scale of his political and economic reforms. While the Polish leaders worked to eliminate the most oppressive Stalinist features, such as arbitrary arrests, collectivisation of agriculture, Herculean work norms and persecution of the Roman Catholic Church, they also maintained the command economy and the absolute monopoly of the communist party. Gomułka likewise insisted on retaining Soviet troops and membership in the Warsaw Pact. Polish citizens grew disillusioned, but still believed in the late 1950s that Gomułka's policies resulted from Moscow's coercion.

Thus, the proponents of the 'personality thesis' are partly correct in pointing to the difference in individual personalities to explain the Soviet decision to invade. However, one must bear in mind at least two other factors: (1) Soviet apprehension about how to end a military conflict with Poland; and (2) the escalating crisis in Hungary. During the secret meeting on 24 October, Khrushchev reportedly said: 'Finding a reason for an armed conflict [with Poland] now would be very easy, but finding a way to put an end to such a conflict later on would be very hard'.[52]

Given the will of the Polish people to fight, it is possible that any leader with a modicum of popularity would have been suitable to the occasion. In addition, the simultaneous eruption of the Hungarian crisis constrained the Kremlin's military resources and reduced its reaction time. Had there been no unrest in Hungary, might the Khrushchev leadership have decided to intervene in Poland? Might they have judged Gomułka's behaviour differently without having Nagy's actions as a basis of comparison?

Hungarian Crisis, 24 October to 4 November 1956

In contrast to the situation in Poland, the problems in Hungary had been festering over a longer period due to Rákosi's tenacious hold on power. Nagy, who was not even readmitted into the Hungarian party until 13 October, had no real authority to speak for the leadership until 23–24 October, when reappointed Prime Minister. Awareness of his lack of status explains in part why he came across as hesitant in his speech to the student demonstrators on 23 October. The Soviet leaders realised that the initial Red Army intervention on 24 October only exacerbated the situation, bringing on a wave of lynchings of ÁVO agents. After Nagy was voted in as Prime Minister, he issued a plethora of reformist decrees. In fact, from this time on, Nagy did not lead the uprising; he was instead desperately trying to keep up with the accelerating events and ever more radicalised popular demands. The Communist Party was in shambles, with membership rapidly evaporating. Eventually, the Kremlin recognised that Nagy had lost control of the party leadership, which was incapable of reform. It would be useful to review Nagy's fast-paced reformist measures, so antithetical to Gomułka's more cautious approach, in the period between the initial Soviet intervention and the final crackdown on 4 November.

Unencumbered by fears of German revanchism, Nagy announced on 25 October that negotiations on the withdrawal of Soviet troops from Hungary would take place. According to newly declassified diplomatic cables, Soviet Presidium members, Mikoian and Suslov, later scolded Nagy for not informing them in advance, saying they considered this 'a most crude mistake, because the withdrawal of Soviet soldiers will inevitably lead to an intervention by American troops'.[53] Then, in a single day, 28 October, the Nagy government broadcast another declaration, calling for a ceasefire, amnesties for those involved in the uprising, an increase in salaries and pensions, the immediate removal of Soviet troops from Budapest and follow-up negotiations for a full military withdrawal from Hungary. Nagy also rejected previous characterisations of the uprising as a 'counter-revolution', insisting that 'this movement aims at guaranteeing our national freedom, independence and sovereignty, and advancing our society, our economic and political system on the way of democracy'.[54] He also promised to dissolve the ÁVO and create new state security organs, one of the key demands of the demonstrators and something that was bound to cause concern in Moscow.

Two days later, on 30 October, Nagy took the momentous step of formalising the establishment of a multi-party state, with full participation by the Smallholders' Party, the National Peasant Party and the Social Democratic Party, as well as the communists. He also formed an 'inner cabinet', reflecting the new multi-party arrangements. On the same day, a 'revolutionary national defence council' of the Hungarian armed forces was set up, which supported the demands of the revolutionary workers' councils.

It will be recalled that a third group of scholars subscribe to the 'neutrality thesis', maintaining that the Hungarians – in contrast to the Poles – alarmed the Soviet Presidium by going too far, especially by declaring neutrality and withdrawing from the Warsaw Pact. To be sure, Nagy's declarations on 1 November exacerbated the situation. However, it should be noted that other Hungarian leaders had already been calling for neutrality and Warsaw Pact withdrawal well before Nagy did, and that he had opposed the move initially. Moreover, as the newly declassified 'Malin Notes' reveal, the Soviet leaders had already decided to intervene a second time on 31 October, *before* Nagy's appeal for neutrality.[55] Hence, in contrast to Soviet motivation in the 'Polish October', which was to prevent something from happening, or at least to get reassurance that something bad was not going to happen, Soviet motivation in Hungary was to undo the damage that had already occurred.[56]

Reasons for Nagy's Failure to Deter a Soviet Intervention

Why was Nagy unable to deter Soviet military intervention? Clearly, he was extremely popular and, like Gomułka, the Khrushchev leadership was at first willing to rely on him to control the party. In fact, this was the original motive in permitting the Hungarian 'comrades' to elect him as Prime Minister during the all-night Parliament session on 23–24 October. As late as 28 October at an emergency meeting of the Presidium in Moscow, the Kremlin leaders still believed they could count on Nagy. According to Malin's notes, Nikolai Bulganin said: 'In Budapest there are forces that want to get rid of Nagy's and Kádár's government. We should adopt a position of support for the current government. Otherwise we'll have to undertake an occupation. This will drag us into a dubious venture'.[57]

Yet Nagy had a different kind of popularity to Gomułka. His affability encouraged his colleagues, other institutions and press organs to take initiatives without his knowledge or permission. This led to a multiplication of overlapping curfews, ceasefires, reform decrees and a dizzying acceleration of events between 23 October and 4 November that convinced the Khrushchev leadership that Nagy could not control his party leadership and government. Only access to Hungarian archival documents enables us now to envision clearly the utter confusion in Nagy's Parliament in the days leading up to the second Soviet intervention.[58] Indeed, according to Zoltán Tildy, a non-communist member of Nagy's new government: 'There was

utter chaos, helplessness and confusion. The Parliament was flooded with delegates and delegations. People from the street were milling in the hallways, one could hardly walk past them, and one could not get any information as to what the actual situation was in the country.'[59] An examination of three factors in particular is useful in illustrating this miasma: the establishment of curfews, the appearance of new political parties and the declaration of a ceasefire.

At 4.30 a.m. on 24 October a curfew was proclaimed on the radio: 'Citizens are permitted on the streets only between 10.00 a.m. and 2.00 p.m.' Later at 4.24 p.m., the announcer said: 'Citizens are prohibited to go out between 6.00 p.m. and 6.00 a.m. the following morning.' The next day, at 5.38 a.m., the radio broadcast a message urging all citizens to go back to work. That same day, at 10.47 a.m., the radio warned Budapest citizens not to go out between 6.00 a.m. and 6.00 p.m. 'unless absolutely necessary'.[60] At a session of the party central leadership, one communist leader, Ferenc Nezval, asked incredulously: 'Did the Political Committee know what the situation was like this morning when it informed people they could go to work? Fighting began after that!'[61] Indeed, at 10.30 a.m. ÁVO personnel began shooting from the rooftops at about 25,000 unarmed Hungarians, who had gathered in front of the Parliament building, shouting 'Down with Gerő! The radio is lying, we're no bandits!' After forty to forty-five minutes, about 234 citizens lay dead and the crowd had dispersed.[62] The next day, 26 October, the confusion continued as citizens were told that they could go out only between 10.00 a.m. and 3.00 p.m.

A second factor which helped convince the Soviet leaders that Nagy had lost control was the proliferation of non-communist parties. Whereas Gomułka preserved the power of the Polish party, Nagy reorganised the government on 27 October, appointing non-communists to key posts and formally establishing a multi-party system on 30 October. Although they changed their minds later, the Soviet leaders initially supported Nagy's move, at least according to Malin's notes. At the CPSU Presidium meeting on 28 October, Suslov said: 'Our line is not to protest the inclusion of several democrats in the government'.[63] Between 31 October and 3 November, the Hungarian Council of Ministers' office was inundated with letters by new political parties, asking for official recognition and start-up funds for newspapers and office buildings. These included the Social Democratic Party, the Hungarian Independent Party, the Democratic People's Party, the Christian Democratic Party and the Hungarian Revolutionary Committee.[64] Church and youth organisations also asked for acknowledgement. Moreover, at a Cabinet session of the communist party an extraordinary decision was made – which the Gomułka leadership would probably never have contemplated – to withdraw funds from the party's account in the National Bank and to distribute it among these new organisations. According to Tildy's testimony, 600,000 forints were taken, the transaction being authorised by the Minister of Foreign Trade.[65]

Nagy's issuance of a ceasefire is a third factor illustrating both the lack of coordination of his government and its failure to deter the second Soviet intervention. At

1.20 p.m. on 28 October, Nagy ordered an immediate ceasefire and 'instructed the Hungarian Armed Forces to fire only if attacked'.[66] Western observers have long been reduced to speculation about the discussions at private meetings of the inner councils of the Hungarian Communist Party. We now know that this ceasefire was the subject of a heated debate at the emergency sessions of the party's Political Committee on 27 and 28 October. Kádár emphasised that the ceasefire should not involve branding the participants as counter-revolutionaries. However, he warned: 'If anyone after the declaration should still rise against our People's Republic, then measures [should] be taken against them to the point of their surrender or execution. We have to stand strictly against atrocities that are condemned even by the general public: shooting prisoners, murders, hangings'.[67] Hegedüs countered:

> I support a ceasefire, but not against bandits and looters... There was no ceasefire in Budakeszi when they tallied up the communists and wanted to hack them to pieces... Let's encircle Budapest with 1,000 of our people to start enforcing it, but wherever the rebels are killing, robbing and murdering comrades, I cannot vote for a ceasefire and I believe neither can you.[68]

Kádár retorted: 'A ceasefire cannot be declared in such a manner that it applies to one city but not another... [I]t has to be comprehensive, along with measures taken against looters, murderers and bandits. In other words we need a general ceasefire, plus the use of force against those still attacking us with weapons'.[69]

Antal Apró further cautioned: 'A ceasefire has to be declared without time limits attached. We must be sure that when the Soviet troops are withdrawn, the Hungarian security forces stand by; otherwise there will be a vacuum in their place'.[70] Agreeing with Kádár's suggestion, he added, 'If we did anything else the party would fall apart, vast masses would rise against us, and we'd get isolated.' Nagy then stepped in, saying: 'A ceasefire has to be declared as quickly as possible. There was absolute uncertainty even this morning when they wanted to start a military operation at 6.00.' He fumed at Hegedüs: 'Comrade Hegedüs has a lot to do with the fact that there's serious fluctuation within the leadership. Yesterday morning he agreed with us and now he again contemplates new military operations'.[71]

Nagy was upset. Despite the discussions about issuing a ceasefire, members of his own Political Committee, along with military officials, were secretly plotting an attack on the Corvin Alley insurgents for 6.00 a.m. on 28 October, which they thought could be a turning point in the conflict. Nagy attempted, in vain, to forbid the operation. The attack was launched, but failed.[72] At his trial in September 1957, Nagy protested his innocence, insisting that it was 'groundless' to blame him.[73] To his credit, he was aware of the chaos amidst his leadership. 'In this tragic situation we find ourselves in, the party leadership's total failure is the reason for the fact that these issues arise in such a random fashion'.[74] He stressed the need to focus on the most pressing matters and not get distracted:

There are two options: if we look on this movement, backed up by such substantial forces, as a counter-revolution then we have no choice but to subdue it by tanks and artillery. This is a tragedy... If we're not careful we will be subjected to an intervention. We should lean on, and lead, the huge national forces that are on the move.[75]

Thus, while Gomułka was careful to walk a fine line between appeasing Polish officials and the population and reassuring the Soviet Presidium members, Nagy apparently believed that appeasing the population was the best way to avoid a Soviet intervention. Describing the national movement as 'counter-revolutionary', he reasoned, would be tantamount to calling in Soviet tanks.

After much debate, the Nagy government announced the ceasefire. However, on the same day of the ceasefire (28 October), the Soviet Union was planning an attack on the Corvin Theatre where one of the worst 'hotbeds of resistance' was located. As Nagy told his interrogators a year later:

The Political Committee held a session on 27 October. It decided that a ceasefire should be declared, so we shouldn't start an offensive action or military operations. Where we are attacked by armies, we will destroy it with armies. During this time the Soviet leaders were working out a plan for the liquidation of the group in the Corvin passage.[76]

The Nagy government and Soviet military units were thus working at cross-purposes. It is easy to see how the Soviet leaders may have concluded that the Hungarian leaders and armed forces would not stand in their way in the event of a full-scale invasion, and that they could end the operation quickly in this small landlocked country.

Nagy saw the ceasefire, among other things, as a necessary measure to accelerate the withdrawal of all Soviet troops from Budapest. Indeed, though perhaps unbeknownst to him, the CPSU Presidium met in Moscow later that day (28 October). According to Malin's notes, Khrushchev said: 'We are ready to withdraw troops from Budapest. We must make this conditional on a ceasefire by the centres of resistance'.[77] Yet, while they welcomed the ceasefire, Mikoian and Suslov seemed to interpret it to mean the voluntary surrender of all weapons. The following day they reported from Budapest back to Moscow: 'The insurgents declare that they will give them [weapons] up after the Soviet troops leave Hungary. Thus, the peaceful liquidation of this hotbed is excluded (i.e. impossible).' They went on to say:

We will achieve the liquidation of these armed Hungarian forces. There is just one fear: the Hungarian army has occupied a 'wait and see' position. Our military advisers say that the relationship of the Hungarian officers and generals to Soviet officers in the past few days has worsened. There is no trust as there was earlier. It could be that the Hungarian units sent against the insurgents could join these other Hungarians, and then it will be necessary to once more undertake military operations (with Soviet forces).[78]

These fears were confirmed by KGB boss Serov in his cables to Moscow: 'The political situation in the country is not getting better; it is getting worse. This is expressed in the following: in the leading organs of the party there is a feeling of helplessness. In the party organisations there is a process of collapse. Hooligan elements are seizing regional party committees and killing communists.'[79] By 31 October, Moscow leaders made the final decision to invade a second massive time.

Conclusion

In short, the 'historical', 'personality' and 'neutrality' theses all retain some validity in elucidating the Soviet decision to invade Hungary, but not Poland, in 1956. Neither one, however, is sufficient. While the recently accessible archival sources do not call for a radically new interpretation of events, they do yield important insights and heighten the relevance of multi-causal explanations of Soviet interventionism: the particular interplay of leading communist personalities, the mood of the masses and the overall sequence of events themselves. Nagy may not have been as 'innocent' and progressive, given his initial opposition to the very decisions for which he has gone down in history as having made. Moreover, the Poznań revolt probably had greater impact on Polish decision-makers than originally thought. Finally, while Alfred Thayer Mahan may have been correct in stating that force is more operative when it is known to exist but is not brandished, Gomułka's bold stance on 19 October 1956 seems not to have impressed the Kremlin bosses to the extent hitherto believed. Thus, Gomułka was arguably less successful in deterring the Soviet leaders during their brief sojourn in Warsaw and less secure politically in his own country than historians have generally surmised.

Notes

*This chapter is a shortened and revised version of an article first published in the *Australian Journal of Politics and History*, vol. 48 (2002), pp. 369–95. We are much obliged to the copyright holders, Blackwell Publishing Ltd, for granting us permission to reprint this revised version. Research for the article was supported by grants from the International Research & Exchanges Board (IREX) and the Woodrow Wilson Center.

1. Alfred Thayer Mahan, *Letters and Papers of Alfred Thayer Mahan, 1840–1914*, eds. Robert Seager II and Doris D. Maguire (Annapolis, MD, 1975), p. 134.
2. Adam Bromke, 'Poland', in Béla Király and Paul Jones (eds), *The Hungarian Revolution of 1956 in Retrospect* (Boulder, CO, 1978), p. 89; and György Litván,

'A Forty-Year Perspective on 1956', in Terry Cox (ed.) *Hungary 1956 – Forty Years On* (London, 1997), pp. 19–20.

3. G.H.N. Seton-Watson, 'Introduction', in Király and Jones (eds), *The Hungarian Revolution*, p. 3.

4. Paul Kecskemeti, *The Unexpected Revolution: Social Forces in the Hungarian Uprising* (Stanford, CA, 1961), p. 144; Konrad Syrop, *Spring in October: The Story of the Polish Revolution, 1956* (New York, 1957), pp. 188–9; and Mark Kramer, 'The Soviet Union and the 1956 Crises in Hungary and Poland: Reassessments and New Findings', *Journal of Contemporary History*, vol. 33 (1998), p. 170.

5. M.K. Dziewanowski, *Poland in the Twentieth Century* (New York, 1977), p. 182; and Bromke, 'Poland', p. 88.

6. Kecskemeti, *The Unexpected Revolution*, p. 135.

7. For example, Ferenc Fehér and Agnes Heller, *Hungary 1956 Revisited* (London, 1983), p. 9; and György Litván (ed.), *The Hungarian Revolution of 1956: Reform, Revolt and Repression, 1953–1963* (London, 1996), p. 51.

8. For example, David Pryce-Jones, *The Hungarian Revolution* (New York, 1970); and Charles Gati, *Hungary and the Soviet Bloc* (Durham, NC, 1986).

9. Syrop, *Spring in October*, pp. 42–54; Dziewanowski, *Poland*, p. 177; R.F. Leslie (ed.), *The History of Poland Since 1863* (Cambridge, 1980), pp. 349–51.

10. On the rumours, see Archive of New Documents, Warsaw (AAN), 237/V-237, Polska Zjednoczona Partia Robotnicza (PZPR), Komitet Centralny (KC), Sekretariat, s. 9.

11. Edward Jan Nalepa, *Pacyfikacja Zbuntowanego Miasta. Wojko Polskie w Czerwcu 1956 r. w Poznaniu w świetle dokumentów wojskowych* (Warsaw, 1992), p. 22.

12. AAN, PZPR KC, Biuro Listów i Inspekcji, Biuletyn, s. 24.

13. Nalepa, *Pacyfikacja*, p. 27.

14. Cited in Paul Zinner (ed.), *National Communism and Popular Revolt in Eastern Europe* (New York, 1956), pp. 166–8.

15. AAN, 237/V-237 PZPR, s. 6–7.

16. Declassified Polish documents show no mention of possible Soviet 'assistance'. Classified documents may still reveal that the idea was raised, although it is highly improbable.

17. Cited in Tony Kemp-Welch, 'Khrushchev's "Secret Speech" and Polish Politics: The Spring of 1956', *Europe-Asia Studies*, vol. 48 (1996), p. 206, n. 148.

18. Syrop, *Spring in October*, p. 51; Nalepa, *Pacyfikacja*, p. 22.

19. Włodzimierz Jastrzębski, 'Bydgoski Październik 1956 r. jako przejaw oporu społecznego przeciwko totalitarnej władzy', in Włodzimierz Jastrzębski (ed.), *Rok 1956 w Bydgoskiem* (Bydgoszcz, 1996), p. 57.

20. AAN, 237/V-324, PZPR Komitet Centralny, Sekretariat, s. 3.

21. Russian State Archive of Contemporary History (RGANI), f. 3, op. 12, d. 1005, ll. 2–2ob.
22. RGANI, f. 3, op. 12, d. 1005, ll. 49–50.
23. Much popular hatred was directed against the dominant 'big four' Hungarian communist leaders, all of whom happened to be Jewish: Rákosi, Gerő, Mihály Farkas and József Révai.
24. Hungarian National Archive (MOL), 1676/2000/XX-5-h, dob. 1, k. 1, old. 137.
25. RGANI, f. 5, op. 28, d. 394, l. 256.
26. Státní Ústřední Archiv (State Central Archive, Prague), fond 07/16, svazek 3, 'Zpráva o jednání na ÚV KSSS 24. října 1956 k situaci v Polsku a Mad'arsku.' Originally cited in 'Az 1956.október 24-i moszkvai értekezlet', *Évkönyv I* (Budapest, 1992), pp. 149–56. For an expertly annotated English translation, see Mark Kramer, 'Hungary and Poland, 1956: Khrushchev's CPSU CC Presidium Meeting on East European Crises, 24 October 1956', *Cold War International History Project Bulletin*, no. 5 (1995), pp. 1, 50–6, quote at p. 54.
27. See Archive of the Institute of Political History (PIL), H-168, 867.f.m-284 and 867.f.f.-215.
28. Foreign Policy Archive of the Russian Federation (AVP RF), f. 059a, op. 4, p. 6, d. 5, l. 1. See my English translation of this telegram in *Cold War International History Project Bulletin*, no. 5 (1995), pp. 23, 29.
29. János Rainer, 'A Parlamenttől a Fő utcáig. Nagy Imre gondolati útja 1956. november 4.-1957.április 4', *Évkönyv I* (Budapest, 1992), p. 125.
30. Kramer, 'Hungary and Poland', p. 51.
31. The formal request did not actually arrive in Moscow until five days later. See AVP RF, f. 059a, op. 4, p. 6, d. 5, l. 12.
32. AVP RF, f. 059a, op. 4, p. 6, d. 5, l. 1.
33. The analysis of political personalities is an exercise in relativity, of course. Gomułka was certainly less skilled in communist *realpolitik* than GDR leader Ulbricht, and his naivety eventually led to his downfall in December 1970.
34. RGANI, f. 89, per. 45, dok. 79; dok. 82; and dok. 80, l. 2. On Nagy's past, see my articles and KGB document translations: 'Imre Nagy, Hesitant Revolutionary' and 'Imre Nagy aka "Volodya" – A Dent in the Martyr's Halo?', in *Cold War International History Project Bulletin*, no. 5 (1995), pp. 23, 28, 34–7.
35. János Rainer, 'The Life Course of Imre Nagy', in Cox (ed.), *Hungary 1956*, p. 144.
36. MOL, XX-5-h, dob. 13, k. 8, old. 99.
37. MOL, XX-5-h, dob. 1, k. 1, old. 193(b).
38. MOL, XX-5-h, dob. 1, k. 1, old. 191(a)–191(b), 194(a), and 199(a).
39. AAN, KC PZPR, paczka 15, tom 58, s. 172–4.
40. See János Tischler's unpublished English translation of a paper presented at the conference 'Hungary and the World, 1956: New Archival Evidence', Budapest, September 1996.

41. AAN, PZPR KC, 237/V-241, s. 166.

42. Ibid.

43. Kramer, 'Hungary and Poland', p. 53.

44. *Trybuna Ludu*, 25 October 1956.

45. Strobe Talbott (ed.), *Khrushchev Remembers: The Last Testament* (New York, 1974), p. 205.

46. Gomułka Family Private Papers. Cited in L.W. Gluchowski, 'Poland, 1956: Khrushchev, Gomułka, and the "Polish October"', *Cold War International History Project Bulletin*, no. 5 (1995), p. 42.

47. Teresa Toranska, *'Them': Stalin's Polish Puppets* (New York, 1987), p. 78.

48. The Malin Notes, as well as other Russian documents, have been published, in Russian in V.K. Volkov and V. Iu. Afiani, *Sovetskii Soiuz i Vengerskii krizis 1956 goda: Dokumenty* (Moscow, 1998). For English versions, see Mark Kramer's masterful translation and analysis, 'The Malin Notes on the Crises in Hungary and Poland', *Cold War International History Project Bulletin*, nos 8–9 (1997), pp. 385–410 and 358–84 respectively; and Csaba Békés and Malcolm Byrne, *The 1956 Hungarian Revolution: a History in Documents* (Budapest, 2002). See also my English translations of still other Soviet telegrams sent from Budapest in 1956, in *Cold War International History Project Bulletin*, no. 5 (1995), pp. 23, 27–8, and 28–37.

49. RGANI, f. 3, op. 12, d. 1005, ll. 49–50. This and the other Malin documents noted below are cited in Volkov and Afiani. Malin's notes are brief, often consisting of sentence fragments, so it is not clear what is meant here. Presumably, the Kremlin planned to undertake military manoeuvres and install a committee of pro-Soviet officials to eventually take over the Polish government.

50. Kramer, 'Hungary and Poland', pp. 50–1.

51. Jastrzębski, 'Bydgoski Październik', p. 57.

52. Kramer, 'Hungary and Poland', p. 54.

53. RGANI, f. 3, op. 64, d. 483, l. 128.

54. Zinner (ed.), *National Communism*, pp. 428–32.

55. RGANI, f. 3, op. 12, d. 1006, ll. 15–18ob.

56. According to the Malin Notes of the Presidium meeting on 28 October, Khrushchev was also concerned that the 'imperialists' might invade Hungary if Moscow did not, concluding that the Kremlin leaders were 'weak'. See RGANI, f. 3, op. 12, d. 1005, ll. 54–63.

57. Ibid.

58. Many otherwise excellent secondary works in English fall short of depicting the actual disarray of the Nagy Parliament from 24 October to 4 November. These include Litván (ed.), *The Hungarian Revolution*; Cox (ed.), *Hungary 1956*; and Jenő Györkei and Miklós Horváth, *Soviet Military Intervention in Hungary* (Budapest, 1999).

59. MOL, XIX-5-h, dob. 25, k. 3, old. 13.

60. MOL, 1676/2000/XX-5-h, dob. 1, k. 1, old. 141; and 'Gyorsirói feljegyzés az MDP Központi Vezetőségének Ülésérol, 1956.október 25, [I] a', in *Ötvenhat októbere és a hatalom: a Magyar Dolgozók Pártja vezető testületeinek dukumentumai 1956 október 24–október 28* (Budapest, 1997).

61. *Ötvenhat októbere és a hatalom*, p. 42.

62. MOL, 1676/2000/XX-5-h, dob. 1, k. 1, old. 143.

63. RGANI, f. 3, op. 12, d. 1005, l. 62.

64. MOL, 3541/2000, XX-5-h, dob. 13, k. 8, old. 72.

65. MOL, XIX-5-h, dob. 25, k. 3, old. 2.

66. *Ötvenhat októbere és a hatalom*, p. 114.

67. PIL, 290, f. 1/15. ő. e. old. 57–68. It should be noted that, until the moment Kádár decided to serve as the Soviet Union's quisling, he strongly supported Nagy's efforts.

68. *Ötvenhat októbere és a hatalom*, p. 102.

69. Ibid., p. 105.

70. Ibid.

71. Ibid.

72. Miklós Horváth, *Maléter Pál* (Budapest, 1995), pp. 97–105.

73. MOL, XX-5-h, dob. 13, k. 8, old. 101.

74. PIL, 290, f. 1/15. ő. e. old. 57–68.

75. Ibid.

76. MOL, XX-5-h, dob. 13, k. 8, old. 101.

77. RGANI, f. 3, op. 12, d. 1005, l. 59.

78. RGANI, f. 89, per. 45, dok. 12, l. 1.

79. Ibid.

Part II

–5–

Romania, 1945–89: Resistance, Protest and Dissent

Dennis Deletant

Overt challenges to communist rule in Romania were uncommon and none threatened to overthrow the regime.[1] As Nicolae Ceauşescu's despotic excesses increased in the 1980s, so people asked, not only in the West, but in parts of the Soviet bloc: why don't the Romanians resist or rebel? Four explanations were usually given. One was that there was no focal point for opposition. A second was that Romanians were by nature timorous and passive, conditioned by their history under the foreign imperial rule of the Ottoman Turks, the Habsburgs, the Romanovs and the Soviet Communists to adopt a defensive stance rather than come out in open revolt. Such a stance involved apathy, duplicity and a reliance on the individual rather than the group. The third explanation was that passiveness was engendered by the Orthodox faith, to which more than 80 per cent of Romanians belong. This life, necessarily, is a tale of tears, a judgement of God upon the people. Justice would come in the afterlife. The fourth explanation was that the secret police, the Securitate, were extremely efficient. This should not be underestimated. The Securitate knew that it could reckon on 'passivity', especially if the regime espoused at least one popular cause, for example, an anti-Russian stance. All four explanations have some truth in them, but they are not entirely valid, either in themselves or as a complete answer to the question.

Let us take the first explanation. The absence of a focal point of opposition was a feature of post-war Romania. At the time of the imposition of communist rule, Romania was a predominantly agricultural country with little industry and only a small working class. Organised labour did not represent a significant force in Romanian politics before the Second World War and there were no traditional links between the intellectuals and industrial workers. The weakness of the pre-war Romanian Communist Party, which was proscribed between 1924 and 1944, explains the few challenges to the communist regime from within Marxist circles. Although Romania's intelligentsia was one of the most sophisticated in Central Europe, and one of the most powerfully influenced by French literary currents, it remained untouched by the French passion for leftist values. Without a tradition of working-class activism, and a social group that espoused egalitarian principles, there was no drive for revisionist initiatives.[2] The notable exception was Lucreţiu

Pătrășcanu, a leading figure in the party, who was purged for 'nationalist deviation' in 1948 and executed in April 1954.

The accusation of timidity was largely based on what appeared to be a complete absence of challenge to the communist regime in Romania; unfavourable comparisons were made with the popular uprisings in East Germany in June 1953 and in Poland in summer 1956, the revolution in Hungary in 1956, the Prague Spring in 1968, and the Solidarity movement of the early 1980s in Poland. The unchallenged acceptance of this charge was itself confirmation of the validity of the explanation regarding the efficiency of the Securitate, for it provided a measure of the secret police's success in preventing information about resistance to the regime from leaking to the outside world. The first major collective protests against the regime in Romania were prompted by the example of the Hungarian uprising in October 1956, but there was a news blackout in Romania and little information about them reached the West, where the Suez crisis and the events in Hungary dominated the headlines. The failure of the Romanian media to report the strike of miners in the Jiu valley in south-western Romania in August 1977 characterised its role as a tool to be manipulated by the regime. There were a number of isolated, small-scale workers' protests in provincial towns in Romania in the 1980s about which nothing was generally known until almost a decade later. Even today, little has appeared in print about them.

Access to information was as essential for individuals to defend themselves against authority as was manipulation of it for the government to protect itself. This control of the media and the 'sanitising of news' was very effective in containing protest and inculcating a sense of isolation and frustration among protestors, and played a self-fulfilling role: if no opposition to the regime was reported, then most of the public not only assumed that there was none, but, guided by this assumption, questioned the point in displaying any.

Moving on to the role of the Church, the Romanian Church was completely subservient to the communist regime. Following the suppression of the Uniate (Greek Catholic) Church – which derived its authority from Rome – in 1948, the Orthodox Church could claim to represent the spiritual needs of the great majority of Romanians, but its direction was entirely subordinated to the interests of the Communist Party. Finally, the peasant was politically emasculated, first through the arrest of the leaders of the National Peasant Party and their imprisonment after trial in the winter of 1947, and then through the detention of thousands – 80,000 on the admission of Party Secretary Gheorghiu-Dej in 1962 – who resisted the programme of forced collectivisation initiated in 1949.

It is not enough to ascribe the lack of resistance to communism in Romania solely to the efficiency of the Securitate, or to 'Orthodoxy'; other factors, such as the linkage between formal and informal systems in Romanian society and duplicity, played a major part.[3] Strong family links enabled people to deal with the crisis in Ceaușescu's Romania. Networks of relatives or friends were used to map a way through the maze of state bureaucracy; on the culinary level – so dear to Romanians

– meat from the state abattoirs was sold under the counter to relatives and friends of the slaughterhouse manager.

It was only after the overthrow of Ceauşescu in December 1989 that details emerged of how several small bands – twenty to thirty persons – of self-styled 'partisans' took to the Carpathian mountains in the late 1940s and escaped arrest by the authorities. The last member of the longest-surviving group was not rounded up until 1960. This 'armed anti-communist resistance', as it has been called, was a spontaneous phenomenon and there were no links between the different groups, but they were driven by a common aim, namely not to submit themselves to the consequences of the communisation of their country. The groups, composed on average of between twenty and forty individuals, did not pose a major threat to communist power; yet, as long as they remained at liberty, they undermined the regime's claim to have total control of the country.

Resistance

The first examples of armed opposition to the communist role in the government had surfaced in the winter of 1944, and had been given a more cohesive form in summer 1945 by General Aurel Aldea – the Interior Minister in the coalition government that had been sworn in by King Michael after the latter had ordered the arrest on 23 August 1944 of the pro-German dictator Ion Antonescu. As a result of Aldea's own arrest in May 1946 by the communist authorities, this opposition crumbled. In fact, Aldea's so-called 'National Resistance Movement' posed little direct threat to the pro-communist government of Petru Groza, its principal activities being the distribution of primitive anti-communist propaganda; but the attacks it had carried out during the winter of 1944 on Hungarians, in revenge for murders of Romanians by Hungarian policemen during the period of Hungarian rule of Northern Transylvania (1940–4), had raised the spectre of civil strife in Transylvania behind the Soviet front line, and showed that it offered a potential nucleus of armed resistance to communist rule.

At the beginning of 1949, the Central Intelligence Agency (CIA), through its Office of Political Coordination (OPC) under the direction of Frank Wisner, began to recruit Romanians from refugee camps in southern Germany, Austria and Yugoslavia. Preference was shown for young men who knew those regions in which partisan activity had been reported. Gordon Mason, the CIA station chief in Bucharest from 1949 to 1951, revealed that these agents were instructed to contact the resistance groups and to deliver light weapons, ammunition, radio transmitters and medicines to them. The agents had three objectives. First, they were to encourage the partisans to carry out acts of sabotage on railways and factories; this would also offer proof of their existence and of their activity. Second, the agents were to monitor Soviet troop movements, especially those which might indicate preparations for an attack on Yugoslavia or on Western Europe. Finally, they were to encourage the partisans to harass Soviet troops should a war break out.[4]

The OPC set up training schools in France, Italy and Greece. Recruits were instructed in parachute drops and in the use of radio transmitters. Gratien Yatsevich, who directed CIA covert operations in the Balkans at the time, disclosed that in terms of resources allocated and agents recruited, the operations in Romania came second only to those in Albania. Among the Romanians recruited at the beginning of 1951 were Constantin Săplăcan, Wilhelm Spindler, Gheorghe Bârsan, Matias Bohm and Ilie Puiu. Their interrogation by the Securitate after their capture revealed that they had been recruited in Italy by a former Romanian pilot, and introduced to two American agents code-named 'Charles' and 'Gunter'. They were given their training in enciphering at the Franciscan Frascatti convent in Rome, and were then taken first to the Netherlands and subsequently to Frankfurt-am-Main, where they were given parachute training at an American airbase. After completing this, they were flown to Athens, from where they took off for Romania. They were dropped on the Negoiu mountain on the night of 18–19 October at a prearranged spot. They tried to make radio contact, but their sets failed to work and they were caught within a month. Bârsan committed suicide on being arrested and his colleagues were tried and executed in 1952.[5] A protest note was delivered by the Romanian Government to the Americans on the basis of an admission by the two men that they had been 'sent to carry out acts of terrorism and espionage against the Romanian army.' The US Government denied any connection with Spindler and Săplăcan, but former CIA officers have since admitted that the group was made up of American agents.[6]

Several groups of 'partisans' had taken to the Carpathian mountains in the late 1940s.[7] The groups were formed in the villages in the mountain foothills and were composed of peasants, former army officers, lawyers, doctors and students. Ill-equipped, they relied on an assortment of rifles, revolvers and machine-pistols left over from the war, and were always faced by an acute shortage of ammunition. They received support from villagers who brought them food and clothing, and often gave them shelter. The communist propaganda of the period dubbed these anti-communist partisans 'legionaries', that is, members of the extreme right-wing movement known as the Iron Guard, and indeed several of them had been members of it. However, the partisans were by no means exclusively 'legionaries', as the Securitate's own statistics show. A Securitate report of 1951 states that the political affiliation of 804 persons arrested for either belonging to, or aiding, seventeen groups, was as follows: 88 former members of Iuliu Maniu's National Peasant Party, 79 members of the left-wing Ploughmen's Front, 73 former legionaries, 42 former members of the Communist Party, 15 members of the National Liberal Party and others.[8]

The most resilient group was the *Haiducii Muscelului* (The Outlaws of Muscel). Composed of between thirty and forty people, it was formed by two ex-army officers, Gheorghe Arsenescu (1907–62) and Toma Arnăţoiu (1921–59), in their native district of Muscel in the foothills of the Carpathians. They avoided arrest by the Securitate for nine years, from 1949 to 1958. From the recent accounts given by contemporaries, Arsenescu seems to have put his faith in a general armed insurrection, which was to be led by other former army officers in the west of the country, but which never materialised. The Ministry of the Interior was clearly worried that the symbol of resistance posed by the band might be contagious, and it was for this reason that it poured troops and Securitate officers into the region. Helped by their local knowledge of the difficult mountain terrain and by several families in the commune of Nucşoara, notably Gheorghe and Elisabeta Rizea, Ion Săndoiu and Ion Sorescu, the group secured provisions and escaped arrest. On the night of 18 June 1949, members of the group were ambushed as they came to collect supplies and in the ensuing gunfight two Securitate officers were killed. The group's escape under cover of darkness through a security cordon thrown around the area resulted in a massive search being carried out for them by two army batallions and units of the Securitate, and the arrest of families suspected of aiding them.[9] Among those arrested was Elisabeta Rizea. She was taken to the mayor's office in Nucşoara, where she was beaten with a heavy stick by a Securitate officer. Eighteen months passed before she was put on trial. While in detention she was beaten on several occasions; she was finally tried and sentenced in December 1950 to seven years' imprisonment for helping the partisan group.[10]

After the ambush of 18–19 June 1949, Arsenescu decided to split his men into two bands, one under his command, the other under the leadership of Arnăţoiu. The members of the first band were soon rounded up, but Arsenescu fled from the area and led a hermit-like existence in the hills for ten years until he was finally caught in 1960. Two years earlier, on 20 May 1958, Toma Arnăţoiu, his brother Petre and Maria Plop, who had given birth to a daughter two years earlier – the surviving members of the second group – had been tracked down and forced to submit.[11] The trial of the brothers took place the following year. Toma and Petre Arnăţoiu were sentenced to death and executed by firing squad at Jilava prison in Bucharest on 18 October 1959, along with thirteen persons found guilty of rendering them assistance. Maria Plop received life imprisonment and died in jail in 1962.[12] Arsenescu's trial took place in February 1962, two years after his capture. He was sentenced to death and executed at Jilava on 29 May 1962. His wife Maria and his father Gheorghe were also tried for assisting him, and were given prison terms of ten and fifteen years respectively.[13]

A second notable resistance group was that led by Ion Gavrilă-Ogoreanu in the Făgăraş mountains. Gavrilă-Ogoreanu, a student at Cluj University, formed his group of eleven from his university colleagues in 1948. For seven years they tied up several companies of Securitate troops before they were captured and sentenced to death in 1957. Gavrilă-Ogoreanu avoided arrest and, with the help of friends, escaped detection until June 1976, when he was finally picked up in Cluj.[14] Unlike Arnăţoiu and Arsenescu, Gavrilă-Ogoreanu was spared the death penalty and survived the communist era.

In Romania today there are attempts to play up this anti-communist resistance. To do so is important in re-establishing self-esteem and national honour. Resistance helped to rekindle the flame of national honour after the ignominy of the Ceaușescu regime. An overcompensatory emphasis on resistance can also be explained by the fact that it was covered up for so long by communist writers. But as Gavrilă-Ogoreanu is honest enough to admit in his riveting autobiography, published in 1993, he and his friends were isolated examples of resistance and of no military importance. They posed no threat to the stability of the new regime because few followed their example. This he ascribes to the passivity of much of the population: 'They are so down-trodden and conditioned to their down-trodden state that they cannot and will not look beyond. Their eyes are those of a mole'.[15]

This assessment, coming from such a venerable figure in the resistance to communist rule as Gavrilă-Ogoreanu, has a more convincing ring about the attitude of much of the local population to resistance groups than the tendency towards hyperbole which characterises some of the writing about the 'armed resistance' which has appeared since 1989.[16] It is as though some authors feel embarrassment at the fact that challenges to communist authority in Romania under Gheorghiu-Dej were not as widespread or serious as in some other Soviet satellites, and seek to overcompensate by exaggerating the scale of resistance in Romania. The publication of memoir literature and the opening of the Securitate files have dispelled the general impression that there was no opposition to communist rule, but at the same time they have revealed the true dimension of resistance. It was not widespread, as Gavrilă-Ogoreanu points out; and therefore his activity, like that of Arnăţoiu and Arsenescu and others, appears all the more valiant and poignant.

Collective Protest

The first major collective protests against the regime in Romania were prompted by the example of the Hungarian revolution in October 1956. The repercussions of the revolt, which began with a massive popular demonstration in Budapest on 23 October 1956 during which the Stalin monument was destroyed, were soon felt in Romania. On 27 October there were student and workers' demonstrations in Bucharest, Cluj, Iaşi and Timişoara. The Communist Party leader, Gheorghiu-Dej, and a Romanian delegation cut short a visit to Yugoslavia on 28 October to address the crisis. On the following day, railwaymen at the Griviţa yards in Bucharest held a protest meeting calling for improved conditions of work; and in Iaşi, the chief city in Moldavia, there were street demonstrations in support of better food supplies. To placate the workers the government announced on 29 October that the minimum wage would be raised, and special concessions were given to railwaymen in the form of free travel. The emphasis of the student protests was on the abolition of the teaching of Russian in schools and universities. On 30 October, more than 1,000 students attended a meeting at Timişoara polytechnic, at which the Communist Party representatives were jeered and forced to leave the hall, whereupon army units were called in to seal off the polytechnic campus and hundreds of arrests were made. The protests, however, made their mark. On 5 November, Miron Constantinescu, a Politburo member, addressed a student meeting in the Transylvanian capital of Cluj, and promised that the compulsory classes in Russian at universities would be abolished and living conditions raised. Two weeks later he was made Minister of Education.[17] There were no further collective demonstrations against communist rule under Gheorghiu-Dej.

The miners' strike of 1977 in the Jiu Valley, in south-western Romania, was the most important challenge posed by a group of workers to communist power in Romania since the 1956 protests. The strike was sparked off by legislation introduced in July 1977 discontinuing disability pensions for miners and raising the retirement age from fifty to fifty-five.[18] A strike was called at the Lupeni pit, and on 1 August 35,000 miners crammed into the grounds of the mine to hear Ioan (also known as Constantin) Dobre, a pit brigade chief from the Paroseni mine, and G. Jurcă, an engineer from the Lupeni mine. They attempted to calm the spirits of the miners, who were demanding a meeting with party leader, Nicolae Ceauşescu. Dobre and Jurcă agreed that the former, being a miner and therefore closer to his colleagues, should draw up a list of the miners' demands and present them to a mass meeting at the Lupeni mine. These were a reduction in the working day from eight to six hours, a restitution of retirement at fifty, a reassessment of the criteria for sick leave, employment for miners' wives and daughters, the recruitment of competent medical personnel to work in the mines, and the objective presentation by the media of the strike. Dobre put these points to the mass meeting on 3 August and they were approved unanimously.

Ceauşescu hastily convened a government commission to deal with the crisis and it was decided to send Ilie Verdeţ, the member of the Politburo responsible for the economy, and other officials to talk to the miners. They no doubt intended to persuade them to call off their strike but they were not given the opportunity to do so. They were jostled by the miners and even punches were thrown as they tried to make their way to the mine manager's office. Verdeţ was told that the miners had no confidence in him since he had deceived the Central Committee as to the true situation in the Jiu Valley, and he was instructed to contact Ceauşescu with the demand that the Secretary General should come to Lupeni to discuss the miners' grievances with them directly. Ceauşescu arrived the same day in a convoy of cars which tried to force a passage through the masses of miners. They failed and Ceauşescu was obliged to get out of the car and make his way to the mine manager's office, from where he addressed the crowd.

Clearly shaken, and visibly angered, he descended to the level of threats: 'if you do not go back to work we'll have to stop pussyfooting around!' Prolonged booing and the cry of 'Down with Ceauşescu' met these menaces and it was only when

Dobre appealed for calm and urged the miners to let the Secretary General finish what he had to say that the atmosphere became less charged. Ceauşescu seized the opportunity to strike a more conciliatory note, conceding a reduction in the working day to six hours throughout the whole Jiu Valley, and agreeing to build factories which would offer work to miners' families. He promised that no retaliatory measures would be taken against those who had organised the strike, and that all those who were to blame for the miners' discontent would be brought to account.

After these promises were made the miners dispersed and some even returned to work on the evening shift of 3 August. But the next day, in spite of Ceauşescu's assurances, the Jiu Valley was declared a 'restricted area', the army sent in, and the Securitate began their work of repression. An investigation was launched to discover where the core of support for the strike lay and in the months following the strike several hundred miners were moved to other mining areas, among them Dobre, who was detained by the Securitate on 30 August and given compulsory domicile in the town of Craiova, in southern Romania.[19] Most of Ceauşescu's other promises were not respected either: the eight-hour day was reinstated, and only those miners who had worked underground for more than twenty years were allowed to retire at fifty. The only concessions made were in the provision of improved medical care in the mines and in the creation of jobs for the miners' families.

Growing economic hardship, produced by Ceauşescu's determination to pay off the country's foreign debt of $10.2 billion by 1990, led miners in seven metal mines in the Maramureş region of northern Transylvania to go on strike in September 1983, in protest at pay cuts introduced under a new wage law. Security police were sent in to break up the strike. Following a reduction of the daily bread ration to 300 grams per person and pay cuts of up to 40 per cent for failure to fill output targets, Romanian and Hungarian workers went on strike at the Heavy Machine Plant and the Refrigeration Plant in Cluj, and at the glass factory in Turda. Leaflets in both languages demanding 'meat and bread' and 'milk for our children' circulated in Cluj, thus demonstrating inter-ethnic solidarity. Party officials rushed food to the factories and promised to meet the workers' grievances, whereupon the strikers returned to work; but just as in the Jiu Valley in 1977, the Securitate launched an investigation into the organisation of the strike and several workers were moved to other areas.

Within three months unrest had spread to the east of the country, encompassing for the first time in decades both workers and students. Once again, wage cuts imposed for failure to meet production targets and food supply problems were the trigger. On 16 February 1987 some 1,000 employees at the Nicolina rolling stock works in the Moldavian capital of Iaşi marched on the party headquarters, protesting at the pay cuts. Their demands were quickly met. On the following day, in what appears to have been an uncoordinated action, several thousand students from the university and polytechnic marched through the centre of the city in protest at the power and heating cuts imposed in student hostels, chanting 'we want water to be able to wash, and light to be able to study'. The authorities again gave in and no repressive action was taken against the students. At the Nicolina plant, however, 150 of the most prominent strikers were dismissed after the customary Securitate-directed post mortem.

Behind this string of protests against Ceauşescu's economic policies lay the introduction of draconian measures designed to reduce food and energy consumption, and wage reductions. Yet instead of heeding the warning signs of increasing labour unrest, Ceauşescu plunged forward blindly with the same measures, seemingly indifferent to their consequences. A sign that the cup of privations had filled to overflowing came on 15 November 1987 in Braşov, the country's second largest industrial centre, in southern Transylvania. The trouble started only five days after the implementation of a decree from Ceauşescu, reducing heating quotas for domestic consumption by 30 per cent and instituting punitive charges for exceeding the quotas. Coming on top of the imposition of wage cuts for the second consecutive month for failure to meet production targets (they could not be met because of a shortage of orders since the internal market was stagnant and there had been a drop in exports), and chronic food shortages, particularly of potatoes which were an essential part of the diet of Braşov's inhabitants, the heating restrictions were the last straw for the working population. Several thousand workers at the *Steagul Roşu* (Red Flag) plant, with a workforce of 22,000, came off the night shift and assembled, ostensibly to vote in the local elections taking place across the country that Sunday. They marched off from the plant at about nine o'clock in the morning in the direction of the party headquarters in the centre of the city singing the anthem of the revolution of 1848 and chanting 'Down with the dictatorship' and 'We want bread'. They were joined by workers from the Braşov Tractor Plant (a workforce of 25,000) and by many townspeople, as they made their way to the city centre where they forced entry into the party headquarters. A number of arrests were made after the disturbances and sixty-one persons were sentenced for periods ranging from eighteen months to three years in prison on charges of 'hooliganism'.[20]

The fact that this protest took place in a major industrial centre, whose production of lorries and tractors was largely for export and whose workers were formerly among the best-paid in Romania, showed to what depths discontent with Ceauşescu's policies had sunk. But what was even more striking, perhaps, about the Braşov protests, was the failure of Romanian intellectuals to react to the events. This lack of solidarity between workers and intellectuals characterised the forms of opposition to the Romanian regime and distinguished Romania from Poland and Hungary.

Only three individuals of public standing spoke out about the events in Braşov. Mihai Botez, a mathematician and erstwhile economic adviser, and a prominent critic of Ceauşescu, issued a statement emphasising that the protests signalled a 'rejection of the leadership's economic and political strategies' and constituted 'a severe warning to the leaders' from the working class. Botez warned that 'repression would be the costliest option, with disastrous implications for the country'.[21] Even more significant, and unprecedented, was the intervention of Silviu Brucan, deputy editor of the party daily *Scînteia* from 1944 to 1956, and Romanian Ambassador to the United States (1956–9) and the United Nations (1959–62). In the evening of 26 November Brucan invited two Western journalists, Nick Thorpe from the BBC and Patricia Koza of UPI, to his house and handed them a statement to Western correspondents in Bucharest, invoking the authority of the party and alerting Ceauşescu to the fact that 'a period of crisis has opened up in relations between the Romanian Communist Party and the working class'. After a rise in the standard of living in the 1960s and 1970s, 'the situation of the workers has deteriorated and the explosion in Braşov is a sign that the cup of anger is now full and the working class is no longer prepared to be treated like an obedient servant.' He warned that 'repression may result in total isolation, this time not only from the West, but also from the East'.[22] Excerpts from Brucan's declaration were broadcast the following evening on BBC World Service News, and the whole text in Romanian was transmitted on the BBC Romanian Service, Radio Free Europe and Voice of America, thus enabling millions of Romanians to hear for the first time a warning to Ceauşescu delivered from a senior party figure.

The third person to speak out was Doina Cornea. Cornea, in a series of open letters to Ceauşescu, which had been broadcast on Radio Free Europe since 1982, did more than any other Romanian to draw attention to Ceauşescu's draconian internal policies. On learning of the workers' demonstration, Cornea made some leaflets, which she distributed on 18 November with her son Leontin Iuhas outside the university and factories in Cluj, calling on workers to show solidarity with those in Braşov. Both were arrested the following day and held by the Securitate until the end of December, when they were released as a result of the public outcry reported in the Western media, and in particular of a documentary about Romania under Ceauşescu by Christian Duplan, transmitted on French TV on 10 December, which included a previously recorded interview with Cornea.

Dissent

When asked by a Western diplomat in the mid-1980s about the incidence of dissent in Romania, a senior official of the Romanian Communist Party replied: 'Corruption is our dissent'.[23] Before discussing 'dissent' in the Romanian context, some clarification of the meaning of the term is advisable. Several Romanian observers confuse dissent with nonconformism on the one hand, and with what they have called 'resistance through culture' on the other.[24] I take a dissident to be a person who operates outside the system, who poses a challenge to it, whereas a nonconformist operates from within. Both express opposition to a regime, but the degree of opposition is greater in a dissident than in a nonconformist. Moreover, dissidence involves a public act, such as a protest, whereas nonconformism is a discreet stance. Nonconformist attitudes manifested by writers in the Ceauşescu period have been presented since 1989 as 'resistance through culture'. If we take 'resistance' to imply a public *act*, the term 'resistance through culture' is an inappropriate term for those who sought through their literary work to extend the boundaries of official tolerance, either by adopting a line considered by the authorities as ideologically suspect, or by highlighting certain contemporary social problems, or both.[25] To pass judgement on such writers is difficult, for in their eyes their works were in themselves acts of resistance to the Ceauşescu regime, albeit that they often entered the public domain with the acquiescence or collusion of the censor. But there is a sense of culpability felt by the community of writers over their compliance with the Ceauşescu regime, which led some of them after its overthrow to present their posture during the Ceauşescu era as they would like it to be seen, rather than as it was. The pages of the literary review *România literară* and the cultural journal *22* abounded with such views in 1990.

How rare open dissent among intellectuals was during Ceauşescu's rule is suggested by an affirmation made to Michael Shafir in the early 1980s. 'Romanian dissent', he was told, 'lives in Paris and his name is Paul Goma'.[26] This is, as Shafir recognises, an exaggeration, but it is symptomatic of the relative absence of challenge to the regime's authority in Romania until the 'Goma affair' broke out in the spring of 1977. The platform for Goma's exposure of human rights abuses in Romania came from the signing in 1975 of the Final Act of the Conference on Security and Cooperation in Europe (the Helsinki Agreement). Article VII of the 'Declaration on Principles Guiding Relations between Participating States' bound the signatories to 'respect human rights and fundamental freedoms, including the freedom of thought, conscience, religion or belief, for all without distinction as to race, sex, language or religion'. Ceauşescu's signature on this agreement, together with Romania's ratification a year earlier of the International Covenant on Civil and Political Rights, provided instruments in international law to which the Romanian regime could be held to account. But the direct stimulus for Goma's action came from the example of the Charter 77 movement in Czechoslovakia, which itself took inspiration from the Helsinki process.

In the euphoria accompanying Ceauşescu's condemnation of the Warsaw Pact invasion of Czechoslovakia in August 1968, Goma joined the Communist Party.[27] Several months earlier he had submitted for publication the manuscript of his first novel, *Ostinato*, based on his experiences at the hands of the security police, but the reader claimed to recognise Elena Ceauşescu in one of the characters and a ban was placed on further publication of Goma's writings. *Ostinato* appeared, nevertheless, in German translation in 1971, and as a result its author was dismissed from the party. Frustrated by the ban on his writings and encouraged by the initiative of Pavel Kohout in Czechoslovakia, Goma wrote a letter to Kohout and the other Charter 77 signatories in January 1977 expressing his solidarity with their movement.[28] Exasperated by his failure to attract support among his friends for this letter, he wrote a few days later to Ceauşescu, inviting him to sign it on the grounds that 'By doing this, you will show that you are consistent with your declarations of 1968, you will prove that you are fighting for socialism, democracy, and mankind'.[29]

Shortly after sending this letter Goma persuaded seven others[30] to sign with him an open letter to the 35 participating states at the Conference on Security and Cooperation in Europe (CSCE) meeting in Belgrade, which had signed the Helsinki Final Act, drawing attention to human rights abuses in Romania and the government's failure to respect its international undertakings in this domain. The open letter was an unprecedented act. Goma's protest subsequently attracted the signatures of over 200 Romanian citizens (despite a campaign of intimidation against Goma and the other initial signatories carried out by the Securitate), and was the first publicly disseminated criticism of the regime in Romania since the imposition of communist rule. However, only a handful of intellectuals signed the appeal and the vast majority of the 200 signatories actually wanted a passport to emigrate to the West.[31]

Goma's courageous move was immediately denounced by Ceauşescu. On 17 February 1977 Ceauşescu delivered an ill-tempered speech, attacking 'traitors of the country' – clearly a reference to Goma's two letters – and that same evening the writer began to receive a string of threatening telephone calls. Every telephone call of support was interrupted, whereas those containing insults and threats went undisturbed. On the following day, a police cordon was thrown up around the block of flats where Goma lived and only residents were allowed through. Passports were given to several of the signatories of the open letter, but Goma and his wife refused this 'offer' to emigrate. On 1 March Goma sent a second, more admonitory letter to the President, which was profoundly prophetic. Goma urged Ceauşescu not to break that bond that his condemnation of the invasion of Czechoslovakia had created with his people. On the following day the psychiatrist Ion Vianu brought Goma a letter expressing his support. Vianu had published in the previous October an article in the Writers' Union journal, *Viaţa Românească*, pointing out the ways in which his discipline was being abused by the regime. On 3 March the literary critic Ion Negoiţescu wrote to Goma, also expressing his support. By now 75 signatures had been gathered. On 19 March, Horst Stumpf, a former boxer, broke into Goma's flat and attacked him. The police, despite being summoned, did not appear. Stumpf repeated the attacks on two occasions just a few days later. Goma was interviewed on 28 March by French television network *Antenne 2* reporter Henri Gallais as he was barricading himself in his flat with the help of some fellow signatories, whose numbers had now risen to 180.

Goma was arrested on 1 April. A day later, Vianu was brought by Securitate officers to the amphitheatre of the Institute of Pharmacy in Bucharest, where he was subjected to the anger and abuse of 200 persons, led by the rector, who dubbed him a 'bandit', a 'Fascist' and a 'pig'. He was dismissed from the Institute and from the hospital at which he worked. In the meantime Negoiţescu was detained for questioning by Securitate officers, and, under pain of a charge of 'homosexual practices' being brought against him, retracted his support of Goma, signing an article about patriotism in *România literară* on 14 April. In fact, Negoiţescu and Vianu were the only two intellectuals to support Goma. Two other signatories, Ion Ladea and Gheorghe Sandu, were savagely beaten by Securitate interrogators. Within a few days, international concern about Goma's arrest snowballed with appeals for his release being made by Eugen Ionescu, Jean-Paul Sartre, Arthur Miller and Edward Albee, among others. The growing chorus of protest threatened to overshadow the centenary celebrations of Romanian independence on which Ceauşescu set great store; his image as the plucky defender of that independence against the great Russian bear to the north was losing some of its gilt as a result of the Goma affair, and on 6 May 1977, four days before the anniversary, Goma was released from custody. After persistent official harassment, he was allowed to leave Romania with his wife and child on 20 November 1977.

Their settlement in Paris, however, did not remove them from the long arm of the Securitate. Goma's successful defiance of the regime clearly rankled with the Securitate and their foreign intelligence arm, the CIE, assumed the task of silencing him and other critics. Goma was one of three Romanian émigrés to whom parcel bombs were addressed from Madrid in February 1981. Matei Pavel Haiducu, a CIE agent based in France to carry out industrial espionage, claimed that he received orders on 13 January 1982 from the CIE head Nicolae Pleşiţă to murder both Paul Goma and another dissident writer, Virgil Tănase, by injecting them with a special poison designed to provoke cardiac arrest. Instead of obeying orders, Haiducu turned himself over to the French authorities.

No Romanian did more to draw attention to Ceauşescu's draconian internal policies than Doina Cornea. Cornea, a university lecturer in the Transylvanian city of Cluj, was dismissed from her post in September 1983 for having used Western philosophical texts in her lectures. In a series of open letters to Ceauşescu, which were broadcast on Radio Free Europe between 1982 and 1989, Cornea denounced the indignity to which the Romanian leader had brought the population. At first sight, one might interpret her string of protests as purely political acts, containing as they did proclamations for democratic reform, denunciations of the demolition of villages under Ceauşescu's systematisation programme (a policy designed to reduce the number of villages in Romania by more than half) and expressions of solidarity with fellow dissenters. Yet they also had a deep moral content. At the heart of Cornea's messages stood the belief that every individual should feel responsible for their actions and should recognise that any failure to act responsibly had repercussions for society at large.[32]

Cornea was placed under house arrest in 1988, a restriction which was only lifted on 22 December 1989, the day of Ceauşescu's overthrow. Her treatment at the hands of the regime remained unique until March 1989,[33] when she shared her predicament with such writers and political figures as Mircea Dinescu and Silviu Brucan, but she had taken her stance long before the changes in the Soviet Union offered a political umbrella, however pervious, to those whose professional or family ties linked them to the home of communism. Cornea remained for almost seven years a largely isolated figure, and yet because her views were formed from her own experience of daily life, one shared by her audience, her message gained in power. The gravest crimes committed by the Ceauşescu regime were, in her eyes, to strip people of their human dignity; to reduce them to an animal state where their major daily concern was the struggle to find food; to institutionalise misery; and to atomise and homogenise the peoples of Romania. That few of her fellow citizens responded to this message should not be regarded as a failure on her part, but confirmation at once of the enormity of the task she set herself, and of Ceauşescu's success in brutalising his people.

Cornea was one of a number of dissidents briefly detained in early December 1987, following the workers' protest in Braşov. They included Mariana Celac, an urban planner who was a critic of the urban and rural resettlement programme; Ion Puiu, a veteran National Peasant Party politician and critic of the regime; Florian Russu, the leader of the outlawed National Peasant Party youth group; Radu Filipescu, a young electronics engineer who had been sentenced in September 1983 to ten years imprisonment for printing and distributing anti-Ceauşescu leaflets, but was released in April 1986; Nicolae Stăncescu and Ion Fistioc, both party members, who had submitted proposals for reform to the leadership and to the Soviet Embassy in Bucharest with the request that they be forwarded to Gorbachev; Nelu Prodan, a young Baptist; and Gabriel Andreescu, a 36-year-old geophysicist, who sent an open letter to a human rights conference sponsored by Solidarity in Kraków at the end of August 1988, calling on Romanian citizens to adopt a policy of non-cooperation with the regime, and to 'refuse to go along with harmful decisions by the authorities'. Other outspoken critics of Ceauşescu included Gheorghe Calciu, Vasile Paraschiv, Dorin Tudoran, Dan Petrescu and Mircea Dinescu. Considerations of space do not allow me to present an exhaustive list.

The most significant act of personal defiance of the Ceauşescu regime proved to be that of a Transylvanian Hungarian. Among the persistent critics of the Communist Party's interference in the affairs of the Hungarian Reformed Church in Transylvania were István Tőkés, a former deputy bishop, and his son László, a pastor, who had been appointed initially to a parish in the Transylvanian town of Dej. Laszlo was a contributor to *Ellenpontok* (Counterpoints), a clandestine Hungarian-language journal produced in Oradea in 1981 and 1982, and the only major *samizdat* printed in Romania. Among his articles was one on abuses of human rights in Romania and this led to his harassment by the Securitate. He and his friends were placed under surveillance, and eventually Tőkés was dismissed from his parish in Dej by order of Bishop Nagy, and assigned to the village of Sânpietru de Câmpie, some forty kilometres from Cluj. Tőkés refused to go and instead went to his parents' house in Cluj, where he spent two years unemployed. He used part of this time to launch a letter-writing campaign in 1985 among the Hungarians of Transylvania to gather statistics about facilities for education in Hungarian.[34] His plight was brought to the attention of the Foreign Relations Committee of the US Senate, and as a result Bishop Papp was instructed by the authorities in 1986 to appoint Tőkés assistant pastor in the city of Timişoara, one of mixed Romanian, Hungarian and German population.[35]

As Ceauşescu's village systematisation programme gathered momentum, so Tőkés used his sermons to encourage resistance to it. He called for solidarity between Hungarians and Romanians, who were both suffering at the hands of the regime, and made no special pleading for Hungarian villages. In the summer of 1988 he talked with representatives in all thirteen deaneries of the Reformed Church to organise resistance to proposals to destroy villages; and at his own deanery meeting in Arad in September, he and three other Hungarian pastors spoke in favour of a statement denouncing the programme.

The statement was sent to Bishop Papp and within twenty-four hours every signatory had been visited by Securitate officers and cross-examined about the meeting. Tőkés's own file was handled by the head of the Timişoara Securitate, Colonel Traian Sima, who authorised visits to Tőkés's church flat by anonymous visitors who would hurl insults and threats. A cultural festival organised with the Catholic Church in Timişoara on 31 October 1988 led to threats of expulsion being made against those students who had participated. Bishop Papp sent a letter to Tőkés banning all youth activities in the Oradea diocese, which included Timişoara, but, undeterred, Tőkés decided to hold another festival in the spring of 1989 with the Orthodox Church, whose metropolitan agreed. On 31 March, at the instigation of the Department of Cults and the Securitate, Bishop Papp instructed Tőkés to stop preaching in Timişoara and ordered him to move to Mineu, an isolated parish in northern Transylvania. Tőkés refused to comply with the order and his congregation expressed its support for him. The bishop then began civil proceedings to evict him from his church flat. Since he was no longer deemed by the Timişoara authorities to be a resident of the city, his ration book was withdrawn and power supplies to his flat were cut off. Tőkés's parishioners rallied round, bringing him and his wife and young child food and fuel. Their action contrasted with that of his fellow pastors. Fear of incurring Bishop Papp's displeasure – 70 per cent of the 200 pastors in the diocese had never been promoted from probationary status and were still directly answerable to Papp – coupled with a feeling that Tőkés's defiance was pointless, meant that the authors of an open letter appealing to the bishop to put an end to the harassment of Tőkés could not find one pastor who was prepared to add his signature.[36]

A court order was made for Tőkés's eviction on 20 October 1989. Tőkés lodged an appeal. Tudor Postelnicu, the Minister of the Interior, ordered the Securitate to enforce the order. On 2 November, four attackers armed with knives broke into the flat, while Securitate agents looked on, but fled after Tőkés and his friends managed to fight them off. After this incident, in which Tőkés was cut on the forehead, the

Romanian Ambassador was summoned to the Hungarian Foreign Ministry and told of the Hungarian Government's concern for the pastor's safety.

Parishioners continued to smuggle in food and firewood for Tőkés to the sacristy of the church, despite the attention of Securitate agents. On 28 November Tőkés was informed that his appeal had been turned down and that his eviction would be enforced on 15 December. As Christmas approached, parishioners brought gifts of food to the sacristy in groups and afterwards gathered outside Tőkés's flat next to the church to show their support. The two guards were unable to move them along and this gave hope to his supporters. On the day fixed for the eviction a human chain was formed around the block in which he lived and the militia were unable to gain access. Tőkés leaned out of his window and thanked the crowd but advised them to leave. His advice was met with cries of 'we won't leave' and several hundred stayed in groups close to the flat. Throughout the following morning their numbers grew, swelled by young Romanians who were attracted by the sight of such a large crowd and the rumour that the Securitate was unable to disperse it.[37] Tőkés pleaded with the crowd to go home, but they were convinced that he was acting under threats from the Securitate and refused. Some called on him to come down into the street and lead them, but Tőkés realised that this might play into the hands of the regime, who could put the blame for the protests on the Hungarian minority.

By seven o'clock in the evening the crowds filled several streets extending from the church. Many students from the local polytechnic and university were present. Around the church Romanians linked hands with Hungarians in a human chain and hymns were sung. About thirty minutes later the first bars of *Deşteaptă-te Române* ('Romanians awake!') – a Romanian national song which had been sung for the first time in a public place during the Ceauşescu era in the Braşov protests of November 1987 – were taken up falteringly. Unknown in the Hungarian community, the song was an anthem of resistance to oppression and a sign that a Hungarian protest had now become a Romanian revolt.

The vigil held in support of Tőkés turned into major demonstrations in the city on 16 and 17 December. They were brought to a halt by the intervention of the army, which opened fire on the crowd. The number of casualties was initially estimated at several thousand, but subsequent investigations put the figure at 122.[38] On Elena Ceauşescu's orders, forty of the dead were transported by lorry to Bucharest and cremated to make identification impossible. Here was a clear sign of her cruelty and ruthlessness. On 18 December industrial workers in Timişoara staged peaceful protests in their tens of thousands within the factory gates, but on 20 December these overflowed into the streets and effectively brought an end to communist rule in the city. The crowds proclaimed Timişoara a free city – this two days before Ceauşescu fled from Bucharest. On the streets of Timişoara there were chants of 'Today in Timişoara, tomorrow throughout the whole land', and the fervour there was gradually transmitted to all those who had been waiting for years for the end of the dictatorship. The Romanian revolution had begun.[39]

Speaking only five days after the Ceauşescus' execution on Christmas Day 1989, the literary critic Dan Hăulică attributed Romania's torment under the dictator directly to passivity and a lack of resistance. Paraphrasing the words of the painter Goya, Hăulică declared that 'the sleep of a nation brings forth monsters'.[40] After twenty-five years of shame, he argued, Romania had recovered its self-esteem. Dignity and freedom – words whose meaning had become so debased under Ceauşescu – had been given back their true value by the revolution.[41] What Romania would find more difficult to shake off was the legacy of compliance towards a dictatorship. In one sense, there is a link between Romania's submissiveness to Ceauşescu and the slow pace of reform in Romania since the collapse of communism: the high degree of centralisation and the unchallenged 'wisdom' of rapid industrialisation under Ceauşescu denied the country the flexibility of response required to promote economic and political reform. It could be argued that 'a higher degree of rebelliousness under Communism made the difference between the countries in East-Central Europe that experienced a more rapid transition to democracy, i.e. the Czech Republic, Hungary and Poland, and those where the process was more tortuous and painful, i.e., Bulgaria and Romania'.[42] Yet, as Dragoş Petrescu contends, 'the issue is not so much the legacy of anti-Communist dissidence in Central and South-Eastern Europe, but the rapid adoption by the West of the so-called rebellious Central Europeans'.[43] But this is a subject for another paper.

Notes

1. For a broader presentation and analysis of resistance, protest and dissent in Romania, see Dennis Deletant, *Ceauşescu and the Securitate: Coercion and Dissent in Romania, 1965–89* (London, 1995).
2. Vladimir Tismaneanu, *Stalinism for All Seasons. A Political History of Romanian Communism* (Berkeley, CA, and London, 2003), p. 35.
3. Steven L. Sampson, 'Muddling Through in Rumania (or: Why the Mamaliga Doesn't Explode)', *International Journal of Rumanian Studies*, vol. 3 (1981–3), pp. 165–85.
4. Elizabeth W. Hazard, *Cold War Crucible: United States Foreign Policy and the Conflict in Romania, 1943–1953* (Boulder, CO, 1996), p. 207.
5. Archive of the Romanian Security Service (SRI), Fond D, dosar 10716. I am grateful to Marius Oprea for this reference.
6. Elizabeth Hazard, 'Războiul rece a început în România', *Magazin Istoric*, vol. 30 (1996), pp. 58–9.

7. For a useful sketch of the activity of these partisan groups, together with a bibliography, see Ştefan Andreescu, 'A Little-Known Issue in the History of Romania: The Armed Anti-Communist Resistance', *Revue Roumaine d'Histoire*, vol. 33 (1994), pp. 191–7. This article can be supplemented by first-hand accounts from survivors of groups which have appeared in the review, *Memoria*, published by Fundaţia Culturală Memoria since 1990. See also *Cartea Albă a Securităţii* (Bucharest, 1994), vol. II, August 1948 to July 1958. For an account of the partisan group, led by a forester Nicolae Pop, in the Ţibleş mountains in Maramureş, see Ştefan Bellu, *Pădurea răzvrătită* (Baia Mare, 1993).

8. *Cartea Albă a Securităţii*, p. 82.

9. A. Marinescu, 'Pagini din rezistenţa armată anticomunistă', *Memoria*, no. 7 (1992), pp. 47–51.

10. *Povestea Elisabetei Rizea din Nucşoara* (Bucharest, 1993), pp. 118–25.

11. Plop's daughter, Ioana Raluca, was taken into care and brought up in an orphanage in Câmpulung. She was only able to discover who her mother was after the overthrow of Ceauşescu (personal communication to the author).

12. Marinescu, 'Pagini', pp. 57–8.

13. M. Arsenescu-Buduluca, 'Sunt soţia "teroristului" Gheorghe Arsenescu', *Memoria*, no. 8 (1993), p. 59.

14. Ion Gavrilă-Ogoreanu, *Brazii se frâng, dar nu se îndoiesc*, vol. 2 (Timişoara, 1995), p. 264.

15. Ibid., vol. 1, p. 268.

16. See, for example, Filon Verca, *Paraşutaţi în România vândută. Mişcarea de rezistenţă 1944–1948* (Timişoara, 1993); and Marinescu, 'Pagini'.

17. Khrushchev himself alluded to the demonstrations in an address to the Moscow Komsomol on 8 November 1956, when he said that there were 'some unhealthy moods' among students 'in one of the educational establishments in Romania', and he congratulated the RCP on having dealt with them quickly and effectively. See Ghiţa Ionescu, *Communism in Rumania, 1944–1962* (London, 1964), p. 272.

18. The first eyewitness account of the strike was given by István Hosszu, a miner from the Jiu Valley who left Romania in 1986, in an interview with Radio Free Europe on 17 July that year; see 'La Grève des Mineurs Roumains en 1977: Un Témoignage', *L'Autre Europe*, nos 11–12 (1986), pp. 154–6.

19. *România liberă*, 13 January 1990.

20. For details, see Marius Oprea and Stejărel Olaru, *The Day We Won't Forget, 15 November 1987, Braşov* (Bucharest, 2003).

21. Vladimir Socor, 'The Workers' Protest in Braşov: Assessment and Aftermath', *Romania Background Report, no. 231, Radio Free Europe Research*, 4 December 1987, p. 3.

22. Silviu Brucan, *Generaţia Irosită* (Bucharest, 1992), pp. 168–9.

23. Both figures involved wish to remain anonymous.

24. I take as my starting point Sorin Alexandrescu's essay, 'A gândi altfel, a fi disident, a acţiona în rezistenţă', *Identitate în ruptură* (Bucharest, 2000), pp. 227–40.
25. Ibid., p. 231.
26. Michael Shafir, *Romania. Politics, Economics and Society* (London, 1985), p. 168.
27. Cristina Petrescu makes the highly original point that Ceauşescu's condemnation of the Warsaw Pact invasion made him a notable 'dissident'. See her afterword to Dan Petrescu and Liviu Cangeopol, *Ce-ar mai fi de spus: Convorbiri libere într-o ţară ocupată* (Bucharest, 2000), p. 319.
28. For the original text, see *Limite*, nos 24–25 (September 1977), p. 9.
29. Ibid., pp. 9–10. Author's translation.
30. Adalbert Fehér, a worker, Emilia and Erwin Gesswein, instrumentalists in the Bucharest Philharmonic Orchestra, Carmen and Sergiu Manoliu, both painters, Ana Maria Năvodaru, a translator and wife of Goma, and Şerban Ştefănescu, a draughtsman.
31. Dragoş Petrescu, '"Rebellious" vs. "Non-Rebellious" Nations. British Perceptions of Romanian Anti-Communist Dissidence in the 1980s', *Romania and Britain: Relations and Perspectives from 1930 to the Present*, proceedings of the British-Romanian Symposium, New Europe College, British Council (Bucharest, 2005), p. 153.
32. For the texts of these letters, see Doina Cornea, *Scrisori deschise şi alte texte* (Bucharest, 1991).
33. Unique at this time in that she was placed under house arrest for over a year as opposed to being briefly detained.
34. László Tőkés, *With God, For the People*, as told to David Porter (London, 1990), pp. 65, 79.
35. Martin Rady, *Romania in Turmoil* (London, 1992), p. 86.
36. Ibid., p. 88.
37. Tőkés, *With God*, pp. 147–8.
38. *Adevărul*, 21 December 1991, pp. 2–3.
39. This is not the place to describe the subsequent events. This has been done admirably by Peter Siani-Davies in his path-breaking study *The Romanian Revolution of December 1989* (Ithaca, NY and London, 2005).
40. Goya's original words were: 'The sleep of reason brings forth monsters'.
41. Round-table discussion, Romanian TV, 30 December 1989.
42. Petrescu, '"Rebellious" vs. "Non-Rebellious" Nations', p. 163.
43. Ibid.

–6–

The Prague Spring: From Elite Liberalisation to Mass Movement
Kieran Williams

Well before the opening of the archives, the Czechoslovak crisis of 1968 – commonly known as the Prague Spring – had already been examined on a scale matched only by the rise of Solidarity in Poland. If we combined even a select sampling of the literature, such as the works of Dawisha,[1] Golan,[2] Kusin,[3] Skilling,[4] Tigrid[5] and Valenta,[6] the reader would be facing almost 3,000 pages of sophisticated analysis and magisterial empirical sweep. Out of this comprehensive investigation into every conceivable aspect of the short-lived experiment in reform communism erupted a few controversies that were still awaiting resolution when the regime crumbled in 1989. In this chapter I shall summarise the answers that new archival materials have provided to outstanding Cold War questions, and also how they have reshaped our understanding of the Prague Spring and the subsequent 'normalisation'.

For general orientation, I should distinguish at the outset between three Prague Springs: the one that happened before the Soviet-led invasion of August 1968; the one that was supposed to happen after August 1968, but was prevented by the invasion; and the one that did happen after August 1968, despite the invasion. The first, initiated by a faction of the party elite led by new First Secretary Alexander Dubček as a response to economic and social malaise, was marked by the semi-planned breakdown of censorship; the replacement of discredited officials with younger, more popular figures (many of whom had been Stalinists in their youth, but had since mellowed); the shutdown of political surveillance by the secret police; the appearance of new formations clustering dissident intellectuals and former political prisoners; the first mixing of plan and market; and preparations for conversion of the unitary state into a federation. The second would have introduced even deeper structural changes, such as relaxation of the Communist Party's internal discipline to allow greater dialogue; the addition of corporatist chambers to the reinvigorated national legislature to represent key economic sectors; and semi-free elections. The third, lasting from the invasion until its first anniversary, saw the quick evaporation of the elite-driven reforms (except federalisation), but also the emergence of a mass movement of students and workers that was absent from the first Prague Spring. Archives have shed light on all three, but the third, in particular, has benefited from the new sources.

The Soviet Decision to Invade

Without a doubt, the subject on which scholars were most eager for new information was the Soviet decision to send the armies of five Warsaw Pact states into Czechoslovakia on 20 August 1968.[7] The terms of the debate were set in the late 1970s when Jiří Valenta combined close reading of official statements, defector and *samizdat* memoirs, journalists' rumours and political science frameworks to argue that the Soviet Politburo had divided into two clear factions: one so disturbed by what was happening in Czechoslovakia that they favoured massive intervention; and the other preferring to give Czechoslovak communists more time to restore the rigid order Moscow preferred. On this view, General Secretary Leonid Brezhnev vacillated between the two groups until the hawkish faction prevailed in a Politburo showdown in the middle of August.[8] Although Karen Dawisha dealt this argument a serious blow in her 1984 book,[9] it was very hard to resist the temptation to seek evidence of factional conflict and ordinary politics in the Kremlin before Gorbachev's rise to power. Now that such matters are less timely, we can afford to accept that crises such as 1968 more united than divided the Soviet command.

Differences of emphasis and tone certainly existed; KGB Chairman Iurii Andropov and Ukrainian party boss Petro Shelest' argued sooner and more adamantly than most of their colleagues for the use of force. No doves, however, can be found in the Politburo records, diplomatic cables or new memoir material released since 1991. Brezhnev and chief ideologue Mikhail Suslov emerge as very much in charge of foreign relations and the flow of information from satellite countries, and not needing to be prodded into action by a coalition of hawks. By midsummer 1968 there seems to have been consensus in the Politburo that the situation in Czechoslovakia was grave, and military intervention very likely.[10] Instead, the documents declassified (and we cannot exclude that they were selected to have this effect) direct us away from the internal dynamic of the Politburo and towards the relationship between a few Soviet leaders and their Czechoslovak counterparts. Particularly striking in the transcripts released of conversations between the leaders at numerous summits and on the telephone is the Soviets' preoccupation with the trustworthiness of their interlocutors and with the keeping of promises. Moscow had wasted no time in communicating its unhappiness with many of the changes that had occurred so far, and pressed Dubček to act. They wanted him not only to clear up the things they already did not like, but also to reassure them by his response that he would be able to stay in control once bigger structural reforms were enacted.

Out of the transcripts steps a Dubček different from the one mythologised in the West and in post-1989 Slovakia (his homeland). We encounter a career party functionary, emotionally very attached to the USSR, in which he had spent a large part of his youth, and sincere in his frequent promises to do something about the developments that displeased the Soviets. As the months passed, however, these promises seemed to be going unfulfilled. (I will argue below that I believe Dubček did intend to keep them, but was following a timetable very different from the sort Moscow expected.) In an emergency summit at the Slovak border town of Čierná nad Tisou at the end of July 1968, Dubček undertook a private and quite detailed pledge to Brezhnev to restore censorship, sideline the more radical reformers, disband new political formations and preserve the secret police.[11]

In the outwardly quiet, but decisive first half of August, Brezhnev and his trusted associates monitored Czechoslovakia closely for signs that the pledge was being carried out. Brezhnev called Dubček twice, on 9 and 13 August, and these conversations played a major part in pushing the Soviets to invade.[12] Dubček struck Brezhnev as edgy, unstable and irresolute, seemingly in no hurry to clear up the matters identified at the Čierná summit. These impressions, combined with alarmist dispatches from the Soviet embassy in Prague and other streams of intelligence, convinced Brezhnev and his peers that Dubček would be unable to manage the upcoming party congress – at which a new Central Committee would be chosen and major policies decided – and that only the strength of arms could prevent Czechoslovakia's capture by revisionists and counter-revolutionaries. The decision to invade was taken by the Politburo unanimously on 17 August, apparently without a formal vote.[13]

One other aspect of the Soviet decision that exercised not just historians, but also, after 1989, the public prosecutor and courts, was the question of who on the Czechoslovak side formally invited the invasion, in return for assurances of elevation into the places to be vacated by Dubček and others. At the time, the Soviets informed the world that their intervention was coming at the urgent request of unnamed Czech and Slovak comrades. Over the decades, speculation in the West (fuelled by the odd whisper out of Prague or Bratislava) had identified the most likely signatories of any such invitation, but confirmation of the names had to wait until 1992. Russian archives divulged not just one letter of invitation, but two: the first, a solo shot from hardliner Antonín Kapek, delivered to Brezhnev at the end of July, was followed by a joint appeal from five of Dubček's former allies, handed over on 3 August.[14] A third letter, to be signed by dozens of collaborators, was being prepared and would have been published had the invasion gone as planned and resulted in a change of leadership. Instead, a couple of minor but essential members of the conspiracy defected back to Dubček at the last minute, and the bigger players lost their nerve.

The Importance of Auto-normalisation

The rollback of reform in the Soviet bloc was commonly known by the euphemism 'normalisation'. In Czechoslovakia, of course, it occurred largely because the occupying Soviet forces would not allow the Communist Party to risk any departure from the received Leninist political model. The new archival sources, however, convey the significance of the less coerced aspect of the rollback, what I call 'auto-normalisation' for lack of a pleasing word. By this I mean the contribution by the reformers themselves, namely the centrists around (and including) Dubček, who had originally accepted that changes had to be made to prevent a systemic crisis and to reset the country's sights on honourable goals long forgotten. These centrists wanted to democratise, not demolish Leninism; they were disquieted by some of the ways in which their countrymen were using new freedoms, and they were willing to curtail them.

As I indicated above, I believe that Dubček and his associates shared many of the Soviets' concerns and at the time of the invasion were preparing restrictive legislation. The key difference between the Soviet and Czechoslovak leaders lay in their perceptions of authority: the Soviets, believing that the protection of socialism legitimated immediate action, saw no reason to hesitate, whereas the Dubček team felt that they had gradually to acquire and deepen the public's trust before reimposing limits on the rights of expression and association. For the reformers, the watershed would be the very event the Soviets so dreaded, the upcoming party congress, which would remove embarrassing hold-overs of the Stalin era and grant the leadership a new licence to act.

One of the most striking revelations of the Czech and Slovak communist archives is the advanced state of these preparations to reverse the changes that had occurred so far. As early as 7 May 1968, only four months after Dubček rose to power, the party leadership (the Presidium) was searching for new ways to restore censorship of the media, and discussion began of making the further existence of any new organisation contingent on its acceptance into the National Front, the communist-controlled clustering of satellite political parties, trade unions, youth unions and assorted recreational groups. Zdeněk Mlynář, the architect of political reform, assured nervous local party functionaries that he favoured a thorough police investigation of the new formation K-231, representing victims of Stalinism, on the grounds that he was sure that some of its leaders had deserved their prison sentences in the 1940s and 1950s.[15] On 20 June the Presidium instructed the government to draw up plans for the suppression of any unrest, and on 18 July the interior ministry set up a special 'operational staff' to monitor public order.[16] Three days earlier, the defence ministry had similarly discussed plans for using the army to suppress 'anti-socialist' protests.[17] Prime Minister Oldřich Černík set in motion the establishment of detention camps for, as Dubček later put it, 'the political isolation of people in the event of open uprisings against socialism'.[18]

The upshot of all this is that we can now better appreciate how little the Czechoslovak reformers tried to refute the Soviet version of what was happening, given that they shared much of Moscow's anxiety. When the invasion failed to install an alternative, harder-line leadership and the Soviets were forced to negotiate with Dubček (who, along with several colleagues, had been abducted to the USSR), most of the points set down in a secret protocol and implemented in subsequent weeks were exactly those which Dubček had promised on previous occasions and were already in the works.

Students and Workers in the 'Prague Winter'

The invasion and auto-normalisation had the unintended consequence of mobilising entire sectors of Czechoslovak society that hitherto had been interested but restrained spectators. Through the archives we can rediscover the lost treasure of civic activism in the autumn and winter of 1968–9, which in so many ways anticipated the combination of forces that finished off communist rule twenty-one years later.

Often forgotten today is the mood of the Czechoslovak public in the wake of the invasion. Far from crushed, the people felt that they had won, since the collaborators had failed to overthrow Dubček's team, and the spontaneous campaign of non-violent resistance had dramatically compounded the occupying armies' logistical woes (supply lines broke down quickly). Most were therefore devastated by the behaviour of their leaders on returning from captivity in Moscow, as they set about censoring and suspending periodicals, banning new political organisations (many of whose leaders had fled westwards) and consenting to the presence of 60,000 Soviet soldiers by signing a treaty on their 'temporary' stationing. The great majority of citizens retreated into the subdued, dutiful compliance that Dubček and his colleagues were tirelessly requesting; a small minority, however, held out.

The resistance to 'normalisation' moved in three phases, each with its defining method. The first was street protests, for which the major autumnal anniversaries (independence day on 28 October, the Bolshevik revolution on 7 November) provided ample opportunity. Crowds in Prague and other cities swelled to several thousands on these occasions, and were dispersed violently by the police, with help from the Czechoslovak army and the party's militia; hundreds of students and young workers were arrested, and one died of his injuries. The second phase moved the protests indoors, as university students launched a nationwide sit-in strike around International Students' Day (17 November) to demand resumption of the reforms and respect for civil and political rights.

The third phase brought together the students and the trade unions. The latter had been quietly establishing their independence, in that Communist Party cells within the unions were defunct by the autumn and unable to influence the enormous turnover taking place in the unions' personnel. Almost 900 local union committees signalled their sympathy for the students and their demands in November by organising fifteen-minute strikes in workplaces. The apogee of the worker–student nexus came in December, when rumours spread that Josef Smrkovský, the popular (and populist) chairman of the national assembly, was to be unseated as part of the impending reorganisation of the legislature to reflect the federalisation of the state. The students' national union sealed a pact with the metalworkers' union (KOVO) to call a general strike should Smrkovský fall.[19] The Soviets had told Dubček that Smrkovský had to go, but rather than confront the matter head-on, Dubček characteristically let the situation deteriorate to the point where Smrkovský offered to settle for the deputy speaker's post in order to prevent a social explosion. Smrkovský personally appealed to the workers not to honour their pact with the students, while Dubček and other top statesmen told them in an open letter, 'What our country needs most now is calm, active and constructive work, practical deeds'.[20]

Smrkovský's self-relegation allowed the metalworkers to stand down without seeming to have reneged on a commitment. Meanwhile, the unions barrelled ahead with a landmark congress in March 1969, only weeks before Dubček's downfall as party leader, at which a seemingly bold coordinating council was freely elected without Communist Party supervision. The congress conceded that the party exercised a 'leading role' in society, but that it would be respected by the unions only if reforms continued. Among the more treasured innovations was the introduction of workers' councils as a feature of enterprise management. By January 1969 councils had been elected in 120 major firms, representing almost 900,000 employees.

Soon after Dubček was replaced as party leader on 17 April 1969 by Gustáv Husák (who had been running the party in Slovakia since the invasion), the communists targeted the students and the trade unions for reconquest. In May 1969 the party's Presidium decided that the university students' union would be banned, while the core of a new, docile union would be recruited from cadets in military academies.[21] The students got wind of this and tried to fight back by invoking their pact with the metalworkers' union, KOVO. On 23 June 1969, KOVO members at the vital ČKD works agreed that they would call a general strike if their leader, Vlastimil Toman, were not given a satisfactory reason for the abolition of the students' union. At this point the limits of the union leaders' radicalism were exposed; under relentless pressure from the party and Soviet counterparts, they were undergoing the same conversion to 'realism' as had many reformers in the Dubček team. Toman found procedural excuses to avoid a general strike, and the wildcat stoppages that did occur lacked any official blessing.[22] A meeting of the KOVO central council on 2 July bitterly denounced the Communist Party's new policies, and reiterated past demands for the withdrawal of Soviet troops and for guarantees of union independence, but again stopped short of coming to the rescue of the students. One week later, the revived party cell attached to the coordinating council of the trade unions held its first meeting, a sign that a significant number of leaders were willing to submit to the party's tutelage. From then on, there was a gradual but steady erosion of independence, for the most part carried out by the same union chairmen freely elected only months before, desperately trying to appease the party and save their jobs under the illusion that at some point the reforms would resume.

The Purge

From the archives we learn that Husák initially did not want to purge the rank and file of the party, only the upper levels. Once a victim of Stalinism, he liked to think of himself as rescuing, not burying, reform, and therefore wanted to get the majority of party members on his side.[23] We also learn, however, that the imperative of reversing the shift to market socialism (the misconceived economic reforms had triggered an ominous wage-price spiral by early 1969) entailed the restoration of the close bond between the party and the economic apparatus. A centrally planned economy needed a reasonably functional party, including active cells in workplaces, to ensure the meeting of targets. Under Dubček, especially by late 1968, the party had fallen into deeper stagnation than under his predecessor, and Husák was eventually persuaded, some time around August or September 1969, by less sanguine colleagues that a purge would get rid of members who could not or would not cooperate, while focusing those who remained on urgent economic tasks.

It is common to talk about the 'normalisation' purge casting out one-third of the party's members, with many losing their jobs as well.[24] Although it is true that the party shrank greatly from its size (1.69 million members) at the time Dubček came to power, we have to be very careful in distinguishing the various modes of exit and in using January 1968 as a baseline. During 1968 itself, more than 22,000 members quit or were expelled and more than 17,000 died, while only 36,649 recruits joined. Most of the departures were resignations in disgust at the direction the party and country took after the leadership returned from Moscow in August 1968. In the first four months of 1969, with Dubček still at the helm, another 12,369 members had left or been expelled; the intake of only 4,035 new members was the smallest since 1952. At the time of Husák's takeover, therefore, the party was already 2.4 per cent smaller,[25] and by the end of 1969 almost 10 per cent smaller than at the start of 1968.[26] Much of the loss had occurred in the party's dwindling working-class membership, since manual workers feared no employment repercussions, whereas white-collar members (who in many cases had joined only to further their careers) clung desperately to their party cards. Another compelling reason for the official purge in 1970, therefore, was to staunch the haemorrhage of proletarian members, or at least to offset it with a matching drop in managerial and service-sector employees.

By the time the purge began in earnest in March 1970, the party already had around 150,000 fewer members than it had had in January 1968. Without this largely voluntary reduction, the purge itself would have been considered a failure. The process was a carefully controlled one, with each member interviewed by a local screening commission; the secret police played no role except in the vetting of army officers.[27] While this ensured that no terror erupted, there was an initial tendency to be too forgiving of colleagues and neighbours, such that superior party committees often had to demand a second round of interviews and impose quotas to get the numbers up. Even so, the vast majority of members, 1.18 million (78.3 per cent of the January 1970 total), were allowed to stay in the party. Almost 260,000 (17.2 per cent) saw their membership cancelled, a lesser sanction that did not necessarily result in job loss, although it might lead to demotion or at least no advancement. (A 1984 study of social stratification turned up a group representing about 10 per cent of the workforce that was reasonably well paid, but excluded from the professions and positions for which they were best suited; many of these were probably thwarted by lack of party membership.)[28] Finally, only around 67,000 (4.5 per cent) were to be expelled outright from the party,[29] which almost certainly meant dismissal and consignment to manual labour; many discharged secret-police officers, for example, ended up helping to build the Prague Metro.

The brunt of 'normalisation' in the party, therefore, was borne by a group that represented only 4 per cent of its January 1968 total, or 0.5 per cent of the country's population (slightly more once we factor in their families). Even within this small fraction we find a subset of expellees, singled out for special monitoring to ensure that they could never again influence public life. This group, numbering 6,335 in March 1972 when a master list was compiled by the party's secretariat, was to be watched by local party bodies, not the secret police. Two-thirds had held high office in 1968 or worked in education, the media, the sciences and medicine or the police; most of the rest had been business directors or managers, and only 2 per cent had been workers. The blacklist remained in force until the end of the regime in 1989, albeit whittled down to just a few hundred names.[30]

Slovakia

As in 1947–8 before the communist seizure of power, and then in 1989–90, when that power was lost, so in 1968–70 Slovak politics exhibited its own distinct dynamic. Like Kádár's reforms taking place at the same time across the Danube, the liberalisation in Slovakia in 1968 was more tightly controlled and less offensive to the Soviets; had all of Czechoslovakia followed the Bratislava Spring, the invasion might never have happened. As we can see from archival materials, however, debates in Slovakia were vibrant and diverse, and not restricted to the foremost Slovak wish that the state be federalised.[31]

First of all, Skilling's claim in his encyclopaedic study of 1968 that in Slovakia there were no new political formations akin to those in Bohemia and Moravia turns out not to be true.[32] On 7 April the Slovak Organisation for the Defence of Human Rights was founded, attracting almost 2,000 members, most of them former political prisoners; the Slovak Party Presidium was sufficiently alarmed to authorise propaganda smearing them as malefactors justly convicted under Stalinism of anti-state crimes.[33] Later in the summer, an Association of Non-Party Members formed and, together with fifteen other new formations, applied for membership of the National Front. As in the Czech-speaking lands, the youth union splintered into more specific components for age and social groups, including a university students' union with a radical 400–member parliament. Already in February 1968 the Slovak trade unions, representing 1.2 million workers, began to distance themselves from their superiors in Prague.[34]

One way in which the Bratislava Spring was distinct was the revival of religion. The first study of Slovak world views, conducted in autumn 1968, found that 71 per cent were believers (compared to 13 per cent of Czechs in a 1974 survey); 42 per cent of Communist Party members also identified themselves as Christians, exceeding the share of confirmed atheists in the party of Marx and Lenin by 5 per cent.[35] While the party was always unnerved by the Catholic Church's ability to mobilise hundreds of thousands of the faithful for pilgrimages, in 1968 the greatest tension arose between Orthodox and Greek Catholic (Uniate) congregations in eastern Slovakia. To break the latter's Vatican ties they had been forcibly submerged into the much smaller Orthodox Church in 1950, and the underground remnants were aggressively persecuted by the local party boss of the time, Vasil Biľak, who in January 1968 became leader of the entire Slovak party. Greek Catholics, who had once made up 6.5 per cent of the Slovak population, began to repossess their old churches, and only the mediation of state officials prevented incidents of violence from escalating into full conflict. Despite the intense hostility of the 'normalisation' regime to organised religion, the Greek Catholics were legalised and given 195 parish churches and the cathedral at Prešov, but no bishop could be ordained until 1990.[36]

In high politics, one Slovak event stands out: the party congress of 26–28 August 1968, on the heels of the Soviet-led invasion. The national party's congress had already been held secretly in a factory in Prague's Vysočany district, and few Slovak delegates had been able to attend. The Soviets had objected vigorously to that congress's election of a new, untainted Central Committee, and insisted that it be annulled. Although some of its members were co-opted into the existing Central Committee, the Vysočany congress was overturned. The Slovak congress, on the other hand, was not, even though it too had elected a new 107–member Central Committee containing only nineteen incumbents; the very leader of the party, Biľak, was so disgraced by his collaboration with the invasion that he was not even put on the ballot.

Why were the results of the Slovak congress allowed to stand? First, they were less important for the direction of the country and foreign relations than the outcome of the national party congress, so the Soviets simply were not as interested. Second, Biľak had been succeeded as Slovak party leader by Husák, whom the Soviets had initially mistrusted but now regarded as dependable and effective. Third, the Slovak congress had disavowed the Vysočany elections, owing to the incomplete Slovak delegation. This decision by the Slovak congress has been bitterly denounced as a stab in the back of the Prague Spring, a betrayal equivalent to that of the great powers at Munich in 1938 when Hitler grabbed the Sudetenland.[37] Such a claim is unjustified, since the Vysočany congress had already been abandoned by Dubček and Czech participants in the Moscow negotiations on 24 August, before the Slovak congress even convened. The hitherto unavailable transcript of the Slovak congress shows just how reluctant the delegates were to distance themselves from Vysočany,

and did so only after lengthy cajoling, nationalist pandering and threats from Husák.[38]

As the new leader in Slovakia, Husák was in a position to do what Dubček had been planning to do nationwide before the invasion – use the authority vested in him by the congress to satisfy Soviet demands and bring the reforms back within acceptable limits. Consequently, it is often alleged that 'normalisation' in Slovakia was not as heavy-handed as in the Czech-speaking lands.[39] This is true in that there was slightly more opportunity in Slovakia for differing points of view to be expressed in official venues, and fewer members of the Slovak party saw their membership cancelled during the 1970 purge (13.3 per cent, as opposed to 18.5 per cent in the Czech lands). The frequency of the more serious penalty of expulsion, however, was barely less in Slovakia (4.2 per cent) than elsewhere, and the purge of suspect sectors such as the arts, media and the cultural custodian *Matica slovenská* was just as severe as in the Czech lands.[40] Although so rapidly modernising a society as Slovakia could not afford to dismiss as many professionals and managers as Czech institutions could, this is one area in which the differences between the two nations should not be overstated.

Public Opinion Under the Ice

One of the revelations of the opened archives is the extent to which the regime conducted opinion surveys of the 'normalised' public. Polls had been undertaken in the post-war period until 1950, and then resumed in 1967; the findings of surveys taken during the Prague Spring were quickly published in the West.[41] Under Husák the government's polling agency continued to take regular Gallup-style surveys on a range of issues, but the results were treated as highly confidential and only the topmost officials were privy to them. In these reports we encounter a nation outwardly preoccupied with material pursuits and light entertainment, but on closer inspection we can find the faint pulse of a civic consciousness.

Political and economic 'normalisation' after the turmoil of the 1960s created a society with the means and motivation to turn inwards and savour the privacy of the nuclear family. One prime indicator was the organisation of leisure: between 1964 and 1971 the aggregate number of days spent on vacation more than doubled, from 74.6 million to 162.6 million per year, while the number of days spent on privately arranged vacations (as opposed to group tours laid on by a trade union or the workplace) more than tripled, from 39 million to 116.2 million.[42] A key factor was the expansion of car ownership: in 1960 there was one car per thirty-five citizens; in 1971 it was one per fifteen. In a 1973 poll, 30 per cent of respondents claimed that someone in the family had a car; by 1976 the figure had risen to 56 per cent, and among white-collar employees it was 66 per cent.

Cars, in turn, facilitated travel to country cottages, the cherished *chata* or *chalupa*, the numbers of which boomed from 128,000 in 1969 to 225,000 by 1981.[43] Almost half the residents of large towns (with more than 100,000 inhabitants) regularly fled to weekend retreats, as did 25 per cent of all those with higher education and 30 per cent of those with secondary schooling, compared to only 13 per cent of unskilled workers. Many who lived in the cities escaped on the weekends even if they did not own a cottage, and they did so in small groups, with just a spouse or companion (20 per cent of the time), with spouse and child or other relations (40 per cent) or with friends (20 per cent). They aimed for the hills, lakes and forests to avoid other people and to create enclaves of free speech.[44]

Leisure time in town was similarly atomised, and centred on television. The number of licensed sets had grown from 795,000 in 1960 to 3.3 million by 1972, invading three-quarters of all households. By 1974, 93 per cent of citizens had access to a television.[45] In 1979, 60 per cent of citizens watched television every day (in 1982 the figure rose to 66 per cent), another 26 per cent tuned in three or four times a week, and only 1 per cent never watched.[46] The country's leaders were fully aware of television's narcotic power, so much so that they asked the Soviets for help in starting up a second channel and colour broadcasting because 'postponement of construction would have an unfavourable political repercussion, especially at present when surrounding socialist states are already beginning to broadcast [in colour]'.[47] Although such fears were exaggerated, television was certainly an invaluable tool of distraction: when asked in 1975 how they would spend a free evening, 19 per cent of respondents – the single largest group – replied that they would watch television or listen to the radio.[48] Workers, pensioners and housewives, polled in 1975, all admitted that they preferred to watch television than talk with friends and relations or read. Like radio, it kept the masses at home, diverted from collective experiences such as films, theatre, concerts, exhibitions or even pubs. In 1974, for example, cinemas were used at less than one-third of their capacity.

The lure of electronic pastimes had a downside for the regime, in that many also turned to Western programmes. Although we can assume that respondents were reluctant to answer candidly questions regarding their reception of illegal transmissions, the numbers reported are still high. A 1974 survey found that 8 per cent of Czechs regularly watched West German or Austrian television, and 19 per cent did so sometimes; while in Slovakia, 45 per cent of which was reached by Austrian television, the figures were 13 and 23 per cent respectively.[49] In 1982, 20 per cent of all respondents admitted to watching Western television, with 15 per cent being regular viewers. Information picked up from these sources was then relayed to friends and colleagues – perhaps 70 per cent of the total population. Factoring in the bombardment of foreign radio, the poll-takers concluded that only one-fifth of the Czechoslovak population was untouched by Western reporting.[50]

As a result of the reach of foreign media, the party had its work cut out in inspiring citizens under 'normalisation' to develop a firm socialist identity. A 1974 survey found that half the population had no regular contact with a member of the party; the isolation of the working class was even greater, with 66 per cent claiming no contact.[51] A 1975 poll found only 2 per cent of respondents regularly attending meetings of the party or a trade union, and practically none going to 'political education' classes. Although members of the party were understandably more likely to go to meetings, 20 per cent of them were completely inactive. Only 32 per cent of respondents felt that participation in public and political life was an important aspect of one's existence (among non-party members only 25 per cent thought so), whereas 68 per cent mentioned 'having a well-furnished flat' as very important.[52] A 1979 poll found that respondents considered the five top values in life to be health, having a good partner, good work, living in peace and certainty and raising children. At the bottom of the scale were 'contributing to the blossoming of socialist society' and involvement in sociopolitical organisations.[53]

However, we should not confuse abstention from meetings and institutions for indifference to public affairs. Part of the reason so many turned to Western media was their desire to know more. Only 50 per cent of respondents reported satisfaction with the amount of information they were given by their own government, and only 35 per cent claimed they were more likely to believe something they heard on the news than on the street.[54] In 1979, 38 per cent of respondents said that they thought about 'societal occurrences' every day, and 56 per cent at least sometimes; only 6 per cent admitted to total indifference to the world around them. More than 60 per cent claimed to be as concerned about the welfare of society as about their own. Half of those polled said that 'on average' they were interested in domestic politics, and 19 per cent were 'very' interested; 25 per cent took little interest and 9 per cent none at all. Respondents admitted that they talked about politics frequently with friends: 6 per cent 'almost all the time', 30 per cent 'often', 32 per cent 'sometimes', 24 per cent 'rarely' and 8 per cent 'never'.[55] In 1978, 28 per cent claimed that they always spoke their true opinion of political events, while 51 per cent did so sometimes; only 8 per cent never did. But of those who always or sometimes spoke frankly, one-third did so only among family, and another third around friends, and 19 per cent in the workplace; only 17 per cent claimed to speak their minds everywhere, including public meetings. Czechs were slightly more likely than Slovaks to speak freely only in private.[56]

From these polls we can deduce that in the 1970s only one-third of the adult population was truly apathetic (confirmed by a 1983 survey reporting that 34 per cent had no interest in politics)[57] and that the majority was more socio-tropic than the 'normalisation' image of an unthinking, escapist lifestyle would suggest. The ease with which hundreds of thousands of outwardly conformist socialist consumers could be mobilised against the regime in November 1989 can be explained if we take these polls as revealing an interior world of quiet political awareness awaiting an outlet.

Conclusion

If I were to venture one overarching effect that the opening of archives has had on perceptions of the Czechoslovak crisis of 1968, it is that the new materials obscure the categories into which the political actors of the day would once have been placed. Shorthand descriptions, such as reformer and hardliner, liberal and conservative, lose their purchase the more one works through the transcriptions of protracted Presidium meetings and is struck by how little the participants – those who would later collaborate with the invasion and those who would oppose it – diverged in their political language and outlook. The apparent ease with which the changes could be reversed and replaced by Husák's 'model byre of the Grand Inquisitor'[58] becomes understandable on discovering how uncommitted and equivocal most of those around Dubček were towards grand reform, its implications and possible direction. The drama of the invasion, and the courage of those who resisted it peacefully, remain unaffected by the new sources, but one now winces when reading how the crowds declared their fervent devotion to Dubček, Černík, President Svoboda and other men who in private barely resembled their public personae.[59]

The history of the various Prague Springs should now move on from the focused narrative of elite politics and even the mass responses of the first year after the invasion, and delve deeper into the longer-term transformation of Czechoslovakia that was occurring at the time, from industrial to consumer society. As the declassified opinion polls show, the turmoil of the late 1960s was part of a deeper cultural shift taking place across Europe – West and East – in lifestyle, expectations and preferences. Dubček's reforms were one way of trying to accommodate and take charge of that change, but so was Husák's 'normalisation'.

Notes

1. Karen Dawisha, *The Kremlin and the Prague Spring* (Berkeley, CA and London, 1984).
2. Galia Golan, *The Czechoslovak Reform Movement: Communism in Crisis, 1962–1968* (Cambridge, 1971), and *Reform Rule in Czechoslovakia: The Dubček Era* (Cambridge, 1973).
3. Vladimir V. Kusin, *The Intellectual Origins of the Prague Spring: The Development of Reformist Ideas in Czechoslovakia, 1956–1967* (Cambridge, 1971), and *Political Groupings in the Czechoslovak Reform Movement* (New York, 1972).
4. H. Gordon Skilling, *Czechoslovakia's Interrupted Revolution* (Princeton NJ, 1976).

5. Pavel Tigrid, *Why Dubček Fell* (London, 1971).

6. Jiří Valenta, *Soviet Intervention in Czechoslovakia, 1968: Anatomy of a Decision* (Baltimore, MD, 1979).

7. The five invading states were the USSR, East Germany, Poland, Hungary and Bulgaria.

8. Valenta, *Soviet Intervention in Czechoslovakia*.

9. Dawisha, *The Kremlin and the Prague Spring*.

10. I discuss these issues, and the relevant sources, at length in Kieran Williams, 'New Sources on Soviet Decision Making During the 1968 Czechoslovak Crisis', *Europe-Asia Studies*, vol. 48 (1996), pp. 455–68; and *The Prague Spring and its aftermath: Czechoslovak politics, 1968–1970* (Cambridge, 1997), pp. 29–38, 63–125.

11. Dubček always denied the existence of such an undertaking, but the evidence from contemporary sources is overwhelming; see Williams, *The Prague Spring and its aftermath*, p. 102; and Jan Pauer, *Prag 1968. Der Einmarsch des Warschauer Paktes* (Bremen, 1995), pp. 166–7.

12. Translations of these conversations appear in Jaromír Navrátil (ed.), *The Prague Spring 1968: A National Security Archive Documents Reader* (Budapest, 1998), pp. 336–8, 345–56.

13. Rudolf Pikhoia, 'Chekhoslovakiia, 1968 god, vzgliad iz Moskvy. Po dokumentam TsK KPSS', *Novaia i noveishaia istoriia*, no. 1 (1995), p. 44.

14. The five were Vasil Biľak, leader of the Communist Party of Slovakia, Kapek, Alois Indra, Drahomír Kolder and Oldřich Švestka. For a translation, see Navrátil (ed.), *The Prague Spring 1968*, pp. 324–5.

15. Archive of the Central Committee of the Communist Party of Czechoslovakia (A ÚV KSČ), fond 018, 1968 (stenogram of the meeting of leading secretaries of district and regional committees, on 12–13 May 1968).

16. Archive of the Federal Ministry of the Interior of Czechoslovakia (A FMV ČSFR), k. 41, 73/7–8, č.j. IMV 003/ZO-70.

17. A ÚV KSČ, fond G. Husák (unnumbered; report by Defence Minister Martin Dzúr for the Communist Party Central Committee's Oversight and Review Commission, 9 June 1970).

18. See Dubček's November 1985 letter to the editors of the party's national daily, *Rudé právo*, its Slovak equivalent, *Pravda*, and the Slovak trade unions' *Práca*, reprinted in the émigré periodical *Listy*, no. 15 (1985), p. 7.

19. A ÚV KSČ, fond 02/1, P5197. Similar promises were made by the lumber industry and agricultural workers' unions, and by workers at the vital North Bohemian electricity plant, the shutdown of which in the depths of a bitter winter would have been devastating.

20. *Rudé právo*, 9 January 1969.

21. A ÚV KSČ, fond 02/1, P5695.

22. A ÚV KSČ, fond G. Husák (unnumbered; information from Prague City Party Committee, 24 June 1969, 1300 hours).

23. This emerges in the discussion at the May 1969 session of the party's Central Committee; see *Zasedání ústředního výboru Komunistické strany Československa dne 29.-30. května 1969. Stenografický zápis*, part 1.

24. Anna Grzymała-Busse, *Redeeming the Communist Past: The Regeneration of Communist Parties in East Central Europe* (Cambridge, 2002), p. 34 (claiming that 'following the Prague Spring, over 28% of KSČ members were expelled from the party within a year').

25. A ÚV KSČ, fond 02/1, P5660.

26. A ÚV KSČ, fond G. Husák (unnumbered; information on party membership, 31 March 1970). During 1969, almost 97,000 members had quit or lost their membership.

27. A FMV, fond A30, i.j. 408, č.j. 001783/120-1971. In 1969–71, 7,473 officers were discharged from the armed forces, 3,228 of these for political reasons. Another 4,200, whose party memberships were cancelled, were kept in service but monitored by military counter-intelligence (VKR). In the VKR itself, around 70 per cent of the commanders were replaced, and 20 per cent of all VKR officers at some point came under investigation.

28. Pavel Machonin, 'Změnil se typ společenského uspořádání v letech 1967–1984?', *Sociologický časopis*, no. 28 (1992), pp. 73–83.

29. A ÚV KSČ, fond 02/1, P8709/32.

30. A ÚV KSČ, fond 02/1, č.j. P8854; A ÚV KSČ, fond 02/1 (unnumbered; annex to Secretariat material, 25 June 1974). See also Jan Šubert, 'Tajný plán', *Lidové noviny*, 12 November 1991. Of the 6,335, almost 1,000 had not been in the Communist Party or one of its satellites, and almost 600 had been involved in various new political formations in 1968.

31. Declassified documents regarding federalisation, which are essential to understanding the breakdown of Czech-Slovak coexistence after 1989, are available in Jozef Žatkuliak (ed.), *Federalizácia československého štátu 1968–1970* (Brno, 1996).

32. Skilling, *Czechoslovakia's Interrupted Revolution*, p. 244.

33. Archive of the Central Committee of the Communist Party of Slovakia (hereafter, A ÚV KSS), fond 03 (uncatalogued decree of the eleventh meeting of the KSS Presidium, 7 June 1968).

34. A ÚV KSS, fond 03, ar.j. 8.

35. Komisia vlády SR pre analýzu historických udalosti z rokov 1967–1970, *Slovensko v rokoch 1967–1970: Výber dokumentov* (Bratislava, 1992), pp. 419–20.

36. Jan Pešek and Michal Barnovský, *Pod kuratelou moci: Cirkvi na Slovensku v rokoch 1953–1970* (Bratislava, 1999), pp. 187–213, 238–50.

37. Petr Pithart, *Osmašedesátý* (Prague, 1990), p. 87; Barbara Jancar, *Czechoslovakia and the Absolute Monopoly of Power* (New York, 1971), p. 178.

38. A ÚV KSČ, fond KSS, sv. 3, ar.j. 7.

39. Petr Pithart, 'Towards a Shared Freedom, 1968–89', in Jiří Musil (ed.), *The End of Czechoslovakia* (Budapest, 1995), pp. 210–12.

40. A ÚV KSČ, fond 02/1, sv. 148, ar.j. 228, b. 14.

41. Jaroslav Piekalkiewicz, *Public Opinion Polling in Czechoslovakia, 1968–1969* (New York, 1972).

42. Office for Public Opinion Research (hereafter, KVVM), č.j. 50744/74-20, č.v. 74-1.

43. Vladimir V. Kusin, 'Husak's Czechoslovakia and Economic Stagnation', *Problems of Communism*, vol. 31 (1982), p. 28. For more details on the *chata*, see Paulina Bren, 'Weekend Getaways: The *Chata*, the *Tramp* and the Politics of Private Life in Post-1968 Czechoslovakia', in David Crowley and Susan Reid (eds), *Socialist Spaces: Sites of Everyday Life in the Eastern Bloc* (Oxford, 2002), pp. 123–40.

44. KVVM, č.j. 57/76-5, č.v. 76-4. In the summer of 1976, for example, only 13 per cent of respondents said they would be vacationing in hotels, motels or a facility owned by an enterprise. All the rest would be using private accommodation.

45. KVVM, č.j. 14 772/75-1, č.v. 74-9.

46. Institute of Public Opinion Research (hereafter, ÚVVM), č.j. 55/79-6, č.v. 79-5; ÚVVM, č.j. 23/82-7, č.v. 82-3.

47. A ÚV KSČ, fond 02/1, P6364. Such fears were unfounded, since a 1973 poll found that 63 per cent of the viewing public did not intend to purchase a new television set just to receive colour broadcasts, because the price was still too high. See KVVM, č.j. 506 24/73-9, č.v. 73-5.

48. KVVM, č.j. 14 162/75-19, č.v. 75-4.

49. KVVM, č.j. 14 772/75-1, č.v. 74-9.

50. ÚVVM, č.j. 23/82-7, č.v. 82-3. In 1978, 25 per cent of respondents admitted that they regularly listened to Western radio, especially for news, and in Slovakia the rate was 35 per cent. In 1982, 41 per cent of those with university education were regular listeners of Western radio.

51. KVVM, č.j. 19722/74-2, č.v. 74-11.

52. KVVM, č.j. 14 162/75-19, č.v. 75-4.

53. ÚVVM, č.j. 23/79-7, č.v. 79-3.

54. ÚVVM, č.j. 55/79-6, č.v. 79-5.

55. ÚVVM, č.j. 55/79-6, č.v. 79-5.

56. ÚVVM, č.j. 46/78-3, č.v. 78-6.

57. ÚVVM, č.j. 117/82-7, č.v. 83-2. Slovaks were slightly more apathetic (38 per cent) than Czechs (33 per cent).

58. Erazim Kohák, *Národ v nás. Česká otázka a ideál humanitní v údobí normalizace* (Toronto, 1978), p. 10.

59. The myths that sprung up around the unworthy Svoboda are expertly dismantled in Jan Pauer, 'Exkurs o úloze L. Svobody v srpnových událostech, 1968', in Jindřich Pecka and Vilém Prečan, (eds), *Proměny Pražského jara, 1968–1969* (Brno, 1993), pp. 187–204.

–7–

Solidarity, 1980–1: The Second Vistula Miracle?[1]

Bartosz Kaliski

The activists and supporters of Solidarity, the multimillion-strong Polish independent trade union movement, perceived its creation, in hindsight, as something as surprising and unpredictable as the fall of the Soviet Union.[2] It was hardly an accident that a leading Polish political journal headed its twentieth-anniversary special issue devoted to Solidarity with a quotation from Joseph de Maistre: 'a miraculous fruit-producing tree in the middle of winter'.[3] Nevertheless, recent advances in knowledge enable us to conclude that a great social conflict was likely in 1980. Some form of 'Solidarity' was bound to be created because Polish civil society, increasingly dissatisfied, frustrated and alienated, had matured to such an organisational extent. The historiography of the Polish People's Republic emphasises great watershed moments, which shook the political order and at times caused fundamental personnel changes in the communist hierarchies. These cataclysmic moments are dubbed 'Polish Months', and the following are the most important: October 1956, March 1968, December 1970, June 1976, August 1980, December 1981 and June 1989.

Historical Context

The events of the 'Polish October' 1956 seemed a most profound revolution, signalling the rejection of the Stalinist model of socialism: the termination of secret police terror, a widening of intellectual freedom and the rehabilitation of the legendary, wartime, anti-communist Home Army (its soldiers filled state prisons soon after the war). Władysław Gomułka, a leading communist imprisoned during the Stalinist era for 'national deviationism', triumphantly returned to power. He was not disingenuous when he claimed that Polish socialism should take its own path, without slavishly copying the Soviet model. Releasing Primate Stefan Wyszyński, detained without trial since 1953, was a visible sign of change towards the Catholic Church and had tremendous importance for Polish national identity. In the January 1957 polls, a group of non-socialist Catholic MPs was elected to parliament to represent the interests of believers. The year 1956 also brought a permanent opening to the West, a temporary suspension of censorship, increased production of consumer commodities and the liquidation of the despised collective farms. Individual land ownership would remain an important distinctive feature of Poland compared to the other countries of the Soviet bloc. However, the crushing of the Hungarian Revolution in October–November 1956 dramatically demonstrated the limits of change acceptable to the Soviet leadership.[4]

Young people were the most active participants in the 'Polish October' – especially the intelligentsia, educated after 1945, broadly receptive to socialist principles and acting largely within the Polish United Workers' Party (PZPR) and its numerous discussion clubs. The youth's acceptance of the system, however, was not unconditional, and their attachment to left-wing thought was tempered by openness to other views. The 'revisionists', as they were called, craved a continuation of the democratic evolution of the system, in stark contrast to the interests of the conservative party bureaucracy, but nobody as yet considered the introduction of a Western model of parliamentary democracy. After a few years, 'revisionism' became the main heresy in official Marxism and was vehemently resisted by Gomułka. In October 1964, Jacek Kuroń and Karol Modzelewski composed 'An Open Letter to the Party' – the most important intellectual diagnosis of 'revisionism' and at the same time its last cry – which cost its authors several years' imprisonment. At the mass level, the movement of workers' councils, so widespread in 1956, was administratively smothered soon after October. Hence, popular dislike for Gomułka grew, compounded by an economic stagnation that took its toll in the years to come.

The 1960s witnessed increasing rivalry between the party and the Catholic Church and a gradual reduction of intellectual freedom. In 1966, the millennium of Christianity in Poland was accompanied by numerous celebrations, indicating the strength of popular Catholicism and the attachment of the masses to religion. In response, the communists organised competitive celebrations of the millennium of the Polish state: the People's Republic, in their view, was the crowning of all progressive currents in Polish history. This ideological duel in 1966 was ultimately inconclusive. It showed the dimensions of secularisation among certain social strata, but also the freshness and strength of Catholic faith, even among the young.

In March 1968 tempestuous student demonstrations were held against censorship and cultural stagnation, and in defence of university autonomy. The contemporaneous 'Prague Spring' was not without importance, since it reawakened dreams of 'socialism with a human face', similar to those of October 1956. However, the students' movement was soon smashed, many were dismissed from university and some were imprisoned. The communist authorities did not hesitate to engage in 'dirty propaganda', directed against leading activists of the movement, such as Adam Michnik and Jacek Kuroń. For several months a press campaign catered to the lowest social instincts, instigating an anti-intelligentsia phobia. It portrayed the main leaders of the student rebellion as the sons and daughters of Stalinist apparatchiks of Jewish descent. For university circles and nonconformist writers, the anti-Semitic overtones in the March propaganda were a profound shock. The participation of the Polish Army in the Soviet-led invasion of Czechoslovakia in August 1968 was an additional harsh lesson of realpolitik and surrender to Moscow. These dramatic experiences also proved that the ideology and practice of the Communist Party differed from the values traditionally associated with the left. It was no surprise that after 1968 members of the PZPR were often perceived as morally suspect. In this sense, March 1968 was a breakthrough. It became a constitutive experience for a new generation – people who would create a conscious opposition movement ten years later.

The 1960s was also a period of numerous clandestine (but on the whole minor) conflicts between workers and the sole employer, the communist state. The workers' revolt of December 1970 represented the peak of this social confrontation. The wave of protests – the result of increased food prices announced just before Christmas – mainly affected the Baltic coastal cities of Gdańsk, Gdynia and Szczecin. Attacks were directed against public buildings, often provincial party committees and the headquarters of the militia. The authorities, as in June 1956 in Poznań, used live ammunition. At least seventy-five were killed and many more injured. The scale of the strikes shook the Gomułka leadership and led to its dismissal. Edward Gierek, head of the party organisation in industrial Silesia, became the new party boss. He enjoyed a solid reputation, looked better than the caustic and gloomy Gomułka, and, even though poorly educated, spoke better French than Russian (before the war he had worked as a miner in France and Belgium). Nevertheless, the tense social climate settled only in February 1971, when Gierek revoked the price increases.

In the 1970s, dissident intellectuals resurrected the tradition of the liberal-leftist intelligentsia, who had played the role of spiritual guide of the nation in the long period of loss of independence after 1795 and in the interwar years. This pattern included respect for democratic procedures and legalism, and underlined values such as tolerance towards believers and 'other thinkers'. Its adherents sought to purge national history of lies and fill in the 'blank spots', especially in relations with the USSR. Leszek Kołakowski's essay, *Theses about Hope and Hopelessness* (1971), became the theoretical basis for the activity of post-1968 proto-opposition groups. Starting from the undeniable fact of the mutability of the communist system, Kołakowski inferred the moral principle of acting in order to advance change. The signing of the Helsinki Final Act (1975) by the countries of the Soviet bloc and the ratification of international treaties on UN human rights (1977), gave an additional justification for nonconformist attitudes.

The 'KOR' Period

The early 1970s brought a change in the concept of economic progress. The party leadership decided to seek enormous loans from abroad, purchase numerous

Western technologies, increase the production of consumer goods and start the mass building of flats. Poland entered the path of 'fast' modernisation and giant investments, and future generations were to pay for them. The drive was typified by the manufacture of a 'car for everybody', and Coca-Cola, a drink previously assoc-iated with 'American imperialism'. Western films appeared more frequently in the cinemas. Large numbers of people joined the PZPR out of conformism, careerism and opportunism. These short-sighted policies were to cost Gierek dearly. The loans were indeed primarily spent on consumption, and society lived for a few years in a false sense of welfare. But the authorities were under the illusion that they had the undeniable right to pursue any political agenda. When it was announced in 1975 that a number of new articles were to be introduced to the Constitution (for example, the formal recognition of the leading role of the Communist Party in the state, Poland's fraternal alliance with the USSR and the tying of citizens' rights to the fulfilment of duties towards the state), many intellectuals and students, together with the episcopate of Poland, protested. The propagandist illusion of consensus was demolished. And even though the authorities carried out the proposed changes, the protests united many of the discontented. Involvement in writing petitions was for many people the first step to opposition.

The 'prosperity' of the Gierek era had to break. In June 1976 the government decided on a drastic increase of food prices, up till then kept at an artificially low level. On 25 June strikes broke out. There were 111 strikes in the country as a whole, involving 80,000 participants.[5] In Płock the workers went on the streets. Employees in Ursus (near Warsaw) stopped traffic on the important railway route to the capital. In Radom there was a full-scale revolt – the crowd burnt the provincial party committee building. The response of the Security Services (SB) and the militia was quick and ferocious. Many workers were dismissed from work, severely beaten, and put on trial. In the opinion of one expert, 'the Communist authorities showed weakness and incompetence combined with brutality towards the workers'.[6] The increased prices were soon revoked, but the June events brought only a minor correction of economic policy.

At the same time, tiny intelligentsia groups in Warsaw started to collect money for the persecuted in Ursus and Radom. Defence lawyers with oppositional leanings proffered legal assistance to condemned workers. This self-help activity could not be overt and was countered by the Security Services. Moreover, those offering help and money were initially mistrusted by the workers, who (up to that time) generally associated educated people with the hated factory bureaucracy. The party slogan about the alliance of workers, farmers and the so-called 'working intelligentsia' was a fiction in the times before Solidarity.

After a few weeks it was clear that coordinated activity was necessary, and hence, on 23 September 1976, fourteen people established the Committee for Workers' Defence (KOR). This fragile body aimed to offer succour to the persecuted and inform world public opinion about the contravention of human rights in Poland.

The committee consisted of members with diverse ideological pedigrees. Among the founders were those formerly infatuated with Stalinist ideology (the pedagogue Kuroń and the writer Jerzy Andrzejewski), the protagonists of the agnostic current of socialist thought (the literary critic Jan Józef Lipski and the economist Edward Lipiński), veterans of March 1968 (Michnik) and national ideologists (such as the poet Stanisław Barańczak). Perhaps owing to this heterogeneity, KOR quickly attracted new adherents, Kuroń's apartment serving as its organisational centre. The significance of the Committee was that it seriously undermined the propagandist image of Poland as a developed country, open to Western values and without political prisoners, focusing as it did on numerous human rights abuses, including restrictions on religious freedom and trade union activity. The murder by the SB in May 1977 of Stanisław Pyjas, a student co-worker of KOR from Kraków, sparked university protests and the establishment of a local Students' Solidarity Committee (SKS). In response, a large number of KOR co-workers were arrested; but after a few weeks of concerted protest Gierek ordered their release. What is more, despite persecution, Students' Solidarity Committees were organised at other universities, in the struggle for greater academic freedom.

Not surprisingly, the authorities reacted by harassing members of KOR and SKS. The catalogue of repressions included 48-hour detentions (according to the law, citizens could be arrested for this period without any specific charge), beatings by 'unknown culprits', dismissal from work, threatening phone calls and confiscation of property. Undeterred, in autumn 1976 the first non-censored publications of KOR appeared. The following summer saw the creation of the Independent Publication House, which published books and papers in large circulations. The oppositional landscape was further diversified in March 1977, with the emergence of the Movement for the Defence of Human and Citizens' Rights (ROPCiO), established on the basis of overt national values and dislike of the USSR. In September 1979 the first opposition party was created from ROPCiO: the Confederation of Independent Poland, which was small, but radically and vocally anti-Soviet.

KOR deemed its action on behalf of the repressed workers from Radom and Ursus over by September 1977. However, it decided to continue to defend those universal human rights endangered by the totalitarian state, taking the name Committee of Social Self-Defence (KSS-KOR). One of its initiatives was the so-called 'flying university', the first lectures of which took place in autumn 1977. This was an educational undertaking, independent from the authorities, and reminiscent in form to the underground university from before the Great War, when Poland was a province of the Russian Empire. The classes were held most often in private flats and were conducted by intellectuals connected with KSS-KOR. In February 1978 the 'flying university' was renamed the Society of Scientific Courses (TKN), covering within its reach many self-education and student groups. Lectures in Polish history enjoyed the greatest popularity. The militia closed meetings of the TKN under the pretence that the law concerning public gatherings had been broken, and detained lecturers for forty-eight hours. Participants were also beaten by student paratroopers organised by officers of the Security Services.

Two other important initiatives emerged in 1978. First, self-defence committees of farmers were organised. Private farmers were legally discriminated against and treated as second-class citizens in the communist system, and it is not without significance that they constituted the main social base of support for Catholicism. Second, the Free Trade Unions were established on the inspiration of KOR. They were most prominent in the Baltic ports of Gdańsk, Gdynia and Sopot, where (among others) the crane driver Anna Walentynowicz and the electrician Lech Wałęsa, soon to be world-renowned, were involved. The official, centralised trade unions had long been part of the system of power as a 'transmission belt' to the masses, and hence failed to defend employees from the possessiveness and exploitation of the communist state. The sociological diagnoses of Polish society from this time make for grim reading. The average Pole felt identification only with the family circle and national community, perceiving state institutions as hostile and unable to represent and solve their interests (the syndrome of 'social alienation'). This 'amoral familiarism', as it was later called, flourished on the level of the production site, where theft and using materials for one's own private ends were commonplace. Work discipline and efficiency were very low. The giant investments came in handy for the party apparatchiks, who gained huge profits, building villas from state money and selling scarce materials on the free market. Nepotism and corruption were rife. Apart from that, production was interrupted due to the lack of raw materials, electric energy and spare parts for the machinery, and the average Pole spent more and more time queuing in front of grocery stores. The socialist 'welfare state' was proving a great lie.

If this were not bad enough for the communist authorities, the election of Karol Wojtyła – a cardinal from Kraków – to the papacy in October 1978 caused yet more consternation. The Politburo concluded that it was better to have Wojtyła as Pope in Rome than as the Primate in Warsaw (Primate Wyszyński was already seventy-eight years old), but it was a worrying consolation prize.[7] It took the first pilgrimage of the Pope to his homeland in June 1979 to show the scope of the threat to the communist power monopoly. Millions of people voluntarily and enthusiastically attended the masses conducted by Pope John Paul II, and church celebrations were organised most effectively. Only the sociologist Jan Szczepański, in a critical analysis prepared for the party leadership, had the courage to anticipate then that the Catholic masses, hitherto asleep and disorganised, would soon crave participation in power.[8] In the following summer these predictions were confirmed almost in their entirety.

Miraculous August

In response to yet another increase in food prices in July 1980, strikes started in many factories in the south-eastern regions of Poland – first, on 8 July, in Swidnik.

In contrast to 1970 and 1976, the strikers did not go out on to the streets, but stayed in their factories. The regional authorities eased the situation with concessions, but this merely encouraged other workforces to put forward similar claims. On 16 July railway workers went on strike in Lublin. This strike had been prepared by politically conscious workers in contact with KSS-KOR representatives,[9] and soon took on the dimensions of a general strike. The Lublin area calmed a little on 19 July after the financial demands of the strikers had been met. The population was informed of these events by Radio Free Europe, which reported on the passive, subdued stance of the authorities.

On 14 August 1980 a small activist group of the Free Trade Unions of the Coast called for strike action at the Lenin Shipyard in Gdańsk. They claimed that Anna Walentynowicz, dismissed from work a few days earlier and subsequently persecuted, should be allowed to return to work; and they demanded pay increases and the introduction of a money bonus to offset the hike in prices. Lech Wałęsa, sacked from the shipyard in 1976, stood at the head of the movement. Although the strike was temporarily suspended on 16 August, when the board of directors decided to concede, workers from other firms protested, counting on the help of the Lenin Shipyard in the realisation of their own *cahiers de doléances*. That day proved a turning point – the shipyard did not go back to work, but continued a solidarity strike. The Gdańsk Inter-factory Strike Committee (MKS) was created, which quickly elaborated a uniform list of twenty-one motions. The right to create free trade unions, independent from the party, was the first of them. The workers also demanded the right to strike, a guarantee of security for strike supporters, as well as freedom of speech and of the press, and the abolition of repression and the release of political prisoners. By 18 August the Gdańsk MKS grouped as many as 156 factories. The following two weeks astonished the world. By the end of the month, 700,000 people were on strike in 700 factories across the whole country. Their interests were represented by three Inter-factory Strike Committees in Gdańsk, Szczecin and Jastrzębie (Silesia). Discipline and order reigned; there was no violence or rioting. The Gdańsk Committee prohibited the sale of alcohol in the city, contributing to a drop in the crime rate during the last two weeks of August.[10]

Almost from the onset, the strikes were covered by foreign press and TV journalists – their Polish counterparts being treated with much less confidence, as it was not certain whether the censor would 'pass' anything from them and how much truth their reports would contain.[11] Photographs of Gate No. 2 to the Lenin Shipyard, surrounded by women and children, decorated with national flags and portraits of Pope John Paul II and the Holy Virgin, circulated throughout the world. The workers were encouraged by the presence of intellectuals, who created a Committee of Experts led by the future Prime Minister, Tadeusz Mazowiecki, to advise the MKS. Press materials were prepared by printers associated with KSS-KOR. Masses were celebrated close to the gate and information about family members exchanged. Farmers brought food. Everything happening nearby took on the atmosphere of a festival. Strike songs were sung, and the negotiations of the presidium of the MKS with the government emissaries were transmitted through the intercom.

After a few days of tense talks, Deputy Prime Minister Mieczysław Jagielski and Wałęsa signed an historic agreement on 31 August, ending the strike. The first paragraph of the document stated that: 'Trade unions in the Polish People's Republic have not lived up to the hopes and expectations of employees. It is necessary to form new, self-governing trade unions, as authoritative representatives of the working class'.[12] For the first time since the late 1940s, the communist authorities permitted the existence of an independent mass social organisation. A week later Gierek resigned as party First Secretary, and Stanisław Kania became his successor.

The 'Self-limiting Revolution'

The British historian and journalist Timothy Garton Ash, who witnessed the crisis in Poland between August 1980 and December 1981, later described it as 'the most paradoxical of European revolutions'.[13] This can be seen on several different levels. The first paradox was the role of Catholic belief, which seemed to galvanise the workers and provide a bridge to unite them with other social groups, especially intellectuals and peasants. The photographs of the Lenin Shipyard not only provided the world with a powerful image of revolution, but also gave visual form to the fusion of religion and national identity that had long shaped Polish history. In part, this unique mix also reflected the late origins of industrialisation in Poland, so that many Baltic coast and Silesian workers – including those who were forcibly resettled from areas lost to the Soviet Union in 1945 – came from peasant backgrounds and brought with them a strong sense of tradition and continued attachment to the land and the Church.[14] Even so, it is also clear from Garton Ash and other accounts that the Poles, while worshipping the Pope as one of their own, did not always regard the Vatican's teachings on private morals as totally binding. For instance, alcohol – which had done so much harm to the Polish economy and society – was frowned upon, but sex outside marriage and the use of contraception were not. In other words, for the first time in Polish history, the industrial working class – a product of the communist era – was redefining morality and national interest in its own image, conscious too that the world was watching and waiting for further developments. This moral dimension to the Polish revolution was symbolised, above all, by the actions of the shipyard workers at Gdańsk, who, in spite of winning a relatively generous pay offer from their managers on 16 August, opted for a solidarity strike so that all wage earners would benefit from the right to form independent trade unions and engage in free collective bargaining.

A second paradox was the 'self-limiting' nature of the Polish revolution.[15] In order to persuade the communists to enter peaceful negotiations – the central aim of Solidarity – it was vital to show that there would be no repeat of Hungary in 1956, or even of Gdańsk in 1970 and Ursus and Radom in 1976: that is, no civil disturbances ending in violence; no mass demonstrations in front of party buildings or newspaper offices; and no direct challenge to the party's hold on power or its control over the police and security apparatus. In part, this strategy reflected Solidarity's view of itself as a trade union which did not interfere in politics, but simply represented the workers vis-à-vis their employer (the Polish state). It also reflected memories of the early Polish 'success' in October 1956 in avoiding a Soviet invasion. Yet as time went on, it became increasingly clear that the chief material demands of Solidarity – lower prices, higher wages, 'work-free' Saturdays – were impossible to realise without substantial and painful reforms to the Polish economy, including the abolition of the corrupt *nomenklatura* system. Indeed, the Poles, even after achieving their own independent trade union, were still worse off in material terms than their fellow workers in East Germany and Czechoslovakia, both of whom lived under harshly repressive regimes, but nonetheless enjoyed the highest living standards in the Soviet bloc and worked only a five-day week. Thus the big risk for the revolutionary movement in Poland in 1980–1 – perhaps an even bigger risk than Soviet military intervention – was that the authorities might seek to co-opt Solidarity as a partner in a new austerity programme, forcing it to share responsibility for reforming and restructuring the economy, without exercising any real power. Yet power was exactly what the younger, more militant members of Solidarity wanted and yearned for.

The third and final paradox is that the older and more experienced members of Solidarity, including Wałęsa, still saw the current Polish leadership under Kania as a lesser evil, which in some circumstances might have to be protected against the impact of internal and international developments. In other words, no matter how 'foreign' or 'un-Polish' the current state of affairs was, it was still possible to imagine something worse – in particular the type of communist dictatorship prevailing in Poland during the final years of Stalin's rule (1948–53), or in contemporary Romania or Albania under Ceauşescu and Hoxha respectively. It was also possible to envisage civil war, or a complete collapse of living standards to a level below that even of the USSR itself. For all these reasons, Wałęsa and his advisers were willing to compromise at key junctures, in other words, to impose limits on the revolution which they themselves had created. Even the demand for freedom of speech and opinion was tempered by self-imposed limitations: the complete abolition of censorship was not called for lest it threaten perceived Soviet military interests, while repeated promises were made to uphold (or at least not to challenge) the sanctity of Poland's treaty obligations with neighbouring socialist countries.[16]

In spite of these restraints, Solidarity did score some notable, if largely symbolic, victories in the period after the Gdańsk agreement of 31 August 1980. For instance, in the autumn of 1980 the communist authorities resorted to their usual tactic of divide and rule by choosing to interpret the Gdańsk agreement as if it applied to the Gdańsk region only; but they were defeated when local Inter-factory Strike

Committees were formed across the country and warning strikes were called to gain the same rights for all workers, irrespective of their trade or political affiliation. This led, in September 1980, to the formation of the Solidarity National Coordinating Committee (KKP), led by Wałęsa, who also remained head of the Gdańsk Inter-factory Strike Committee.[17] Second, on 10 November Solidarity won a lengthy and complex battle in the Polish Supreme Court to secure legal registration without having to accept any limits on its right to strike. This decision overturned a previous ruling by the Warsaw Provincial Court on 24 October, but added, with the consent of Solidarity's own lawyers, a seven-point appendix, which included Solidarity's recognition of the 'leading role of the Party in the state'. Third, when a prominent Solidarity activist from the Warsaw region, Jan Narożniak, was arrested at the end of November, the mere threat of a general strike was sufficient to secure his release three days later. Demands were even raised for the punishment of those responsible for his arrest, thus raising for the first time the question of the legitimacy of the party's hold over the police and security forces.[18]

Finally, not only did Solidarity succeed in getting a monument erected to the dead workers of December 1970 in front of the Lenin Shipyard gates in Gdańsk, but they also organised an official ceremony on 16 December 1980 to mark the tenth anniversary of these events, at which the titular head of state, Henryk Jabłoński, and the Gdańsk Communist Party secretary, Tadeusz Fiszbach, appeared with bowed heads alongside Wałęsa and the Archbishop of Kraków, before a crowd of 150,000.[19] Two weeks later the Gdańsk memorial was also visited by Kania himself.[20] This was an event of immense and unique importance: it would have been quite impossible to imagine a similar monument appearing in East Berlin or Prague to the victims of June 1953 or August 1968, let alone such a monument receiving an official visit from the party First Secretary. More generally, of course, the idea that an independent trade union could claim to represent the workers vis-à-vis the party and state was a pivotal moment in post-war Eastern Europe, and marked the beginning of the end of communist rule, both in Poland and further afield.

The Attitude of the Party

How did the Polish Communist Party react to these events? Certainly the evidence is that the 'appeasers' or 'modernisers' had a slight edge over the hardliners at first. Among them was Kania himself, who told the Central Committee on 4 October that the August strikes were caused by genuine worker discontent and by errors committed by the PZPR and government, which could only be rectified through the democratisation of internal political processes and a greater stress on economic rationality.[21] His long-term aim, it is now believed, was some kind of 'enlightened despotism', with the legitimacy of communist rule strengthened by co-opting Solidarity and forcing it to share responsibility for running the country, without conceding it any real power.[22] In the meantime, dozens of corrupt party bosses were sacked and there were some very slow attempts to reform the party itself by introducing so-called horizontal structures to complement the vertical ones.[23] The purpose here was to stem the exodus of ordinary party members into the ranks of Solidarity by giving the party itself a stronger regional and local base, without thereby infringing the basic Leninist requirement of 'democratic centralism'.

Even so, it would be wrong to see any real consistency in party thinking. Hardliners like Stefan Olszowski also had an important voice in the Politburo, and their position was strengthened by continuing threats from outside, especially when the Red Army decided to begin preparations for military manoeuvres close to the Polish border in early December 1980. Already in October the GDR and Czechoslovakia had closed their frontiers to normal traffic with Poland, and party newspapers in Prague and East Berlin frequently made reference to parallels with the situation in 1968, thus hinting at imminent invasion. On 5 December, at a meeting of Warsaw Pact leaders in Moscow, both Honecker for the GDR and Zhivkov for Bulgaria were harshly critical of the Polish leadership, while Kádár, for Hungary, spoke in milder terms. However, Brezhnev had the final say, and, for reasons that remain unclear even today, he ruled out armed force in a conversation with Kania after the meeting.[24] One explanation for Soviet hesitancy was the 'Afghanistan factor', making military strategists reluctant to launch a war on two fronts; another was the tough warnings issued by the outgoing Carter and incoming Reagan administrations in the USA (the Polish-American lobby exerted far more influence in Washington than the Hungarian- and Czechoslovak-American lobbies were able to do in 1956 and 1968 respectively). Nonetheless, the most compelling factor was the apparent unity of the Poles and the strength of their millions-strong movement. As Raymond Pearson puts it: 'As the largest state of eastern Europe, Poland was a much more formidable proposition than Hungary ... [and its] glorious tradition of nationalist military resistance [stood] in marked contrast to nationally divided and traditionally unheroic Czechoslovakia'.[25]

Meanwhile, communist hardliners inside Poland had ensured that there would be no legal recognition of Rural Solidarity (the farmers' collective) or of independent student unions, on the grounds that only wage earners had a right to form self-governing trade unions, not independent producers or members of the intelligentsia. Further attempts were made to create divisions within Solidarity, for instance by isolating so-called 'anti-socialist elements' like KOR, while going partway to implementing some of the new 'social accords' as set down in the Gdańsk and other regional agreements.[26] Leading figures in the Polish episcopate were also leant on to discourage popular protests and strikes at crucial moments, causing strains in the relationship between the Catholic Church and the independent workers' movement, which were undoubtedly exploited for all they were worth.[27]

In practice, though, there was no clear direction from the PZPR; and while negotiations continued between representatives of the regime and Solidarity delegates, behind the scenes figures in the Ministry of Interior were already preparing for a major crackdown, including discussions with their Soviet counterparts on plans for the instigation of a military coup and the mass arrest of Solidarity activists.[28] Both Wałęsa and the millions of ordinary members of Solidarity were unaware of this double game played by the Communist Party leaders, although, given the precedents of 1956 and 1968, they might have had some inkling of what was coming. In November 1980 the security services in Gdańsk had already launched operation 'Klan' against individual trade union leaders, which meant, in practice, heightened surveillance and control of the Solidarity leadership by recruiting new informers or by activating existing ones in its ranks. By the beginning of 1981, 1,800 agents were active in Solidarity at different levels of that organisation's hierarchy, including 13 in its National Coordinating Committee.[29]

It is now accepted, however, that General Wojciech Jaruzelski, the Defence Minister and Politburo member who went on to become Prime Minister in February 1981 (and from October 1981, party First Secretary too), was not at first one of the hardliners; nor was he party to any coup plots emanating from Moscow. As Defence Minister since 1968, he was widely regarded as a 'moderate' who had opposed corruption and mismanagement in the armed forces. It was also rumoured that he had advised against armed intervention by the state during the strikes of December 1970 and August 1980. Like Kania, he seemed to be looking for a political rather than a military response to the current crisis, and even risked provoking the ire of his Warsaw Pact neighbours by promising, in his inaugural speech on 12 February 1981, to speed up legislation implementing the Gdańsk accords. In the meantime, along with his deputy, Mieczysław Rakowski, he also offered stable government in partnership with the unions, something which even top Solidarity officials like Wałęsa and Modzelewski seemed at first to welcome, albeit cautiously and not without reservations.[30]

The Bydgoszcz crisis

The new spirit of compromise and goodwill was swiftly undone, however, when, a month later, the Bydgoszcz crisis hit the headlines. The background was the continued refusal by the party-controlled courts to register the million-strong Rural Solidarity, leading the latter to organise a mass sit-in at Rzeszów, in the south-east of the country, in early 1981. The issue remained unresolved on 16 March, when independent farmers took over the headquarters of the United Peasant Party in the north-west town of Bydgoszcz, again in order to publicise the case for the full recognition of Rural Solidarity, including the right to strike. Solidarity in Bydgoszcz backed the farmers, but contrary to assurances previously given by local party officials, its activists were not permitted to speak during a meeting of the local council on 19 March, which was suddenly adjourned at two o'clock in the afternoon, without prior warning and before rural grievances could be addressed. The representatives of Solidarity and some of the councillors agreed to stay on in the assembly hall as a form of protest against the action of the authorities, and they refused to leave even after the police were called. Finally, in the evening, the police returned in greater numbers and ejected all the protesters by force. Three people were beaten in the process, including Jan Rulewski, the regional president of Solidarity, who was regarded as a radical. Worse still, the whole incident was recorded on tape, and was soon being broadcast across the country.[31] The reaction of Solidarity's KKP was immediate: they insisted on the punishment of the persons responsible for the police brutality and a guarantee against similar incidents in the future. The KKP rallied for a four-hour 'warning strike' on 27 March and, as a precaution in case talks failed, issued a call for a general strike of unlimited duration to begin on 31 March.

This was a moment of extreme tension for Poland and the whole of the Soviet bloc. If the industrial workers did not make common cause with the victims of Bydgoszcz, then Solidarity itself would no longer exist as a united, democratic and national movement. In the PZPR, on the other hand, conservatives hostile to any further concessions were beginning to round on Kania. On top of this, from 16 March the Warsaw Pact began yet another series of manoeuvres close to the Polish border. The stalemate came to an end on 30 March, when the will to compromise took over. The authorities officially admitted breaking the spirit of the Gdańsk agreement by using the police against Solidarity, while the Solidarity leadership took some of the blame for the escalating tension in the country, and Wałęsa went on national television to announce that the next day's general strike was cancelled. It now seems that the Bydgoszsz crisis was not a deliberate act of 'provocation' by the authorities, but an unfortunate accident caused by hotheads in the local police and militia. For Kania and Jaruzelski, the period of nervous waiting came to an end in early April when Brezhnev ceased to press for the introduction of martial law and agreed to postpone any further military operations. On 7 April the Warsaw Pact manoeuvres were officially over.

The Bydgoszcz crisis was nonetheless a vital caesura in the history of Solidarity. The mode of attaining agreement with the authorities was far from democratic – it was reached by Wałęsa and a handful of his top advisers without reference to the views of the broader membership. Some radicals in the regional Inter-factory Strike Committees felt that the opportunity had been lost for the final crushing of the party's monopoly of power. Criticisms were also levelled at Wałęsa personally, who was accused of isolating himself from the workers, acting like an autocrat and relying too heavily on the advice of members of his inner circle. Modzelewski subsequently resigned from his position as official press spokesperson for the union, although he also appealed for unity and argued that Wałęsa should not be overthrown by a grass-roots revolt against the leadership.[32] It was, of course, obvious that any evidence of splits in Solidarity would be more than welcomed by the communist authorities in Warsaw and Moscow.

The Road to Martial Law

At first, though, it appeared as if Solidarity moderates had emerged strengthened from the Bydgoszsz crisis, and that both sides were now more willing to agree. The process of compromise continued when, in early April, the first issue of the weekly newspaper *Solidarność* was published with official sanction and a circulation of half a million, and on 11 May the court in Warsaw finally registered Rural Solidarity. At the end of May the death of the Catholic Primate, Cardinal Wyszyński, was the occasion for a mass outpouring of grief and further demonstrations, which the authorities met with equanimity. The appointment of Monsignor Józef Glemp as Wyszyński's successor was formally announced on 7 July.

The ninth (extraordinary) congress of the PZPR was held between 14 and 20 July 1981. Contrary to expectations, Kania retained his position as First Secretary in a secret ballot, even though the Soviet leadership had written to key members of the Central Committee beforehand, suggesting that they vote both him and Jaruzelski out of office. More striking still, the former First Secretary Gierek and the former Prime Minister Edward Babiuch were both expelled from the party. The congress also passed resolutions demanding free and secret elections to all party offices, with a maximum period of ten years for those seeking re-election, and insisted on clauses allowing for the instant dismissal of those who proved corrupt or incompetent, without having to go through the usual bureaucratic channels. Meanwhile, a huge change in personnel took place, so that only four out of the fifteen previous Politburo members and less than one in eight of the former Central Committee members remained in post. Extraordinarily, 20 per cent of the new Central Committee were also members of Solidarity, as was one of the eleven new members of the Politburo.[33]

Yet by the late summer of 1981, against the background of a worsening economic crisis and hunger demonstrations in several cities, the party's line became tougher and the will to compromise correspondingly weaker. For instance, in early August 1981 Rakowski, previously regarded as a liberal, attacked Solidarity for instigating 'anti-Soviet, anti-government and anti-Party' actions among the workers and for spreading anarchy and lawlessness.[34] The KKP, in turn, reproached the government for its failure to devise a clear programme for ending the economic crisis, and for its refusal to provide free access to radio and television. Both sides accused each other of breaking the spirit of the Gdańsk agreement, which celebrated its anniversary on 31 August 1981.

The cracks in Solidarity also deepened. For example, at its first (and very much belated) national congress, which took place in two stages in September and October 1981, it became clear that many delegates were no longer willing to recognise the leading role of the Communist Party in the Polish state – a dangerous step, which undermined the position of moderates. Further tensions were caused by the decision to send messages of support to free trade union activists in other Warsaw

Pact countries. This led to ferocious attacks in newspapers published in the USSR and elsewhere in the Eastern bloc. The Soviet news agency TASS condemned the Solidarity congress as an 'anti-socialist and anti-Soviet orgy', while the Soviet navy carried out manoeuvres off the coast of Gdańsk.[35] In the meantime, the congress itself passed a resolution condemning the Solidarity leaders for arranging a compromise deal on self-management and reform of factory administration, without first seeking the views of the union membership.[36]

On 18 October, just a week after the end of the congress, Kania announced his resignation as party First Secretary. The Central Committee now chose General Jaruzelski, the Prime Minister and Defence Minister, as his replacement. The concentration of power in the hands of one man, standing at the head of the party and the army, was of tremendous importance for the coming weeks. During the Central Committee plenum on 18 October, appeals were made to close ranks behind the new party leader in order to stop the decomposition of socialism. General Czesław Kiszczak, the head of the Ministry of Interior, called for radical action against strikers and lawbreakers through the use of extraordinary measures.

Jaruzelski, Wałęsa, and the Catholic Primate Glemp are believed to have met on 4 November to discuss proposals for a new pact to rescue the economy. However, the worsening atmosphere meant that compromise was no longer on the cards. In particular, Solidarity was increasingly wary of being drawn into a new 'Front of National Cooperation', as proposed by the government authorities. It is even possible that the meeting with Jaruzelski on 4 November did not take place at all, as there are no reliable accounts of the agenda or outcome. The different parties to the negotiations simply issued bland statements through their representatives. Even if the meeting did take place, it did little to change the course of events. Months of logistical and legal preparations at the Ministry of Defence and the Interior Ministry were drawing to a close and force was now increasingly used against protestors, as on 2 December, when a Solidarity-backed strike at the Warsaw Fire Officers' School was brutally suppressed. Finally, on 13 December Jaruzelski made his move, announcing the formation of a Military Council for National Salvation (WRON) and the imposition of martial law. Overnight, the right to strike and the activity of independent trade unions was suspended. Phone connections were cut, publication of all but official party newspapers ceased, and a curfew was introduced. Tanks and armoured vehicles appeared on the streets, and a mass round-up of strikers and Solidarity leaders began. The principal motive was to forestall a Soviet invasion, and for this reason at least some Poles were relieved that the period of waiting and uncertainty was finally over.[37] In many towns, however, especially in the mining districts of Silesia, spontaneous strikes were organised against the military coup. They were ruthlessly broken. The carnival of Solidarity was definitely over, to be replaced by more than eighteen months of army rule.

Conclusion

Although the Soldiarity movement lasted only briefly, it left an indelible mark on Polish society and the political system. As it turned out, many of the changes introduced proved irreversible. The independent trade union had broken the barrier of fear towards the authorities. The period between August 1980 and December 1981 was a time of unlimited freedom. The authorities' monopoly on information was curtailed and union publications went to great efforts to retell Polish history, which in turn directly threatened the legitimacy of the Communist Party, since the retelling of history involved the disclosure of sensitive information regarding the Polish-Soviet 'friendship'. The restitution of workers' neglected rights went hand in hand with the revindication of national rights: pride, a right to education without 'blank spots', and open discussion of historical events like the Katyń massacre, which until that moment was forbidden. The moral excess hampered Solidarity in finding a lasting modus vivendi with the immoral state, but it was exactly the moral factor which seduced intellectuals from all over the world and assured Solidarity its legitimate voice.[38]

Pressure from the mass of unionists led to the dismissal of scores of compromised members of the PZPR apparatus from all ranks. Solidarity taught Poles to overlook the authorities.[39] It led to a loosening of censorship (until then, the press, radio and television were above the law). Solidarity woke millions of citizens from their slumbers, allowing them to feel masters of their own country at last. During the final sitting of the National Coordinating Committee in December 1981 the idea was even voiced of brokering an agreement with the Communist Party of the Soviet Union, above the heads of the PZPR. Solidarity, however, was unable to arrest the decline of the national economy. It was unable to test the idea of worker self-government as a panaceum for all the ills of centrally controlled production. The PZPR became weaker and hence sought support in the reliable apparatus of repression, the security services and the army. By 1981 even the militia had links to Solidarity cells. Communist rule was held up by force in December 1981, but it was this same force that ultimately destroyed the regime's credibility. The Catholic Church played a vital role too, as a mediator during the strikes. In return for assistance in stabilising communist rule, it gained an expansion of religious freedoms which was practically unheard of in earlier periods. Evidence of this increased freedom can be seen in the daily broadcasting of Mass on Polish radio, even after the declaration of martial law.

Today Solidarity is the mythological founder of the Third Republic of Poland. This is granted by almost all participants in political life in Poland. The idea that Solidarity began the process that led to the fall of the Berlin Wall and the opening of the Iron Curtain is taken as read. From such certainties, myths are created.

Notes

1. The 'Vistula Miracle', the great victory of the Polish Army over the Red Army in 1920, is so named because it occurred on 15 August, a Catholic festival devoted to the Holy Virgin.
2. This essay is based mainly on Polish sources. Key documents on Solidarity can be found in English translation in A. Kemp-Welch, *The Birth of Solidarity: The Gdańsk Negotiations, 1980* (London, 1983); and W.F. Robinson (ed.), *August 1980: The Strikes in Poland* (Munich, 1980). For secondary English-language literature, see T. Garton Ash, *The Polish Revolution: Solidarity,* 2nd edn (London, 1990); A. Touraine, F. Dubet, M. Wieviorka and J. Strzelecki, *Solidarity. The Analysis of a Social Movement: Poland 1980–81* (Cambridge, 1983); K. Ruane, *The Polish Challenge* (London, 1982); and D. MacShane, *Solidarity: Poland's Independent Trade Union* (Nottingham, 1981).
3. Round-table discussion, 'Krzywa niepamieci', *Res Publica Nowa,* no. 8 (2000).
4. For details on the events of 1956, see the chapter by Johanna Granville in this volume.
5. M. Zaremba, 'Od wojny domowej do solidarnosciowej rewolucji, czyli spoleczenstwo nieprzedstawione dekady lat siedemdziesiatych', *Res Publica Nowa,* vol. 8 (2000), p. 51.
6. J. Holzer, *Solidarność 1980–1981. Geneza i historia* (Warsaw, 1990), p. 24.
7. J. Zaryn, *Dzieje Kosciola katolickiego w Polsce (1944–1989)* (Warsaw, 2003), p. 401.
8. A. Friszke and M. Zaremba (eds), *Wizyta Jana Pawla II w Polsce 1979. Dokumenty KC PZPR i MSW* (Warsaw, 2005), p. 325.
9. M. Jachowicz and J. Pleszczyński, 'Pierwsze ogniwo', *Tygodnik Powszechny,* vol. 36 (2005), p. 4.
10. A. Drzycimski and T. Skutnik (eds), *Zapis wydarzen. Gdańsk – Sierpień 1980. Dokumenty* (Warsaw, 1999), p. 397.
11. J. Jankowska and M. Miller, *Kto tu wpuscil dziennikarzy. 25 lat pozniej* (Warsaw, 2005), p. 222.
12. Kemp-Welch, *The Birth of Solidarity,* p. 168; and J. Gmitruk and J. Sałkowski (eds), *Porozumienia spoleczne 1980–1981* (Warsaw, 2005), p. 15.
13. Garton Ash, *The Polish Revolution,* p. xii.
14. Touraine et al., *Solidarity,* p. 32.
15. The phrase comes the Polish sociologist Jadwiga Staniszkis – see J. Staniszkis, *Poland's Self-Limiting Revolution,* ed. J.T. Gross (Princeton, NJ, 1984).
16. Garton Ash, *The Polish Revolution,* p. 93; Touraine et al., *Solidarity,* p. 65.
17. R.J. Crampton, *Eastern Europe in the Twentieth Century – and After,* 2nd edn (London, 1997), p. 368.

18. Ibid., p. 370; and Garton Ash, *The Polish Revolution*, p. 99.
19. Garton Ash, *The Polish Revolution*, p. 108.
20. Touraine et al., *Solidarity*, p. 198.
21. Garton Ash, *The Polish Revolution*, p. 85.
22. Touraine et al., *Solidarity*, p. 18; Garton Ash, *The Polish Revolution*, p. 115.
23. Z. Włodek (ed.), *Tajne dokumenty Biura Politycznego PZPR a 'Solidarność' 1980–1981* (London, 1992), p. 108.
24. A. Paczkowski, *Droga do 'mniejszego zła'. Strategia i taktyka obozu władzy: lipiec 1980 – styczeń 1982* (Kraków, 2002), p. 113.
25. R. Pearson, *The Rise and Fall of the Soviet Empire* (London, 1998), p. 99.
26. Garton Ash, *The Polish Revolution*, p. 77.
27. Touraine et al., *Solidarity*, p. 47; and Crampton, *Eastern Europe*, p. 370.
28. R. Kukliński, *Wojna z narodem widziana od środka* (Gdańsk, 1987), pp. 33–4.
29. S. Cenckiewicz, *Oczami bezpieki. Szkice i materiały z dziejów aparatu bezpieczeństwa PRL* (Kraków, 2005), p. 467.
30. Garton Ash, *The Polish Revolution*, pp. 150–4.
31. Ibid., pp. 159–60.
32. Ibid., p. 169.
33. Crampton, *Eastern Europe*, p. 373. By October, however, these 'bigamists' were forced to choose between the party or Solidarity.
34. Garton Ash, *The Polish Revolution*, p. 204.
35. B. Kaliski, *'Antysocjalistyczne zbiorowisko'? I Krajowy Zjazd Delegatów NSZZ 'Solidarność'* (Warsaw, 2003), p. 112.
36. Touraine at al., *Solidarity*, p. 200.
37. Pearson, *The Rise and Fall of the Soviet Empire*, p. 98.
38. Z. Stawrowski, 'Doświadczenie "Solidarności" jako wspólnoty etycznej', in D. Gawin (ed.), *Lekcja Sierpnia. Dziedzictwo 'Solidarności' po dwudziestu latach* (Warsaw, 2000), p. 109.
39. S. Kowalski, *Krytyka solidarnościowego rozumu. Studium z socjologii myślenia potocznego* (Warsaw, 1990), pp. 33–44.

Part III

−8−

Negotiated Revolution in Poland and Hungary, 1989

Nigel Swain

The year 1989 was one of 'negotiated revolution',[1] and nowhere more so than in Poland and Hungary, where socialist regimes collapsed, but not a drop of blood was shed and demonstrations were sanctioned rather than suppressed. Indeed, it did not take long for conspiracy theories to emerge in both countries which claimed that no revolution had taken place at all − behind locked doors, power had simply been transferred from one elite to another.[2] Negotiations were at the centre of both revolutions, and both negotiations ended with the demise of communist power. Yet the build-up to the negotiations, the agendas that the opposing sides set themselves and the outcomes that they achieved all differed radically. This study compares these two negotiated revolutions, in terms of origins, agendas and outcomes.

Poland

Origins

By the mid-1980s, Poland was beginning to emerge from the trauma of martial law.[3] Party politicians[4] were realising that concessions were necessary if the huge problems that the regime faced were to be overcome, but they were reluctant to make overtures to the old enemy − Solidarity. After declaring martial law on 13 December 1981, and officially banning Solidarity on 8 October 1982, the government's goal had been to emulate post-1956 Hungary and create a depoliticised, economically prosperous welfare state. The ban on Solidarity was lifted on 22 July 1983, and in its place a new 'official' national trade union council was created in November 1984. Economic prosperity, it was hoped, would emerge from a series of reform measures introduced in 1982; but these reforms were unambitious and stamped by compromise from the start. Although the powers of the Planning Commission and the numbers of branch ministries were reduced, central intervention soon increased again, as did the control of prices.

The government's policy of initiating dialogue with other social actors began by trying to open up channels to the Church, but these were shattered when Father

139

Popiełuszko was murdered by functionaries of the Ministry of the Interior in October 1984. In 1986, the government proposed a Social Consultative Council and put out feelers to the Catholic opposition, including the Catholic Intellectual Clubs. The latter did not accept as an organisation, but key individuals within them did. Furthermore, the government more or less gave up on censorship from 1986 onwards. The underground journal, *Res Publica*, was legalised in 1987, and by 1988 press freedom was virtually complete. The party hoped that the third papal visit of John Paul II in June 1987 might strengthen its image and improve its legitimacy, but this backfired. The Pope declared in Gdańsk that Solidarity's heritage was crucial for Poland and the Poles.

But Solidarity had been weakened badly by martial law, and some members were considering compromise. While still in prison, Adam Michnik, one of the leading 'dissident' intellectuals, had written a book in which he suggested that 30 per cent of parliamentary seats should be freely elected.[5] Solidarity's call for a boycott of the 1985 parliamentary elections had been substantially ignored, with a turnout only a little lower than usual. Even the general amnesty of September 1986[6] and the release of all Solidarity politicians revealed a movement that was deeply divided, and uncertain about whether to act legally or underground, as a union or as a political party. 'By late 1987 Solidarity was on the defensive and in disarray',[7] and, as Padraic Kenney has documented, opposition was channelled through entirely new social movements, with very different goals to those of Solidarity.[8] William Wallace even described Lech Wałęsa at this time as, 'a rather sad and ageing symbol of a once glorious past'.[9] Nevertheless, Solidarity was still in the frame, still a force to be reckoned with, and one that the Catholic Church in particular insisted that the government should deal with.

But a prerequisite of Poland's policy of emulating post-1956 Hungary was successful economic reform, and the 1982 reforms proved a damp squib. By 1987 it was clear that further measures would be necessary. After what one observer termed 'eight wasted years',[10] hard currency debt by 1986 was five times the annual level of hard currency exports and had increased by 35 per cent since 1982; yet the shops were still empty. Mindful that reform under such conditions would be painful, the government announced on 8 October 1987 its decision to hold a referendum on 27 November on whether voters supported 'radical economic reform' and 'deep democratisation'. Some days later, on 13 October 1987, the party initiated talks with oppositionists, which included 'well-known former advisors to Solidarity', but not Solidarity itself. But the party misjudged its support in the November referendum. It set as the measure of confidence in its policies the votes of 50 per cent of the electorate, rather than 50 per cent of those who voted. This created defeat out of victory. Solidarity called for a boycott and the party failed to meet its self-imposed target, if only by 5 per cent. Defeated by its overconfidence, the party felt obliged to push further its search for social partners who might make difficult reforms more palatable.

On 1 February 1988, the most dramatic price increases since martial law were introduced. These included 40–50 per cent increases in the price of basic foods and services, and further increases were promised for May. Hardly surprisingly, in April the strike wave which party analysts anticipated broke out. These strikes were totally independent of the Solidarity movement, yet Solidarity was still strong enough to benefit from them, for, after Wałęsa's intervention, they were called off. The respite was only temporary, however; a second round of strikes broke out in August. By this time Solidarity too felt that compromise was necessary. Both the party and Solidarity had approved the reforms of 1988 and thus were implicitly critical of worker demands. For both, time was running out. In February 1988, Bronisław Geremek, a leading figure in Solidarity, called for an 'anti-crisis pact', even though, by implication, this recognised the leading role of the party within state structures. In August, party leader General Wojciech Jaruzelski received a document written by the Group of Three, a team of party analysts set up in 1986, which suggested the creation of a new political order, to consist of a presidency, a new senate, with three electoral chambers, and a parliament with 40 per cent non-party deputies. Co-opting social partners by means of partial electoral reform seemed to be the way forward.

Agenda

Solidarity leaders and the Minister of the Interior, Czesław Kiszczak, finally sat down to negotiations on 31 August 1988. At this stage the party made it clear that Solidarity representatives had been invited to common talks, but not Solidarity as an organisation. Wałęsa's reply was that he would insist on the legalisation of Solidarity. The consequence of this was that a further five months would elapse before the actual talks began. During this period Wałęsa came under criticism for not imposing prior guarantees and for allowing repression of strikers to continue; while the party came under pressure from hardliners (from the trade unions and regional leaders) for holding talks in the first place. In order to make progress, the government was reshuffled on 27 September, but the new Prime Minister, Mieczysław Rakowski, was hated by many Solidarity members, and his cabinet seemed little more committed to the idea of negotiating. Bargaining over the inclusion of the 'professional anti-Communists', Jacek Kuroń and Adam Michnik, took almost three months.[11] The hiatus was broken on 18 November when the bishop of Gdańsk, Tadeusz Goclowski, persuaded Wałęsa that legalisation of Solidarity might be the result rather than precondition of talks. Nevertheless, Jaruzelski, Kiszczak, Rakowski and Minister of Defence Florian Siwicki all had to threaten to resign before the party finally agreed, at the tenth plenum of the Central Committee in December 1988 and January 1989, to take part in formal negotiations.

The Round Table negotiations started on 6 February and concluded on 5 April 1989, with only two official full meetings on those two dates. The party's agenda was an extension of the policy that had developed over the decade: a compromise with Solidarity which it hoped to co-opt into government as a reluctant ally for socialist reform. Frances Millard is by no means alone in arguing that 'The Round Table may be seen as the final attempt by Polish reform communists to transform the system while maintaining control of the process of change'.[12]

Much of the opposition agenda at the Round Table was made up of unfinished Solidarity business, in particular the legalisation of the organisation. Although this outcome had already been agreed before the talks began, Solidarity felt that this might be the most difficult strand in the negotiations and appointed Tadeusz Mazowiecki, whom they considered their best negotiator, to head the talks. Geremek headed the political reform delegation and Witold Trzeciakowski the economics team. Although Solidarity did not accept the party's agenda of co-option, and doggedly resisted some of the constitutional arrangements suggested by the party, it had entered the talks in the spirit of compromise. As Geremek put it, 'The negotiations aimed at changing the price we were supposed to pay for the legalization of Solidarity'.[13] But partly because of the de facto legitimacy of Solidarity as a representative of the popular will, it was ready to range widely when discussing that price. Its prior espousal of the idea of an 'anti-crisis pact' meant it was prepared to put on the agenda a large number of economic and social issues, even though many of the negotiations in this field eventually came to nothing. Thus, while Solidarity was adamant that the political and constitutional arrangements that it negotiated constituted a one-off solution only, a stepping stone to truer, more democratic elections next round, it was willing to trade the 'unfinished business' of legalising Solidarity for partial acceptance of the co-option agenda – discussion of an economic and social crisis pact, and not entirely free elections. Instead they settled for an open contest in just 35 per cent of the seats in parliament and a freely elected senate. Solidarity's caution in this respect is perhaps best reflected in Geremek's comments that completely free elections would be too radical for the Soviets.[14] As Piotr Pykel has expressed it, what Solidarity wanted was more 'liberalisation' than 'democratisation'.[15]

A political science sub-industry has grown up to consider why it was that the Polish party accepted the deal that it did, so losing the elections of 4 and 18 June so badly.[16] What it reveals is little more than what most people sensed at the time: the party just did not believe it could lose as badly as it did.[17] Indeed, it was the party, not Solidarity, which had pushed for early 'non-contested' elections. Aleksander Kwaśniewski has commented that if the communists had known the outcome in advance, they would not have entered negotiations and embarked on peaceful change; events would have ended up more like those in Romania.[18] Even if the party was not confident of actually winning, it could not conceive of losing 'that badly'. Experts at the time felt it might get a third of the contested seats. As a consequence, it disregarded the expert opinion of political advisors who pointed out the potential pitfalls of both the electoral system for the parliament and the free vote in the new senate. For them, Kwaśniewski's brainwave of a freely elected senate which helped elect the president was a neat way out of a bargaining impasse and allowed them to achieve one of their main goals, namely a strong presidency to be filled by Jaruzelski, while avoiding fully contested elections to the parliament. As in the case of the November referendum, the party grossly overestimated the level of its support.

Outcome

In the event, after a dynamic electoral campaign on the part of Solidarity, and a lacklustre one by the party (which accepted too literally, perhaps, the idea that these were 'non-contested' elections), they did do 'that badly'. In fact, they fared 'much worse'. In the first round of the elections on 4 June, Solidarity won 92 of the 100 senate seats and 160 of the 161 independent seats in the parliament. Furthermore, all but two of the candidates on the National List failed to get the required 50 per cent of the vote because of the Solidarity-inspired campaign to cross off all names on the National List. The immediate upshot was a minor constitutional crisis, since it implied that the senate would be short of its constitutionally defined number of 460 deputies. It caused a political crisis too, because the establishment coalition would command only 60 per cent, rather than 65 per cent, of this smaller parliament. This in turn might prevent the coalition ensuring that its candidate be elected president; yet an 'unwritten clause' (because implicit in its logic, but never spelled out) of the Round Table 'contract' was the election of a communist president. The Round Table had to be reconvened and Solidarity agreed to a fresh election for the 33 vacant seats in a contest where the previous candidates would not stand. After the second round on 18 June, Solidarity emerged victorious in all but one of the 100 senate seats (the odd one going to an independent wealthy businessman), and all 161 of the non-party sector of the parliament. The party and its allied satellite parties controlled, as agreed, 65 per cent of the lower house. But only 38 per cent of these were actual party representatives. Some of the remainder sympathised with Solidarity – those elected on the second National List owed their seats to Solidarity support (one Peasant Party deputy was a member of Solidarity) – and the rest were members of the nominally independent satellite parties. If the latter decided to demonstrate genuine independence after more than forty years of subservience to the party line, the party itself would be in a minority.

In the light of this overwhelming electoral defeat, Jaruzelski's position as president-designate began to be questioned, and a curious coalition of actors came together to defend it. As might have been expected, party members hinted to the American Embassy that removal of Jaruzelski might impact negatively on President Bush's visit, scheduled for 9 July. Military men too intimated that they would be threatened by such a development and might go back on the Round Table agreements. But even Solidarity leaders felt that there was a danger of civil war and Soviet intervention if Jaruzelski were not elected. On the occasion of their invitation to dinner with the American Ambassador, they explained that they felt they could not vote for him themselves as this would contradict promises they had made in the electoral campaign, yet they viewed his non-election with concern. The Ambassador suggested that certain key individuals should fail to attend the electoral session.[19] Exhibiting similar caution, Kuroń acknowledged publicly that, for geopolitical reasons – 'Poland's position at the "heart of the [Soviet] empire"' – a communist president was necessary.[20] Thus, while Jaruzelski did withdraw his candidacy on 29 June, and the election, originally scheduled for 5 July, was postponed, Wałęsa eventually stated openly that he supported him, if only because the other candidate in the offing, Kiszczak, was little preferable. On 10 July President Bush advised Jaruzelski to stand again, and, whether Bush's advice was decisive or not, he announced his candidacy on 18 July. Thanks to judicious voting, six deliberate invalid votes and eleven absences from the chamber by some Solidarity members (in line with, but not necessarily following the advice of the American Ambassador), Jaruzelski was elected by parliament and the senate the following day by the majority of a single vote.

Solidarity's landslide electoral victory also forced the composition of a new government on to the agenda in a way that had not been anticipated originally. As early as 3 July, Michnik had argued that Solidarity should press for taking over the prime minister's office, a formula known as 'your President, our Prime Minister'. Jaruzelski's response, announced on 17 July, had been the idea of a 'grand coalition', in which the party retained control over key ministries, such as the Ministry of Internal Affairs, the Ministry of Defence and the Ministry of Foreign Affairs, while Solidarity would get positions in economic and social ministries, together with a deputy prime ministerial post. Jaruzelski repeated this offer once elected President on 25 July, but Wałęsa rejected it. By this time there were two clear factions within Solidarity: those around Kuroń and Michnik, advocating seizure of executive power; and those supporting Geremek, who stressed the need to respect the Round Table pacts.

There then followed a month of political uncertainty, during which two radical changes took place. First, Solidarity became increasingly confident of the mandate that its electoral success had given it. Second, after forty years of loyalty, Poland's satellite parties did indeed begin to behave as independent parties, although Michnik for one suspected they were acting at Jaruzelski's behest. On 28–29 July the party's Central Committee held its thirteenth plenum. Rakowski became First Secretary and was suggested by Jaruzelski as Prime Minister. On 1 August the United Peasant Party suggested forming a government in coalition with Solidarity. Solidarity originally rejected this, but less than a week later, on 7 August, Wałęsa floated the idea of a coalition between Solidarity, the United Peasant Party and the Democratic Party. It was becoming increasingly clear to him that there was no real danger of a party coup and that Moscow in fact was unlikely to intervene: the Soviet Ambassador had even indicated that he had no objection to such a coalition. Kiszczak, however, stressed in his discussions with the American Ambassador, on 11 August, that a Solidarity government was unacceptable, not only to neighbouring countries and to leaders of the army and police, but also to the Church, noting further that Gorbachev's future was not secure.[21] A week later Kiszczak resigned as Prime Minister, suggesting that the United Peasant Party leader be given the post. On 17 August, after consulting with the leaders of the United Peasant Party and the Democratic Party, Wałęsa countered with the idea of Mazowiecki as Prime Minister. The party Politburo responded to this with a somewhat menacing statement to the effect that such a government would represent a *coup d'état* and a breach of the Round Table agreements, and that it threatened both domestic stability and the East–West relationship. But this was bluff. The party had gone too far to retreat from reform now. Two days later, on 19 August, Jaruzelski charged Mazowiecki with forming a government. His candidature was approved by parliament on 24 August and a grand coalition government, which included four party ministers, was approved with no votes against on 12 September.

By the end of August 1989, nothing remained of the party's co-option strategy. The size of Solidarity's electoral victory had pushed Polish politics well beyond its agenda of only a few months earlier. Solidarity had become the lead party in a coalition government, not the co-opted junior partner that the party had hoped for. Yet the party retained some vestigial influence via its hold of the strong presidency. This might have been worth something if developments in Hungary and elsewhere had not expanded the bounds of the possible even further.

Hungary

Origins

Hungary by the mid-1980s had enjoyed more than twenty years of 'goulash communism' under János Kádár, leader since 1956, and more than fifteen years of the most radically reformed economy of the Soviet bloc.[22] The economy, if not problem-free, at least put goods in the shops. But the limits of Kádár's economic and political reforms were being reached and both government and opposition were considering how things could be changed.

In 1985, the party radically reformed the economic structure again. Further far-reaching measures followed in 1987 in the sphere of banking; and in 1988 in the fields of taxation, price control, subsidies policy and company law, effectively allowing for the re-creation of privately owned companies. More important for political developments, in 1985 the party also introduced multi-candidate, more or less contested elections, which had the unintended consequence of weakening the central apparatus and radicalising the provinces, whose support Károly Grósz, the aspiring 'centrist' communist, needed in his struggle to take over from Kádár.

Under the impact of these reforms the opposition became more visible, yet perhaps more divided. The older 'populists' retained and strengthened their links with the reform wing of the party, in particular with Imre Pozsgay, who played a role in organising the first semi-official meeting of the populist Hungarian Democratic Forum (MDF) in Lakitelek in September 1987. The 'democratic opposition', with its younger, more urban and radical focus, was not invited to take part, but nonetheless observed from the sidelines. On 30 January 1988 the MDF began a series of well-attended public meetings in the Jurta Theatre (a theatre relatively independent of state interference because of its status as a 'small co-operative'), on various aspects of democratic reform. In March the 'democratic opposition' set up its 'Network of Free Initiatives' as an umbrella group for the reform-minded, and the Federation of Young Democrats (Fidesz) announced its formation on 30 March.

The party made little effort to quash these embryonic political actors, although it shocked everyone in April 1988 by expelling four well-known reformers from its ranks. The end of the Kádár era came at the party conference that May. The most important development was a change of guard in the party leadership. Kádár was effectively removed, together with his inner circle and a phalanx of older politicians and key reformers entered the Politburo, including Miklós Németh, Rezső Nyers and Pozsgay.[23] The conference also made a commitment to a vaguely defined 'socialist pluralism'. At first it looked as if there was little substance to this 'socialist pluralism', and the Politburo initially rejected the 'democracy package plan' submitted by fifteen independent MPs, but drafted by Pozsgay's reform socialist allies in July. After a summer of inaction, however, at the beginning of November the Central Committee opted less ambiguously for political pluralism, the lifting of censorship and the transfer of most party privileges to government. Grósz also relinquished the premiership to Németh, while Pozsgay submitted to parliament the 'democracy package' of July. Ominously for the party leadership, the formation of the first grass-roots 'Reform Circle' in Szeged was announced on 29 November. These associations of local party members, incensed by the lack of resources and clientelism at the municipal level, were to become a constant irritant to national politicians throughout 1989: at their first national conference in May, their second conference in September, and through their determining role as a component of the Reform Alliance at the party's October conference.[24] On that same November day, Grósz appeared to be putting the brakes on the reform process, by giving a speech which spoke of a 'white terror'.

Two months later, Pozsgay bounced the party further towards reform. One of the consequences of the reformist victory at the May 1988 party conference (and of the political horse-trading that had preceded it) had been the establishment of a committee, headed by Pozsgay, to review the party's path over the preceding three decades. On 27 January 1989, while Grósz was in Switzerland, Pozsgay stated in a radio interview that its preliminary findings suggested that the events of 1956 had been a 'popular uprising' rather than a 'counter-revolution', the official interpretation.

He also asserted that the party would have to learn to live with a multi-party political system. The tense situation created by this statement was discussed at the Central Committee meeting of 10–11 February. But, perhaps mindful of Pozsgay's high opinion poll rating, Grósz merely described his statement on 1956 as 'premature', and confirmed the decision to move towards a multi-party political system, albeit one 'amenable to influence' and where socialism was accepted as the dominant ideological paradigm. The party had accepted a future based on multi-party politics, and the competing agents in that politics were fast emerging. A second meeting in Lakitelek took place in September 1988 and the MDF became a social movement (not a party); the Federation of Free Democrats (SZDSZ) was formed as a party out of the 'democratic opposition' on 13 November 1988; and the Smallholders' Party reconstituted itself on 18 November.

Thus, while Solidarity and the Polish party spent the five months between August 1988 and February 1989 arguing over the precise composition of negotiations still informed by an agenda of compromise, radical change had taken place in Hungary. Hungary's 'Spring in Autumn'[25] and the following winter witnessed the formation of a more or less formal but divided political opposition, while the ruling party had adopted a vision of a multi-party future, the latter endorsed by the Central Committee only days after the Polish Round Table negotiations began. By February 1989 the party was committed to a framework which included a plebiscite on a new constitution (winter 1989), election of a president (spring 1990) and national elections (summer 1990). In late March Grósz visited Gorbachev and was given the impression that the Soviet Union would not interfere in events in Hungary, while Németh claims he was given an instant and categorical 'No' when he later asked Gorbachev if the Soviet Union would intervene if the party was voted out of power.[26] The party's reform agenda seemed secure.

Agenda

The party's strategy, like that of its Polish counterpart, was to seek acceptable partners which it might co-opt to share the costs of transition; and a necessary condition of such co-option was keeping the opposition divided. It held initial discussions with the MDF as early as January 1989, and followed this up with a variety of ad hoc talks with various opposition groups in early March. But the 'divide and rule' strategy was knocked off course by the events of 15 March and their aftermath.

The anniversary of the Hungarian Revolution of 1848 fell on 15 March. However, it had been supplanted as an official holiday during the socialist years by 4 April, the date in 1945 when Soviet troops finally liberated the whole of Hungarian territory. Thus, 15 March had become an occasion for unofficial demonstrations, culminating in terms of popular consciousness in the 'Battle of Chain Bridge' in 1986. The issue in 1989 was not whether or not the date should be celebrated. This was quickly conceded. The issue was whether there should be joint or separate celebrations.

The party preferred the former, but Hungarians opted massively for the latter. This evidence of mass support for change prompted the Independent Lawyers' Forum – which had been established in November 1988 to give advice to new political clubs and associations – to suggest on 22 March the formation of the Opposition Round Table (ORT), initially made up of eight opposition groupings. The ORT's central remit, indeed its *raison d'être*, was to counter 'divide and rule' tactics. Thus it rejected an invitation to talks with party representatives on 8 April, once it became clear that some ORT members, among them the Young Democrats, were to be excluded.

Unlike Solidarity, the Hungarian opposition had entered 1989 with no 'unfinished business'. Yet it was conscious of its weakness, its lack of legitimacy when compared to Solidarity, and its internal divisions. ORT thus concentrated on a future politics and from the very start constructed for itself a restricted agenda. In their first few meetings they did discuss policy issues, but, inspired by the Free Democrats, the focus was simple and radical: the passing of a limited number of cardinal laws necessary for holding free elections for what would be a legitimate parliament. This parliament could then amend the constitution and elect a president. Wholly free elections were a *sina qua non* from the off. There was no talk of Polish-style electoral compromise. Furthermore, there were to be no concessions to the party over attempts to resolve the economic and social problems that it was responsible for creating.

Despite the impasse of 8 April, the two sides met in preliminary talks on 22 April, where the following key points of difference emerged. ORT wanted bilateral talks, the party multilateral ones. ORT saw the task as passing the cardinal laws noted above, while the party wanted the negotiations to address economic, social and attitudinal problems as well. In further talks on 2 May, ORT agreed to a compromise concerning the consideration of economic and social issues. Despite this, the Central Committee on 8–9 May issued a statement regretting that they had failed to reach agreement on who should participate in the talks. ORT interpreted this as a unilateral breaking-off of negotiations. Such a denouement was curious given that at the same Central Committee session, the party had effectively renounced the *nomenklatura* system of political and other key appointments, so liberating the government almost completely from party control.

Earlier in May, the government, though still not formally free from party domin-ance, had made a decision which would have even more significant repercussions. As Németh tells it, he had been approached as Prime Minister by the person responsible for maintaining the physical border controls on Hungary's western boundary, and asked for a relatively large amount of money to renew them.[27] Given that all Hungarian citizens had had the right since January 1988 to get a passport and travel to the West; that hordes of Hungarian shoppers buying consumer goods on Vienna's *Mariahilfer Strasse* had become the stuff of urban legend; and that an Austrian TV crew had demonstrated in the autumn of 1988 that no electricity ran through the border fences,[28] there was no strong domestic reason to incur this expense. It was also a way of testing whether Gorbachev meant what he said about non-intervention.[29] Therefore, the decision was made not only not to renew the barriers, but to dismantle them. With much publicity (150 journalists, served coffee and sausages by soldiers), the first steps were taken on 2 May 1989, despite furious reactions in East Germany, Czechoslovakia and Romania, and some anxiety in Austria concerning the possibility of increasing numbers of refugees.[30] The first chink in the Iron Curtain had appeared.

Meanwhile, with negotiations stalled, ORT wrote on 18 May to the party's Reform Circles, who were about to hold their first national congress, requesting that they put pressure on the party leadership. The Reform Circles obliged, and two days later called on the party to stop its delaying tactics and negotiate with the ORT. Pressure on the party to return to the negotiating table also came from another issue that dominated Hungarian politics in the spring and early summer of 1989. Pozsgay had reinvigorated the reformist agenda in January by his categorisation of 1956 as a 'popular uprising'. A consequence of this was the momentous decision that Imre Nagy, the hero of 1956, and his associates should be ceremoniously re-interred, and a Central Committee meeting of 29 March further resolved that this should be organised by the government and not the party. The date set was 16 June, the thirty-first anniversary of Imre Nagy's execution. As that date approached, reformists in the party were keen to be part of it. Németh and Mátyás Szűrös (Chairman of Parliament), for example, applied to attend the ceremony in their governmental and parliamentary roles, while the Reform Circle also asked for permission to lay a wreath.

In this climate of heightened expectations, on a question of historical interpretation which was turning into an issue of national identity, it was inconceivable that the party should continue to appear obdurate. The stalemate was broken when the Central Committee meeting of 29 May proposed a solution of four-sided talks: the party, ORT, third-party organisations and observers. After further protracted negotiations, during which the Christian Democratic People's Party (KDNP – established on 17 March) joined the ORT, agreement was reached on 10 June for three-party talks (the party, ORT and a miscellany of other bodies – the old Front organisation, the old trade unions and two new left-wing organisations, but not the Reform Circles). The agenda was the compromise one of establishing the rules and principles for the transition to democracy and addressing the economic and social crisis. The first formal round of National Round Table (NRT) negotiations took place on 13 June, just in time for the Nagy re-interment. Although ORT had given ground on economic and social issues, and accepted the introduction of the third side to the talks, by maintaining their unity they had minimised the danger of co-option, and the agenda still centred on their cardinal laws for progress towards democracy.

Even before serious NRT negotiations were underway, Solidarity's electoral victory strengthened the hand of reformers within the party. The Central Committee meeting of 23–24 June effectively demoted Grósz (who had once been warned by Jaruzelski that martial law 'won the battle but not the war'),[31] by creating a new Presidium, consisting of Nyers, Németh, Pozsgay (all reformers) and Grósz. It also confirmed Pozsgay as the party's prospective presidential candidate. Unconnected, but symbolic of a changing era, Kádár died on 6 July. In the wake of the Polish electoral defeat, it became clear that co-opting the new political opposition was unrealistic. The party was unlikely to prevail in elections; indeed, it was already losing by-elections held over the summer to the MDF. Furthermore, the latter, also at a meeting on 23–24 June, had decided to become a formal political party.

Yet the party might retain the presidency, and with it some continued political influence. Without Poland's rigged parliament, a party candidate would not win if the president were elected by parliament. But a popular reformist like Pozsgay would almost certainly win in direct presidential elections, whatever the party's share of the parliament. What is more, if direct presidential elections were held first, an incumbent reform communist president might actually boost the chances of a reformed Communist Party in free parliamentary elections. The presidency thus became the focus of Party policy as the summer progressed, and it became imperative for the party that elections to that office should be direct and precede parliamentary elections. The reformed Young Communist movement began a campaign for a referendum for early presidential elections, although Pozsgay distanced himself in mid-August. At the same time, the party's negotiating stance on anything that might maintain its advantage in the electoral context became tougher rather than more conciliatory. It made no concessions on its presence in the workplace, its wealth and its armed wing (the Workers' Guard).

If the policy of 'divide and rule' had failed in the spring of 1989, when what was at stake was the structure of talks, splitting the ORT proved more successful when negotiations became substantive. The division which quickly emerged was the historic one – the populists versus those associated with the 'urbanist', 'democratic opposition'. In party terms, this meant the KDNP, Hungarian People's Party (MNP) and the MDF on the one hand, and on the other the SZDSZ and Fidesz. The MNP had been created on 11 March 1989 as the legal successor of the post-war National Peasant Party. The issue that divided them was the presidency – what powers should the office have, and, especially, how and when should it be elected?

Tensions came to a head in August amid a series of tortuous ORT negotiating sessions. It is clear from the record that the populists changed their opinion over the issue of the presidency and came to support the 'your President, our Prime Minister' solution with Pozsgay the favoured candidate for a directly elected presidency. It is evident that this shift took place only two days after Jaruzelski's election to the Polish presidency. It is also well established that Pozsgay and József Antall of the MDF met regularly, and that parties like the MNP were indebted to Pozsgay for their very existence. What remains unresolved from the evidence available is the frequently heard assertion that the populists were simply acting at Pozsgay's behest. Whatever the case, the presidency issue definitively split the ORT in August, although it managed to conceal this fact from the general public until the negotiations were concluded.

While talks in Budapest were reaching their troubled and ultimately bitter conclusion, more dramatic events were taking place in the western provinces. Hungary, unlike Poland, had a border with the West. If its domestic politics impacted on border issues, this could have implications for the whole bloc. East German citizens had long been able to travel relatively freely to Hungary and had regularly holidayed by Lake Balaton, where they could meet up with West German relatives. With the border effectively open, as it had been since May, there was little to stop GDR citizens moving on from Lake Balaton to the border with Austria and thence, via Austria, to West Germany. Over the course of the summer, a trickle of GDR émigrés became a flood, culminating, symbolically at least, in the Sopron Pan-European Picnic of 19 August. At this event, organised by activists from local MDF groups and the Sopron Opposition Round Table, amidst much publicity, many hundreds of GDR citizens crossed the border unscathed as border guards looked on in confusion.[32]

Faced with this orchestrated challenge to the status quo, and cognisant of the fact that Poland was becoming post-communist without Soviet intervention, on 22 August the Hungarian government decided that its future lay with West Germany rather than the GDR.[33] The government made careful preparations with both Moscow and Bonn, which included secret talks in a castle near Cologne. Then, on the stroke of midnight of 10 September, East German tourists began to cross the border to Austria freely. As he recalls in his interview with Misha Glenny, an aid suggested to Németh that there might be some international impact of this decision in the next three years.[34] The Berlin Wall fell within only two months.

Outcome

The National Round Table negotiations reached their climax (but not their formal conclusion) eight days later. Despite the fact that (to the surprise of the party, but not of their ORT partners) the SZDSZ and Fidesz did not sign the NRT agreement of 18 September, they did not use their veto to prevent the others from signing it. To Pozsgay and his supporters, it must have seemed as if the party's fallback agenda of contested elections and a socialist president was holding firm. Pozsgay remained popular and presidential elections were scheduled for 25 November, prior to probable parliamentary elections in March 1990. Furthermore, the party had retained some advantage in electoral competition by stalling on the issues of its presence in the workplace, the Workers' Guard and disclosing its finances – the three other reasons why the SZDSZ and Fidesz did not sign the agreement. What the non-signatories to the NRT agreement had neglected to warn their populist ORT partners about was their plan to counter-attack. At the signing ceremony they announced their intention to call a referendum on all four issues on which they disagreed. The 'your President, our Prime Minister' solution was not yet a done deal.

Indeed, as September moved into October it began to look less secure. The October party congress did result in the expected victory for the reform communists, but there was little enthusiasm for the successor Hungarian Socialist Party, which became almost a bit player in the new politics. Most of the sitting party members of parliament, for example, failed to join it. Parliament, as planned, began to pass the legislation proposed by the NRT. But it also passed legislation depriving the party of the electoral advantages it had sought to maintain. The three questions on the referendum, other than that of the presidency became non-issues. Meanwhile, the non-signatories started their campaign to collect the signatures required for holding a referendum and, after less than a month, claimed 204,152 signatures, although only 114,470 were accepted by the official scrutinisers.[35] The date for the referendum was set for 26 November, and the presidential elections were suspended. The MDF appointed its own candidate for President on 21 October, but, in appointing the relatively unknown Lajos Für, suggested it was only half-serious about challenging Pozsgay.[36]

The final nail in the coffin for the party's presidential strategy came on the day of the referendum. The non-signatories won, if only by a margin of less than 1 per cent of the vote.[37] What perhaps tipped the balance and radicalised the population against the party and the populist opposition was the changed international situation. Following constant haemorrhaging of the GDR population since 10 September and the change of government in the GDR, the Berlin Wall had been breached on 9 November. On 17 November the botched suppression of a student demonstration in Prague triggered a chain of events that would lead to regime change in Czechoslovakia. On the very day of the referendum, Václav Havel, symbol of Charter 77 and the Czechoslovak opposition, and Alexander Dubček, symbol of the reform communist Prague Spring, addressed a crowd of 750,000 in Letná Park in Prague.[38] For Hungarians going to the polls, there was no longer any reason to buy into any sort of party agenda.

Conclusion

Communist power was negotiated away in 1989, in both Poland and Hungary, behind closed doors, but with the help of dramatic displays of anti-regime sentiment on the part of the general public. In Poland, this focused on a single event: the elections of June. In Hungary, pressure was more diffuse, but the demonstrations of 15 March, the public theatre of the re-interment of Imre Nagy in June, and a summer dominated by by-electoral defeat and the Sopron Picnic all convinced the party that change was unavoidable. In both countries these massive popular displays, together with Gorbachev's resolute refusal to intervene, convinced all but a few marginal leaders that the 'Chinese solution' was not an option.[39]

But the negotiations differed in origin and content. The Polish Round Table talks bore the imprint of the past's tragic defeats and were premised on compromise and co-option, while few in the party accepted a reform agenda. The results of the restricted elections that emerged demanded a more radical agenda and stirred the satellite parties into independent action. Yet an element of compromise remained in Poland's final 'your President, our Prime Minister' solution. Hungarian negotiations followed a different and entirely independent agenda. The Hungarian opposition demands emerged from a movement growing in strength. They were more radical from the start and were broadly accepted by a party already committed, both at the leadership and grass-roots level, to a reform path – on paper in February, and, reluctantly, in reality by the early summer. Yet a divided opposition was almost manipulated into a 'your President, our Prime Minister' deal by a community of interest, if not alliance, between the populist opposition and the party. The latter only failed because of the increased radicalisation that followed the fall of the Berlin Wall, itself the consequence of events triggered by Hungary's decision to let East Germans cross its border with the West.

Notes

1. Round-table negotiations between the incumbent party and opposition representatives formed a part of Eastern Europe's 1989 revolutions in every country except Romania and the former Yugoslavia (excluding Croatia). For an assessment of the round-table negotiations that accompanied the collapse of socialism, see Jon Elster (ed.) *The Roundtable Talks and the Breakdown of Communism* (Chicago, IL, 1996).
2. For such views in Poland, see Frances Millard, *The Anatomy of the New Poland* (Cheltenham, 1994), p. 63. In Hungary rumours circulated of a pact in which the Vatican and Israel, as well as the two superpowers, were allegedly involved.
3. This account is based primarily on David Ost, *Solidarity and the Politics of Anti-Politics* (Philadelphia, PA, 1990); Millard, *The Anatomy*; Piotr Pykel, *The Final Stage: A Comparative Study of the Transition from Communist Rule to Democratic Government in Poland and Czechoslovakia* (Florence, European University Institute Ph.D., 2004); and Wiktor Osiatynski, 'The Roundtable talks in Poland', in Elster (ed.) *The Roundtable Talks*, pp. 21–68. Economic points come from Martin Myant, 'Poland – the Permanent Crisis', in Roger Clarke (ed.), *Poland: The Economy in the 1980s* (Harlow, 1989), pp. 1–28; and William Wallace, 'Moving Forward' in Clarke (ed.) *Poland*, pp. 139–49. Only direct quotes or materials from other sources are referenced in what follows.

4. In this contribution, 'party' denotes the incumbent ruling 'communist' party, the Polish United Workers' Party in Poland and the Hungarian Socialist Workers' Party in Hungary.

5. Pykel, *The Final Stage*, p. 45, citing Adam Michnik, *Takie Czasy... Rzecz o Kompromisie* (London, 1985), p. 84.

6. There had been a limited amnesty on 17 July 1986, and Wałęsa had been released as early as 11 November 1982, following the death of Leonid Brezhnev, the Soviet leader.

7. Ost, *Solidarity*, p. 169.

8. Padraic Kenney, *A Carnival of Revolution* (Princeton, NJ, 2002).

9. Wallace, 'Moving Forward', p. 142.

10. Wallace, 'Moving Forward', p. 139, citing George Blazyca in the *New Statesman*.

11. Osiatynski, 'The Roundtable', p. 29.

12. Millard, *The Anatomy*, p. 57.

13. Quoted in Osiatynski, 'The Roundtable', p. 42.

14. Osiatynski, 'The Roundtable', p. 48.

15. Pykel, *The Final Stage*, p. 67.

16. See, for example, Jacquelin Hayden, 'Explaining the collapse of socialism in Poland: strategic misperceptions and unanticipated outcomes', in *Journal of Communist Studies and Transition Politics*, vol. 17, no. 4 (2001), pp. 108–29; and Marek Kaminski, 'How communism could have been saved: formal analysis of electoral bargaining in Poland in 1989', *Public Choice*, vol. 98 (1999), pp. 83–109.

17. The State Department had received far better advice from its ambassador in Warsaw. See National Security Archive, 'Solidarity's coming victory: big or too big', and its eleven related documents (http://www.gwu.edu/~nsarchiv/NSAEBB/NSAEBB42/#docs) NSA, Solidarity, Documents 1 and 2.

18. Osiatynski, 'The Roundtable', p. 26.

19. See NSA, Solidarity. Even before the June elections a total Solidarity victory was viewed as the 'most dangerous scenario' because it could prevent the election of Jaruzelski as president (see Document 2), and this was a concern returned to as soon as the first results were known (see Document 3). The views of the Solidarity leaders are given in Document 4.

20. Quoted in Millard, *The Anatomy*, p. 71.

21. NSA, Solidarity Document 6.

22. This section is based primarily on Rudolf L. Tőkés, *Hungary's Negotiated Revolution. Economic Reform, Social Change and Political Succession, 1957–1990* (Cambridge, 1996); Nigel Swain, *Hungary: the Rise and Fall of Feasible Socialism* (London, 1992); Sándor Kurtán et al. (eds), *Magyarország Politikai Évkönyve 1988/1990* (Budapest, 1989/90); András Sajó, 'The roundtable talks in Hungary', in Elster (ed.), *The Roundtable Talks*, pp. 69–98; and András Bozóki et al. (eds), *A Rendszerváltás Forgatókönyve: Kerekasztal-Tárgyalások*

1989–ben CD-ROM (Budapest, 2000). Only direct quotes or materials from other sources are referenced in what follows.

23. For an assessment of the magnitude of these changes, see Paul Lendvai, *Hungary: The Art of Survival* (London, 1988), pp. 149–50.

24. For an excellent analysis of this story of local level revolt against the party centre, see Patrick O'Neil, *Revolution from Within* (Cheltenham, 1998).

25. *Frühling im Herbst* is the title of a documentary on events in Hungary made by Karl Stipsicz for Austrian Television (ORF) in 1988.

26. For Grósz, see Cold War International History Project, Virtual Archive, Hungary Document No. 3 (http://wilsoncenter.org/index.cfm?topic_id=1409& fuseaction=library.document&id=14943); for Németh, see the interview with Misha Glenny (http://news.bbc.co.uk/1/hi/special_report/1999/09/99/iron_ curtain/458991.stm), 'Round the Table', first broadcast on 7 October 1999.

27. http://news.bbc.co.uk/1/hi/special_report/1999/09/99/iron_curtain/458991.stm, 'Breaking the Bloc', first broadcast on 14 October 1999. Newspaper accounts suggest that the Central Committee had made a decision to this effect back in February 1989 (*Magyar Nemzet*, 3 May 1989).

28. *Frühling im Herbst.*

29. Németh makes this point in the interview with Misha Glenny (http://news.bbc. co.uk/hi/english/static/special_report/1999/09/99/iron_curtain/default.htm).

30. *The Times*, 3 May 1989.

31. As reported by Gyula Thürmer, an adviser to Grósz, to Misha Glenny (http:// news.bbc.co.uk/1/hi/special_report/1999/09/99/iron_curtain/458991.stm), 'Round the Table'.

32. *Magyar Nemzet*, 22 August 1989, reported border guard sources to the effect that as many as 1,000 GDR citizens crossed the border to Austria that weekend, but not all of them on the occasion of the picnic.

33. Németh gives the date in the interview with Misha Glenny (http://news.bbc. co.uk/hi/english/static/special_report/1999/09/99/iron_curtain/default.htm).

34. http://news.bbc.co.uk/1/hi/special_report/1999/09/99/iron_curtain/458991.stm, 'Breaking the Bloc'.

35. *Magyar Nemzet*, 14, 25 and 31 October 1989.

36. Ibid., 23 October 1989.

37. Ibid., 30 November 1989.

38. Bernard Wheaton and Zdeněk Kavan, *The Velvet Revolution: Czechoslovakia, 1988–1991* (Boulder, CO, 1992), pp. 88–90.

39. In Hungary, even the Ministry of the Interior did not come on board Grósz's inconsequential plans for martial law. In Poland, there was opposition, as discussed above, to dealing with Solidarity, yet little basis to fears of a back-lash after the elections, despite occasional hard-line statements by the party. Solidarity topped the polls even among the police and the military.

–9–

'To Learn from the Soviet Union is to Learn How to Win': The East German Revolution, 1989–90

Peter Grieder

For those who experienced it, the revolution of 1989–90 in East Germany was something akin to a miracle. It seemed all the more miraculous because it was so unexpected. The German Democratic Republic (GDR) had always been regarded as the most stable of Moscow's satellites. In July 1987, the Soviet leader, Mikhail Sergeevich Gorbachev, had told the West German President, Richard von Weizsäcker, that Germany might be reunited 'in a hundred years', reducing this to around fifty on Weizsäcker's intervention. In January 1989, Erich Honecker, dictator of the GDR and General Secretary of its ruling Socialist Unity Party (SED),[1] declared that the Berlin Wall might survive for fifty or a hundred years, if the grounds for its existence were not removed.[2] The West German *Bild-Zeitung*'s decision in summer 1989 to end its long-standing tradition of placing the 'GDR' in inverted commas in order to point up its illegitimacy was certainly not taken in the belief that it would be consigned to the dustbin of history in little over a year.[3]

That what took place was a revolution should be beyond doubt. According to Lenin, revolutions occur when 'those above' cannot rule and 'those below' will not be ruled in the old way.[4] He would have recognised this situation in the GDR in the autumn of 1989. Revolution is best defined as 'sudden systemic change'. Within the space of twelve short months, an entire political, economic and social system known as 'communism' was obliterated. More than this, a 41-year-old country ceased to exist, its citizens joining the Federal Republic of Germany (FRG) on 3 October 1990. All this was achieved through popular pressure and with very little violence. However, East Germany would still be with us today had it not been for Gorbachev's retreat from empire, so the events of 1989–90 are better characterised as a revolution wrapped up in decolonisation. This chapter will analyse the relative importance of the internal defects of the GDR, West Germany's policy of *Ostpolitik* ('policy towards the East'), Gorbachev's reforms and the East German people themselves in consummating the first peaceful and successful revolution in German history.[5]

Underlying Indigenous Causes

There are two opposing views of the GDR's trajectory. The first claims that its people were always fighting a latent civil war against the communist authorities and that the state suffered a 'downfall in instalments'. From the popular uprising in the GDR on 17 June 1953, to the Hungarian Revolution of 1956, the building of the Berlin Wall in 1961, the crushing of the Prague Spring in 1968, to the overthrow of the system in 1989, ordinary East Germans showed their contempt for the regime. According to this standpoint, the history of East Germany was one of continuous decline.[6] The second interpretation argues that between 1971, when Honecker became First Secretary of the SED, and 1987, when Gorbachev's reforms in the Soviet Union began to destabilise the GDR, East German society was 'viable' and 'supported by the majority of the population'.[7] Neither view does full justice to the reality of life inside this dictatorship.

Although the first interpretation rightly points up tensions between the population and its communist rulers during the flashpoints identified above, the second convincingly demonstrates that East Germany did not suffer incessant decline, but actually achieved a 'precarious stability' during the 1970s. However, the latter goes too far in alleging that East German society was 'viable' for most of the Honecker era. Vicissitudes in the fortunes of the system notwithstanding, it is safe to say that the GDR would have collapsed at any time in its history had the Soviet Union withdrawn its support. While there was popular appreciation of the additional welfare benefits introduced during the Honecker years, most people grudgingly participated in the communist dictatorship because they could see no prospect of its removal. The existence of an increasingly successful 'social market economy' in neighbouring West Germany necessitated construction of the Berlin Wall to stop the GDR from bleeding to death.

Particularly devastating for the self-styled 'Workers' and Peasants' State' was its failure to win legitimacy in the eyes of its own citizens. This is illustrated graphically by Honecker's abortive attempt to manufacture a new East German 'national identity' from the early 1970s, manifested in a 'policy of demarcation' (*Abgrenzung*), which disassociated the GDR from any notion of a shared German culture with the Federal Republic, and rewrote the country's constitution to remove all references to the goal of German reunification. Most East Germans, however, continued to feel part of a single German nation, thereby undermining communist attempts to insulate them from the West. While the GDR remained an artificial Cold War creation, ultimately dependent for its existence on Soviet bayonets, the Federal Republic was repeatedly legitimised in free elections, and earned the support of Germans on both sides of the Iron Curtain with its impressive social, economic and political achievements.

The GDR is perhaps best classified as a bureaucratic-totalitarian welfare state. In this respect it differed from the totalitarian regimes of Nazi Germany or Stalinist Russia, which can be described more usefully as 'charismatic-terrorist' in character.

The SED's central mission was to oversee as much of East German society as possible, in the name of communist ideology. Indeed, not only the means of production, but society itself was nationalised in the GDR. As for the paternalistic aspects, they were fully integrated into the system of control. Over the past decade some historians have identified 'limits' to this dictatorship,[8] thereby highlighting inefficiencies in certain areas. However, if one employs totalitarianism as a relative historical concept rather than an absolute theoretical one, then East Germany was undoubtedly one of the *most* totalitarian states in the Soviet bloc, even if it failed to reach Orwellian standards of perfection. Besides, totalitarianism should not be taken literally to mean the total control of society by the state, but its *enforced fusion* with state structures, and on this criterion the SED was strikingly successful. The regime's all-embracing remit severely impaired the normal functioning of societal life, stifled public discourse and implicated huge swathes of the population in the dictatorship.

In some respects, the state became more totalitarian following Honecker's assumption of power. Not only was there increased emphasis on the teaching of Marx and Lenin in schools, but military training also became part of the curriculum.[9] East Germany's infamous secret police, known as the Stasi or Ministry of State Security (MfS), hypertrophied to such an extent that, in any given year throughout the 1980s, about one in fifty of the country's 13.5 million adults was working for it on the home front, either as an officer or an informer.[10] Ultimately, the ministry became so bloated that it became a victim of its own omnipotence.[11]

But the most damaging and counterproductive aspect of this dictatorship was its bureaucratic stranglehold on the economy. Honecker exacerbated the problem by abandoning his predecessor's decentralising economic reforms and bringing all remaining private and semi-state-owned businesses under state control in the early 1970s.[12] Although the 'administrative-command' system imposed by the Soviets in the late 1940s had certain advantages for the less developed countries of Eastern Europe, and initially proved reasonably effective in mobilising resources for post-war reconstruction in the GDR, the latter's highly advanced economy and diverse industrial base proved completely ill-suited to this Stalinist model in the long run. Ultimately, the 'administrative-command' system could not keep pace with the scientific-technological revolution. Supply problems became endemic; growth and productivity stagnated. The huge resources allocated to the army, the bureaucracy and the Stasi also took their toll. In many ways, then, East German totalitarianism was self-defeating.

Apart from these systemic defects, other problems began to plague the economy. Honecker had substantially boosted spending on social programmes as part of his so-called 'unity of social and economic policy' after 1971. This new brand of consumer socialism, intended to secure the population's political compliance, was dramatically undermined by soaring oil prices, which hit the GDR particularly hard because of its raw material shortages. The subsidisation of rents, transport and basic foodstuffs was simply beyond East Germany's means. To pay its bills the government had to borrow heavily from the West. By the late 1980s the country was heading for insolvency.

The mounting economic and political problems of the GDR notwithstanding, its leaders continued to boast that it was the tenth most developed industrial power in the world. On 1 December 1988 Honecker even went so far as to claim that 'fundamentally' its living standards were higher than those of the Federal Republic![13] A yawning discrepancy developed between party propaganda and real life, which further alienated the population. This is best illustrated by a joke which circulated among East Germans during the Honecker years:

> A man from Dresden took his courage in his hands and went to the police station: 'I want to leave the country', he says. The police officer asks him: 'Where do you want to go then, young man?' 'To the GDR', he answers. 'But you are already here', exclaims the astonished officer. 'No, no', comes the riposte, 'at long last, I want to move to the GDR which is described in the newspapers'.[14]

Many thousands wished to leave the country, but only a tiny minority actually succeeded in doing so. West German researchers found that political considerations, such as 'lack of freedom to express one's own opinion', slightly outweighed material considerations in causing the 1984 and 1989 refugee waves, but both represented a damning indictment of the GDR's failure to address its structural problems, and to counter the magnetic pull of democracy and prosperity in the Federal Republic.[15] As popular discontent welled up, various peace, human rights and environmentalist groups[16] began to form within the interstices of ossified totalitarian structures. Most of them found sanctuary in the Protestant Churches, which were the only institutions in East Germany not directly under SED supervision. By rekindling civil society, these brave men and women lit a flame which eventually ignited the conflagration of 1989.

Ostpolitik

Ostpolitik is the term used to describe West Germany's decision to open relations with the Eastern bloc in the late 1960s and early 1970s. The role of this policy in bringing about the collapse of the GDR is disputed. Yet, whatever its precise impact, it helped to create some important prerequisites for the 1989 revolution. Its founding father, Social Democrat (SPD) Chancellor Willy Brandt, aimed to subvert Moscow's domination by attempting 'change through rapprochement'. By fostering links with the Soviet Empire, he hoped to penetrate it with Western values and reduce Cold War tensions. With regard to the GDR, this meant improving the everyday life of ordinary East Germans through a 'policy of small steps' that would ultimately lead to reunification. This fresh approach came after twenty years of confrontation, which had only resulted in the construction of the Berlin Wall.

Central to *Ostpolitik* was the West German government's policy of enhancing relations with the Soviet Union. This was indispensable if hopes of German reunification were to be kept alive. Brandt understood very well that nothing could change in Eastern Europe without the Kremlin's approval – hence the FRG's signature of the non-aggression treaty in Moscow on 12 August 1970. This recognised Soviet gains in Eastern Europe, pledged Bonn not to use force to reverse them and paved the way for further agreements with individual satellites, including the GDR. Without the solid relationship between the Federal Republic and the USSR, Gorbachev could never have trusted Chancellor Helmut Kohl's personal assurance in November 1989 that the crowds at the Berlin Wall were ordinary German citizens rejoicing in the fall of the barrier that had separated them for twenty-eight years, and not counter-revolutionary mobs seeking violent confrontation with the Soviet Union. The KGB and East German Stasi had wanted to convince him of the latter, but their version of events was discarded by the Soviet leader in favour of Kohl's.[17] If this had not happened, the East German Revolution might have been drowned in a bloodbath.

Relations between the two German states were formalised when the USSR permitted East Germany to sign the so-called 'Basic Treaty' with the Federal Republic on 21 December 1972. This ratified the existence of 'two German states in one nation' and renounced the Hallstein Doctrine,[18] according to which Bonn denied full diplomatic relations to any country, apart from the Soviet Union, that recognised the GDR. Simultaneously, however, the FRG eschewed any official recognition of East Germany as a sovereign state,[19] thereby upholding its constitutional commitment to reunification, while accepting that this was not yet a realisable objective. The 'Letter on German Unity', handed over by the West German Government on signature of each of the main Eastern treaties, asserted that none of them contradicted the 'political goal' of the Federal Republic to 'work towards a state of peace in Europe in which the German people regains its unity in free self-determination'.[20] Brandt's successors, Helmut Schmidt and Kohl, continued to pursue *Ostpolitik*, even when superpower tensions escalated again after 1981. Between 11 and 13 December of that year, against the backdrop of martial law being declared in Poland, Schmidt visited Honecker at Werbellinsee. Both leaders agreed that 'never again would a war be allowed to emanate from German soil'.[21]

The Helsinki Final Act of 1975 formed a key component of the West's strategy of détente, of which *Ostpolitik* was a constituent part. At the Conference on Security and Cooperation in Europe, held between 30 July and 1 August of that year, Honecker, together with the other Soviet bloc leaders, signed up to Basket Three of the accords, guaranteeing citizens basic human rights. In return for these concessions, the Western allies formally accepted the reality of Soviet hegemony in Eastern Europe since the end of the Second World War. While it is undoubtedly true that Honecker and the other communist dictators had no intention of properly implementing the provisions they had agreed to, that was not the point. When the full text of the Helsinki Final Act appeared in the SED's daily newspaper, *Neues Deutschland*, it sold out for the first time in its history.[22] The human rights stipulations contained therein gave a considerable morale boost to ordinary East German citizens, who now set about using them to hold their communist rulers to account. After the fall of the GDR, the Wittenberg pastor, civil rights and peace campaigner, Friedrich Schorlemmer, recalled his euphoria when reading the terms of the agreement. If the guarantees in Basket Three were put into practice, he thought, that would create 'a totally different state, a totally different country'.[23] For obvious reasons, East Germans were particularly interested in the right to visit friends and relatives in the Federal Republic. Within one year of the accords, over 100,000 people had applied for permission to leave the GDR.[24] Soon the East German government was being pilloried, both at home and abroad, for violating the very human rights provisions it had solemnly signed up to. This undermined the state's legitimacy in the eyes of its own population and the international community.

The SED's need to avoid public displays of repression in the era of Helsinki also influenced its decision to use the Protestant Churches to help control dissent in the GDR.[25] But Honecker's attempt to co-opt them, by means of the Church-state agreement of 6 March 1978, backfired disastrously, as they soon became semi-autonomous spaces in which opposition groups could organise and congregate. The regime's mistake was to assume that the Churches operated according to the same centralising principles as the SED, when, in fact, 'turbulent priests' lower down the hierarchy could not be straitjacketed like Communist Party members.[26] The March 1978 agreement was undoubtedly a key turning point in the history of the GDR.[27]

Over the two decades of its enactment, *Ostpolitik* helped eclipse the much-vaunted 'anti-fascist' credentials of the 'Workers' and Peasants' State', by further improving the popular image of West Germany in the eyes of East Germans. After all, Brandt had fought in the anti-Nazi resistance. When he visited Erfurt in the GDR on 19 March 1970, he was greeted with unalloyed jubilation.[28] The fact that he was awarded the Nobel Peace Prize in October of the following year further eroded the claims of East German leaders that their state was morally superior to the Federal Republic. But *Ostpolitik* did much more than this. It also weakened the prevailing revanchist image of West Germany in the eyes of everyone living in the Soviet Empire. Certainly, the Kremlin would never have sanctioned German reunification in 1990 if Bonn had insisted on restoring the Reich borders of 1937. The fear that the FRG wished to take back land lost to Poland after the Second World War had added credence to communist propaganda in that country. Yet when Brandt dropped to his knees before a memorial to the heroes of the Warsaw Ghetto on his visit to Poland in December 1970, this one poignant gesture did more to win the trust of Poles than his predecessors had managed in twenty-one years. When Germany was reunited, the Oder-Neisse border with Poland was confirmed, in line with Brandt's agreement of two decades earlier. The impact of *Ostpolitik* was particularly important in Hungary's decision to allow East Germans to cross their border with Austria in September 1989. This treachery, as Honecker perceived it, sounded the death knell of the SED dictatorship, yet it would have been impossible had the Hungarian communists still regarded West Germany as the enemy. The East German Foreign Minister, Otto Winzer, had once described *Ostpolitik* as 'aggression in carpet slippers'.[29] Now the carpet itself had been pulled out from underneath the GDR.

East German leaders were desperate to maintain stable relations with the Federal Republic, not only because they craved international recognition, but also because they became more and more dependent on it for economic assistance. The result of this increasingly lopsided relationship was a reduction in overtly oppressive measures taken against the East German population. This can be seen on 24 January 1984, when Honecker apparently responded to external pressure by releasing from prison Bärbel Bohley and Ulrike Poppe, two members of the banned 'Women for Peace' group in the GDR, who had been arrested the previous month. The SED leader liked to pose as a peacemaker on the world stage, so must have been irritated by the negative publicity surrounding their incarceration.[30] When the regime abstained from using force to crush the revolution of 1989, this was partly because it feared losing its hard-won international status and economic aid.

On 29 June 1983, to the astonishment of political observers, Bavaria's right-wing premier, Franz Josef Strauss, arranged for a DM 1 billion credit to be paid to East Berlin. In return, Honecker eased restrictions on travel to the Federal Republic. But as East Germany's hard currency procurer, Alexander Schalck-Golodkowski, testified after reunification, these credits never stood a chance of saving the GDR. Instead, he claimed, they helped achieve the aim of the politicians in Bonn: to make East Germany politically dependent on the Federal Republic.[31] Moreover, such economic assistance made it increasingly difficult for the SED to sustain the traditional image of the 'class enemy' in the West. The Soviet Union would never have tolerated the GDR's collapse in the period before Gorbachev anyway, so any other course adopted by the FRG at this juncture would simply have raised Cold War tensions and endangered world peace. In the long run, East Germany's indebtedness to Bonn rendered it bankrupt – an important factor in the regime's implosion in 1989–90.

The crowning moment of Honecker's political career was undoubtedly his long-delayed official visit to the Federal Republic between 7 and 11 September 1987. This seemed to bestow prestige and international recognition on his regime. Yet there was another side to the event which rotted away at its ideological foundations. The Stasi noted that young East Germans interpreted it as a sign that the Berlin Wall and the traditional negative image of West German 'imperialism' were both redundant.[32] When Honecker made his celebrated remarks in Bonn that 'socialism and capitalism can no more be combined than fire and water',[33] he had no idea that in three years his beloved 'Workers' and Peasants' State' would be erased from the map of Europe. Indeed, the internal prestige which the GDR acquired through his visit contributed to the fact that its leadership ignored the mounting domestic crisis and rejected reform.[34] This doomed the regime to eventual collapse.

While rapprochement brought some improvements in the everyday lives of ordinary East Germans, it also failed to achieve gradual liberalisation in the GDR. Paradoxically, however, it was by triggering an increase in the size of the Stasi[35] and then lulling the regime into a false sense of security, that *Ostpolitik* accomplished a victory of unintended consequences. In the end, the short-term gains made by the GDR, in the form of international recognition and economic assistance, were outweighed by the longer-term corrosive effects.

The Gorbachev Factor

On 12 March 1985 Mikhail Gorbachev became General Secretary of the Communist Party of the Soviet Union (CPSU). His policies of *glasnost* ('openness') and *perestroika* ('restructuring') inaugurated a new era, not only in the countries of the Eastern bloc, but in the whole world. Crushed by the burden of Cold War defence expenditure, the Soviet Empire had become overstretched. The Kremlin therefore decided that its military presence in Eastern Europe diminished rather than enhanced USSR security, and at a CPSU Central Committee plenum in February 1988, Gorbachev conceded the right of every people and every country to 'choose freely its social and political system'.[36] Naturally, at this time he still believed that reform communist governments would replace the discredited totalitarian regimes in the region. But in line with his new doctrine of non-interference in the affairs of the satellite states (later dubbed the 'Sinatra Doctrine', after the American crooner's song, 'My Way'),[37] he also made clear that every Communist Party had the sovereign right to decide all questions for itself.[38]

Gorbachev's desire for disarmament led to heated debate in the SED Politburo. The party's ideological spokesman, Kurt Hager, feared that unilateral cuts would destabilise the situation in the GDR and Eastern Europe. Gorbachev went ahead regardless, announcing Soviet troop reductions at the United Nations in December 1988, and envisaging cutbacks even in East Germany's National People's Army (NVA) in January 1989.[39] Even more galling for the SED was Moscow's increasing acceptance that, irrespective of the existence of two German states, there was only *one* German nation.[40] As far as the SED leadership was concerned, there was no need for reform in East Germany. In 1986 Honecker insisted that the GDR population lived in one of the freest countries in the world.[41] On 9 April 1987, in an interview with the West German magazine *Stern*, Hager made the Politburo's hostility to the reform process in the USSR abundantly clear. When one's neighbour starts changing his wallpaper, he said, one does not necessarily feel obliged to do the same![42] As a consequence of this dismissive remark, Hager's personal office was bombarded with protest letters from East German citizens, including SED members.[43]

Although the SED leadership did not dare to lambaste the reformers in Moscow publicly, it did its best to insulate the GDR against the disruptive neighbour two doors down. On 20 October 1987 the Politburo passed a resolution stipulating that in future the speeches of Soviet leaders would be censored before being published in East Germany.[44] Over the next two years, it took the unprecedented step of banning Soviet journals, articles and films that dealt with the issue of Stalinism. For example, the German-language edition of the Soviet news digest, *Sputnik*, which championed liberalisation, vanished from East German news-stands. Incredibly, it was now easier to obtain contemporary Soviet publications from West Berlin than in the capital of the GDR.[45] SED censorship was counterproductive, however, since it often intensified cravings for the forbidden fruits of *glasnost*. Following the prohibition of *Sputnik* on 18 November 1988, the SED was inundated with angry letters of protest, some of them from party members.[46]

For SED gerontocrats, Stalinism was a strictly taboo subject, since the last thing they wanted was a discussion of the GDR's own repressive history. Tensions with the Kremlin on this issue had already flared up in January 1988, when Honecker informed Moscow's ambassador that the term *perestroika* would henceforth be removed from official Soviet documents distributed in East Germany:

> We are against the practice of the purest slander of the CPSU history and socialist construction in the USSR. We are surprised by doubtful economic experiments, not to speak of the information sphere. For years we educated GDR citizens about the example of the CPSU and the heroic struggle of the Soviet people. Now we learn, however, that it was all a string of failures.[47]

On 17 March 1988 Hager held a conversation with his Soviet opposite number, Alexander Yakovlev, about the history of the communist movement and cooperation between the two parties on theoretical questions. Hager expressed his concern that 'one-sided assessments' of the Stalin era were 'awakening doubts about socialism'. He also expressed his astonishment that the Soviet party newspaper, *Pravda*, could go so far as to claim that 'nobody has a monopoly on truth'. This, protested Hager, meant replacing a 'firm, class-based standpoint' with the idea that 'ultimately nobody is right'. Yakovlev, who was one of Gorbachev's most trusted advisers, answered: 'You emphasise the monopoly; I on the other hand emphasise the truth.' Hager countered that it was inadmissible to allow doubt to be cast on the 'truth' of Marxism-Leninism.[48]

As fraternal relations with the bigger brother deteriorated, the SED leadership began pointing up 'national peculiarities' in East Germany's development, even coining the slogan 'socialism in the colours of the GDR',[49] to highlight its independence. The extent of antipathy to Gorbachev in the leadership was conveyed to me by a personal aide to Hermann Axen, the Politburo member responsible for fraternal relations with other communist parties. In 1992 he claimed that his boss had sincerely believed that Gorbachev was a CIA agent.[50] The GDR leadership was terrified that their captive population would be infected by the democratic virus emanating from Moscow. They were right to be worried. East Germans began demonstrating for reforms similar to those being undertaken in the Soviet Union; and when challenged by police, they flaunted Soviet badges and pictures of Gorbachev.[51] On 8 June 1987 crowds of young people gathered at the Brandenburg Gate in order to listen to a rock concert on the other side of the Berlin Wall. The police, however, moved in and there were violent clashes. The young fans called out 'Gorbi! Gorbi!' and 'the Wall must go!'[52] On 17 January 1988 more than a hundred peace and human rights activists were arrested when they attended the officially sanctioned demonstration to honour Karl Liebknecht and Rosa Luxemburg, the assassinated leaders of the abortive communist uprising in Berlin in 1919. Their crime was to carry banners emblazoned with Luxemburg's motto: 'Freedom is always freedom for dissenters'. Some of those detained were even expelled from the GDR.[53]

Even more terrifying for the Politburo was the prospect that elements inside the SED would start clamouring for liberalisation. After all, the Communist Party was the linchpin of the totalitarian system, so any divisions within its ranks might bring the whole edifice crashing down. It is a common misconception that there was a clear dichotomy between the party and people in the GDR. Some East German communists were as, if not more, enthusiastic than their fellow countrymen about reform in the Soviet Union. Others, however, were much more critical.[54] Every month, all SED regional leaders were required to deliver a report to the Politburo, describing the mood in their respective party organisations. On 22 July 1988 the Second Secretary of the regional leadership in Dresden submitted a report containing a striking passage about attitudes to *glasnost* and *perestroika* in his area. Some older comrades were apparently expressing doubts about whether such open public discussion of all-important questions in the USSR strengthened socialism and the leading role of the CPSU. At the other extreme, party organisations were having to battle with individual comrades who wanted to see developments in the Soviet Union simply 'duplicated' in the GDR.[55] Over the year as a whole, the SED initiated some 23,000 proceedings against its own members, the highest number since its foundation in 1946.[56]

For the majority of East Germans, Gorbachev had come to personify hope and freedom. Opinion data collated by the country's Institute for Youth Research, based in Leipzig, shows that at the end of 1988, 83 per cent of those young people questioned declared a positive attitude towards Gorbachev, 50 per cent a very positive attitude. The figures for non-party members were 82 per cent and 49 per cent; for SED members, 90 per cent and 55 per cent respectively. Even more worrying for the Politburo was the finding that in early 1989 a mere 8 per cent of non-communist youth identified with the policies of the SED, while only 48 per cent of young comrades professed to 'fully identify' with their party.[57] Clearly, developments in the Soviet Union were undermining confidence in the SED and encouraging East Germany's disaffected youth to speak out more freely. By 1989 the Soviet neighbour had done much more than just change his wallpaper; in the name of building a new 'common European home',[58] he had begun demolishing his house and the houses of all those around him. The SED, like the other communist parties in Eastern Europe, would be unable to insulate itself against the advancing bulldozer.

The Revolution

If the GDR entered its fortieth year in the midst of a profound midlife crisis, by the autumn of 1989 it was in the throes of a fatal nervous breakdown. The first sign of trouble came with the local elections in May, which were judged to be fraudulent by the opposition groups that observed them. Afterwards, small demonstrations took place in several places and hundreds of complaints were lodged against the authorities.[59] On 2 May 1989 Hungary, now under reform-communist rule, began to dismantle the Iron Curtain along its frontier with Austria. East German holidaymakers soon besieged the embassy of the Federal Republic in Budapest, hoping to gain permission to travel there. The embassies in Prague and Warsaw were also occupied. Then, on 10 and 11 September, without any prior consultation with its East German ally, Hungary permitted all the refugees to leave for the West, thereby causing the largest exodus from the 'Workers' and Peasants' State' since the building of the Berlin Wall in 1961. Within weeks, Czechoslovakia and Poland had followed suit. The Soviet Union stood by and did nothing.

Meanwhile, in Leipzig, on 11 September there had been mass arrests following a demonstration. This only inflamed the situation, and every Monday more and more people took to the streets there to protest. Between late August and early October, a spate of new opposition groups was established, ranging from New Forum, Democracy Now and Democratic Awakening to the Social Democratic Party in the GDR (SDP). All pleaded for peaceful dialogue with the authorities as a way of solving the country's problems. This combination of refugee exodus and internal dissent began to destabilise East Germany on the eve of its fortieth birthday.

When Gorbachev arrived in East Berlin to attend the official anniversary celebrations on 7 October, he was confronted with a country in ferment. On the official parade the crowds chanted, 'Gorbi! Gorbi!', while the Soviet leader denied Honecker the customary comradely bear hug.[60] To make matters worse, he uttered the fateful words, 'life punishes those who come too late',[61] thereby implying that the SED should instigate reforms or suffer the consequences. He even went so far as to tell East Germans: 'If you want democracy, take it and it will be yours.' This was tantamount to stating that all communist claims about democracy in the GDR were bogus; indeed, it was an open incitement to oppose the SED![62] A decisive impetus was thereby given to the revolution.

Two days later, on 9 October, the mass movement against the SED achieved its breakthrough in Leipzig, when 70,000 people took to the streets. The very real threat of bloodshed was averted when three regional communist leaders declared themselves willing to open a dialogue with the protesters.[63] Meanwhile, in Berlin, the incipient fissures in the leadership turned into open splits after Gorbachev's return home. Honecker was relieved of all his functions on 18 October and replaced by the designated heir apparent, Egon Krenz. His talk of a *Wende* (change) rang increasingly false, as the SED tried to ride the tiger of revolution so as better to control it. By now the demonstrations involved huge numbers of people from nearly all walks of life. The biggest of these took place on 4 November in East Berlin, where approximately a million citizens gathered to demand civil rights and free elections.[64]

The serendipitous opening of the Berlin Wall on 9 November 1989 was the key watershed of the revolution. It only happened because a Politburo member at an evening press conference forgot to mention that the new decree giving GDR citizens the right to an exit visa at any border crossing, including that of Berlin, only applied to the country's four million passport holders. Asked when the new regulations would take effect, he replied, 'immediately, without delay', failing to specify under what conditions. The announcement triggered a rush of people to the Wall.[65] In the absence of any guidance from the country's paralysed leadership, the local guards opened the border on their own initiative. There followed one of the greatest spontaneous street parties in world history, as East and West Berliners celebrated the end of their city's division. The fall of this most potent symbol of communist oppression, which had guaranteed the GDR's stability since 1961, sent the 'Workers' and Peasants' State' racing into history.

After the fall of the Wall, the chant of the revolutionary crowds changed from 'We are the people!' to 'We are *one* people!'[66] If demands for political freedom had dominated until this point, the desire to partake in the economic success of the Federal Republic now took centre stage. Meanwhile, the SED began to implode, as its functionaries lost the will to rule and an unshackled media reported stories of corruption at the highest levels.[67] On 1 December East Germany's parliament deleted the party's 'leading role' from the country's constitution, and the SED called an extraordinary party conference to begin the task of shedding its totalitarian baggage. Soon it had renamed itself the Party of Democratic Socialism (PDS). Krenz resigned as General Secretary on 3 December, along with the entire Politburo and Central Committee. In mid-January 1990, angry citizens stormed the Stasi's headquarters in East Berlin to ensure that the ministry ceased its activities and was brought under some kind of democratic control.[68]

On 18 March 1990 the first and last free parliamentary elections were held in the GDR. The communists were swept from power, marking the final collapse of their dictatorship. 'Alliance for Germany', a conservative coalition sponsored by West German Chancellor Helmut Kohl, won 48.09 per cent of the popular vote (of which the Christian Democratic Union accounted for 40.81 per cent), giving it a mandate to expedite reunification with the erstwhile capitalist enemy to the west.[69] The GDR had effectively voted itself out of existence. Six and a half months later, it joined the Federal Republic of Germany under Article 23 of its Basic Law.

Why was the revolution so peaceful? This was by no means a foregone conclusion. When the Chinese communists carried out their Tiananmen Square massacre on 4 June 1989, East Germany's rubber-stamp parliament issued a statement praising the suppression of the 'counter-revolution' there.[70] This was intended as a warning to the increasingly restive population in the GDR. If there was any doubt about the regime's determination to put down any similar disturbances at home, Margot Honecker, the hard-line Education Minister and wife of the SED General Secretary, provided it. Addressing the ninth Pedagogical Congress in June, she condemned those promoting change in Eastern Europe as 'counter-revolutionaries' who wanted a return to capitalism. She then threatened violence: 'We are now in a period of struggle which needs young people who are willing to fight to strengthen socialism … if necessary, with a rifle in their hands'.[71] On 8 October Erich Mielke, head of the Stasi, ordered a state of red alert for the GDR's security forces.[72] Two days later, Erich Honecker received a high Chinese dignitary and referred to the similarities between the 'counter-revolution' in Beijing and the unrest in the GDR. He then made plans to crush the next Leipzig demonstration with methods not so different to those adopted in China a few months earlier.[73] Since the police were overwhelmed by the huge numbers of protesters, Honecker gave the order to provide the NVA with live ammunition.[74]

That it was not used can be attributed to four factors. First among these was Gorbachev's refusal to countenance violence. In contrast to 17 June 1953, Soviet tanks did not roll. According to some sources, the Commander-in-Chief of Warsaw Pact forces, to whom the NVA was ultimately responsible, ordered the latter's troops to be withdrawn from Leipzig and other GDR cities. Krenz also seems to have had a hand in the decision.[75] If either the Soviet or East German military had been deployed, it would have fatally damaged Gorbachev's credibility with the West, on whom he relied increasingly for the success of his reforms. The second factor relates to the splits in the SED, not only within the leadership, but at regional level. These had the effect of paralysing the party's decision-making capacity. By replacing Honecker with Krenz, the Politburo signalled that it had decided against the use of armed force. Third, some members of the GDR's army, police and 'combat groups' were unwilling to open fire on civilians,[76] thereby weakening the power of the state at the crucial moment. Fourth, the tactics of the revolutionary crowds themselves were anything but provocative. Armed with nothing more than candles, they hardly fitted the description of violent counter-revolutionary mobs that the security forces had been trained to quell. Once the Wall had been breached, the SED was in no position to defend itself anyway, and lost the will to rule.

The final intriguing question is why Moscow decided to abandon its long-standing East German ally altogether and accept reunification. The answer lies in the Soviet Union's desperate need for economic assistance. As Europe's most wealthy country, West Germany was in a position to help. The GDR, by contrast, was on the verge of bankruptcy. The drowning 'Workers' and Peasants' State' ended up being swept away in the tide of history, leaving Gorbachev with a choice: surf the wave or close the floodgates. He chose the former and Germany was reunited as a capitalist democracy at the heart of the European Community and NATO.

Conclusion

That the Soviet Union would give up the GDR had always been the SED's worst nightmare. It had also been the ultimate dream of the majority of Germans on both sides of the Iron Curtain. In the *annus mirabilis* of 1989–90, what nobody thought possible came to pass. How, then, should we rank the relative importance of the GDR's internal defects, *Ostpolitik*, Gorbachev's reforms and the East German revolutionaries themselves in bringing about this remarkable turn of events?

Paradoxically, bureaucratic totalitarianism was both the lifeblood and wasting disease of the GDR. Indeed, this was its tragedy. Any attempt at liberalisation was bound to push it into the magnetic field of the Federal Republic, thereby calling into question its very existence as a state. Simultaneously, however, the increasingly outdated political and social structures to which the GDR was wedded, and its failure to win legitimacy in the eyes of its own citizens, doomed it to collapse in the long run. Even so, dictatorships can last well beyond their natural expiry date, particularly if they have a formidable apparatus of repression and are protected by a superpower.

East Germany was born of the Cold War and died with it. *Ostpolitik* certainly played its part in reducing East–West tensions and created some important prerequisites for reunification. However, the extent of its effectiveness as a Trojan Horse is debatable, even if, in the end, it did do more to undermine the GDR than to stabilise it. The accompanying Helsinki Accords improved superpower relations and provided both East Germans and the international community with a kind of 'Magna Carta'[77] against which SED human rights abuses could be monitored. Some of the most egregious forms of repression were thereby mitigated. Ultimately, however, nobody played a greater role than the Soviet leader, Mikhail Gorbachev, in bringing this ice age in international relations to an end.

But his influence went much deeper than that. The onset of *glasnost* and *perestroika* in the Soviet Union plunged the GDR into existential crisis. As the historian Jeannette Madarász has perceptively noted:

> Gorbachev's reforms challenged most of the basic assumptions of life in the GDR and questioned the validity of compromises that had supported the relationship between

state and society for many years. They undermined the status quo and encouraged parts of the population to discuss more openly…issues lethal to the stability of the state such as the lack of economic success, travel outside the Eastern bloc, and popular input into politics.[78]

By permitting Hungary and Poland to liberalise, Gorbachev showed East Germans that emancipation from Moscow would be tolerated. Without Hungary's decision to open its border with Austria, the SED might have weathered the refugee crisis. The 'Gorbachev effect' was strongest in the GDR because, unlike the other East European states, it depended on the Soviet Union for its very existence. It was not for nothing that the revised constitution of 1974 proclaimed: 'The German Democratic Republic is forever and irrevocably allied with the Union of Soviet Socialist Republics'.[79] Gorbachev not only made the 1989 revolution possible, he actively incited it. Furthermore, once it had started, he refused to crush it, thereby ensuring its success. Rarely in history has so much been owed by so many to one man.

None of this detracts from the immense courage of ordinary East German citizens, who took to the streets in their hundreds of thousands to overthrow the communist system. It was their popular pressure in the face of an uncertain regime response that forced the SED to concede power. Without the 'wave of history' they generated, the GDR would not have been swept away. In the end, however, they had Gorbachev to thank for their success, and for this reason the latter must take most of the credit for the demise of the 'first "Workers' and Peasants' State" on German soil'. Until the mid-1980s, the people of this state had been told that 'to learn from the Soviet Union is to learn how to win'.[80] With the advent of Gorbachev's revolutionary changes in the USSR, they were able to turn this slogan against their rulers. The GDR's dependence on the Soviet Union was ultimately its undoing.

Notes

1. Honecker had been appointed First Secretary of the Socialist Unity Party of Germany on 3 May 1971. He was renamed General Secretary at the party's ninth congress, held between 18 and 22 May 1976. With this new title, he set about further strengthening his position as SED leader. A few months later, on 29 October 1976, he also became East Germany's Head of State, a position formally known as Chairman of the State Council.
2. Timothy Garton Ash, *In Europe's Name: Germany and the Divided Continent* (London, 1993), p. 356.

3. Corey Ross, *The East German Dictatorship: Problems and Perspectives in the Interpretation of the GDR* (London, 2002), p. 126.

4. Wilfriede Otto, 'Angst der Macht vor Visionen, 1980–1989', in Thomas Klein, Wilfriede Otto and Peter Grieder (eds), *Visionen, Repression und Opposition in der SED, 1949–1989* (Frankfurt/Oder, 1997), p. 459.

5. Mary Fulbrook, *Anatomy of a Dictatorship: Inside the GDR, 1949–1989* (Oxford, 1995), p. 3.

6. Armin Mitter and Stefan Wolle, *Untergang auf Raten: Unbekannte Kapitel der DDR-Geschichte* (Munich, 1993).

7. Jeannette Z. Madarász, *Conflict and Compromise in East Germany, 1971–1989: A Precarious Stability* (Basingstoke, 2003), p. 192.

8. Richard Bessel and Ralph Jessen (eds), *Die Grenzen der Diktatur: Staat und Gesellschaft in der DDR* (Göttingen, 1996); and Corey Ross, *Constructing Socialism at the Grass-Roots: The Transformation of East Germany, 1945–65* (Basingstoke, 2000).

9. R.J. Crampton, *Eastern Europe in the Twentieth Century – and After*, 2nd edn (London and New York, 2003), p. 358.

10. Mike Dennis, *The Stasi: Myth and Reality* (London, 2003), p. xi.

11. Ibid., pp. 242–6.

12. Peter Grieder, *The East German Leadership, 1946–1973: Conflict and Crisis* (Manchester, 1999), pp. 160–70.

13. Hermann Weber, *DDR: Grundriß der Geschichte, 1945–1990* (Hanover, 1991), p. 186.

14. Madarász, *Conflict and Compromise*, p. 143.

15. Dennis, *The Stasi*, p. 223.

16. Fulbrook, *Anatomy of a Dictatorship*, pp. 215–36.

17. Helmut Kohl, interviewed for the film documentary, 'Das war die DDR. Teil 4: "Wir sind das Volk"', *Eine Dokumentation über die Geschichte und den Zeitgeist der Deutschen Demokratischen Republik* (1993).

18. Ross, *The East German Dictatorship*, p. 10.

19. M.E. Sarotte, *Dealing with the Devil: East Germany, Détente and Ostpolitik, 1969–1973* (Chapel Hill, NC, and London, 2001), p. 154.

20. Garton Ash, *In Europe's Name*, p. 223.

21. Weber, *DDR*, p. 175.

22. 'Wir sind das Volk'.

23. Interviewed in ibid.

24. Crampton, *Eastern Europe*, p. 358.

25. Fulbrook, *Anatomy of a Dictatorship*, p. 206.

26. Ibid., p. 116.

27. Ibid., pp. 276–7.

28. Sarotte, *Dealing with the Devil*, pp. 46–8, 154.

29. Garton Ash, *In Europe's Name*, p. 204.

30. Ulrike Poppe interviewed in 'Wir sind das Volk'; and Weber, *DDR*, p. 332.

31. Interviewed in 'Wir sind das Volk'.

32. Dennis, *The Stasi*, p. 222.

33. Garton Ash, *In Europe's Name*, p. 172.

34. Gert-Joachim Glaeßner, 'German Unification and the West', in Gert-Joachim Glaeßner and Ian Wallace (eds), *The German Revolution of 1989: Causes and Consequences* (Oxford, 1992), p. 214.

35. Sarotte, *Dealing with the Devil*, p. 54.

36. Martin McCauley, 'Gorbachev, the GDR and Germany', in Glaeßner and Wallace (eds), *The German Revolution of 1989*, p. 164.

37. Timothy Garton Ash, *We the People: The Revolution of '89 witnessed in Warsaw, Budapest, Berlin and Prague* (Cambridge, 1990), p. 140.

38. McCauley, 'Gorbachev, the GDR and Germany', p. 169.

39. Ibid., pp. 170–1.

40. Ibid., p. 178.

41. Weber, *DDR*, p. 197.

42. Otto, 'Angst der Macht vor Visionen', p. 445.

43. Stiftung Archiv der Parteien und Massenorganisationen der DDR im Bundesarchiv (henceforth SAPMO-BA), DY30/vorl.42228.

44. Monika Nakath, 'SED und Perestroika: Reflexion osteuropäischer Reformversuche in den 80er Jahren', *Hefte zur DDR-Geschichte* (Berlin, 1993), p. 17.

45. David Clay Large, *Berlin* (New York, 2000), p. 520.

46. SAPMO-BA, DY30/V2/2.037/36; SAPMO-BA, DY30/JIV2/2A/3178: information on initial youth reactions to the *Sputnik* ban, 29 November 1988.

47. Charles S. Maier, *Dissolution: The Crisis of Communism and the End of East Germany* (Princeton, NJ, 1997), pp. 219–20.

48. SAPMO-BA, DY30/vorl.42343: 'Gedächtnisprotokoll über das Gespräch mit Genossen Jakowlew am 17.3.1988 in Ulan Bator.'

49. Weber, *DDR*, p. 197.

50. Personal interview with Manfred Uschner, 8 December 1992.

51. Clay Large, *Berlin*, p. 520.

52. 'Wir sind das Volk'; and Weber, *DDR*, p. 338.

53. Weber, *DDR*, pp. 193–4, 340.

54. Stefan Wolle, *Die heile Welt der Diktatur: Alltag und Herrschaft in der DDR, 1971–1989* (Bonn, 1998), p. 315.

55. SAPMO-BA, DY3/Büro Honecker 2218.

56. Madarász, *Conflict and Compromise*, p. 193.

57. Nakath, 'SED und Perestroika', pp. 46–7.

58. Garton Ash, *In Europe's Name*, pp. 2–3, 105–7, 113–14.

59. Weber, *DDR*, p. 211.

60. Crampton, *Eastern Europe*, p. 394.

61. Clay Large, *Berlin*, p. 524.

62. McCauley, 'Gorbachev, the GDR and Germany', p. 174.
63. Weber, *DDR*, p. 217.
64. Ibid., p. 219.
65. Maier, *Dissolution*, pp. 160–1.
66. Garton Ash, *We the People*, pp. 69–72.
67. Fulbrook, *Anatomy of a Dictatorship*, p. 262.
68. Ibid., p. 264.
69. Weber, *DDR*, p. 232.
70. Ibid., p. 343.
71. McCauley, 'Gorbachev, the GDR and Germany', p. 170.
72. Fulbrook, *Anatomy of a Dictatorship*, pp. 253–4.
73. Crampton, *Eastern Europe*, p. 394.
74. McCauley, 'Gorbachev, the GDR and Germany', p. 175.
75. Ibid., pp. 175–6.
76. Otto, 'Angst der Macht vor Visionen', p. 459.
77. Glaeßner, 'German Unification and the West', p. 213.
78. Madarász, *Conflict and Compromise*, p. 193.
79. Garton Ash, *We the People*, p. 65.
80. Ibid.

–10–

Revolution and Revolt against Revolution: Czechoslovakia, 1989

James Krapfl

If only because some label is required to discuss the dramatic upheavals that occurred in 'Eastern' Europe in 1989, the question incessantly arises: were they, properly speaking, 'revolutions'? Neither political theory nor historical scholarship has yet produced an undisputed answer. Interestingly, however, the academic debates parallel discussions that took place among participants in the events themselves – at least in Czechoslovakia. In order to shed fresh light on the 'revolution' question, and to suggest new ways of understanding 1989, this essay analyses Czechoslovak rhetoric about revolution between 1989 and 1991, a period when many believed a revolution was occurring.

I examine this rhetoric by reading the diverse utterances of Czechoslovaks about revolution, during the revolution, from the perspective of literary criticism. Czechoslovaks began narrating the history of their revolution almost immediately after it began; by reading these narratives as constituting a single 'text', we learn how Czechoslovaks strove to fix the meaning of events as they unfolded. This approach owes its inspiration to Lynn Hunt, who developed it for the study of revolutionary France. Using Northrop Frye's theory of plot structures, Hunt argued that the French after 1789 first narrated their revolution as comedy, then as romance and finally as tragedy, with attendant political implications in each case.[1] Czechoslovaks shared with their French predecessors the linguistic necessity of framing historical narratives according to some generic plot, but their rhetorical shifts were more complicated. While all protagonists began interpreting the Czechoslovak revolution within the framework of romance, successive attempts to cast the story comically, tragically and, ultimately, satirically were linked to specific groups, none of whose perspectives achieved hegemony. Inescapably, each employment implicitly articulated a programme for future action, upon which Czechoslovaks could not agree. Each narrative shift marked nothing less than a revolt against a particular understanding of revolution, or against revolution *per se*.

Revolution as Romance

> There has been a struggle between good and evil since time immemorial. Our students have come out on the side of good and achieved an utter triumph.
>
> Michal Horáček, December 1989[2]

The revolution began, by nearly all accounts, on 17 November 1989, when special police forces brutally suppressed a peaceful, student-led demonstration in Prague.[3] Accounts of the 'massacre' were the first historical narratives the revolution produced about itself, and they set the tone for a romantic interpretation of subsequent events. Initially these accounts were presented orally, as when drama students burst into Prague theatres on the night of 17 November to tell colleagues what was happening, but in subsequent days witnesses put their recollections into simple, direct texts that circulated throughout Czechoslovakia:

> Special units of the Interior Ministry succeeded in dividing the crowd. I was in the part closed off between the Na Perštýně intersection and Voršilská street. The side street, Mikulandská, was also cut off... The police called us to disperse, but there was nowhere to go. We were closed in.[4]

> Policemen ran amongst the demonstrators and cruelly beat them. The assault intensified and units joined with police dogs. Armoured transports drove into the crowd. Everywhere there were cries for help and the hysterical shrieks of girls and women, drowning amidst the barking of dogs.[5]

> When a policeman raised his truncheon against this girl I put myself in his way without thinking. For this I was dragged away... A storm of blows showered on my head, back, and genitals. I heard men with hatred in their voices shout 'give it to the mother f—ker!' 'On his face!'[6]

> A girl in tears wailed... that they had beaten and dragged away her husband... Policemen beat her, too, though she was pregnant.[7]

Romantic plots, according to Frye, narrate the story of a quest, a heroic struggle between good and evil, where either protagonist or antagonist stands to achieve decisive victory. It posits a world where extraordinary things can happen, and where humans are capable of extraordinary deeds.[8] The texts of witness established this framework by contrasting the non-violence of the demonstrators, and their humane attempts to help one another, with the gratuitous violence and vulgarity of their attackers. The violence they had witnessed was beyond the ordinary experience of most participants as well as of compatriots who heard their story; it stimulated an urgent desire for extraordinary action 'to overcome government by violence' once and for all.[9]

Students and actors made such action possible by inviting all citizens to participate in a general strike on 27 November, setting examples with their own full-time strikes, which they inaugurated on 18 November. They were conscious of taking a great risk. Should their initiative fail, actors could expect to lose their jobs, and university administrators threatened not only to expel students, but to punish their families and 'rinse their hands in students' blood'.[10] Despite the peaceful capitulation of Communist regimes in neighbouring countries, there was no guarantee that Czechoslovak hardliners would follow suit, and 1968 had shown what manner of reprisal could befall individuals who openly defied the regime. Nonetheless, strike initiators felt they had no choice, and as they 'wrote' the revolution, they emplotted it as a romance. 'I don't give a damn whether other schools join or whether you join,' a drama student in Prague exclaimed, 'I can't continue like this any longer, I'm going on strike now, IMMEDIATELY!!!'[11] Such headlong movement and disregard for consequences is characteristic of romantic protagonists. Students vowed to continue their strike until several demands had been fulfilled: (1) a thorough investigation of the massacre and punishment of its perpetrators; (2) free and honest reporting in the media; (3) release of all political prisoners; (4) freedom of assembly; and (5) a 'consequential dialogue with all segments of society'.[12] Realising that their efforts would be fruitless without the support of society at large, students and actors countered media censorship by personally visiting factories, farms and workplaces across the country. They testified to the violence of 17 November, explained that their demands were in everyone's interest, and helped establish workplace strike committees. Most importantly, they gave citizens the sense that their action could be meaningful.

At the same time, broadly based civic initiatives began springing up, from the Hungarian Independent Initiative in southern Slovakia to the Liberec Civic Initiative in northern Bohemia. The most important of these were Public against Violence (VPN), established on 19 November in Bratislava, and Civic Forum (OF), created a few hours later in Prague.[13] Given their location in the capitals, they immediately came to orchestrate much of the popular movement and assume the role of negotiator with the regime; branches of VPN and OF were soon established in municipalities, workplaces and among interest groups throughout Czechoslovakia. In addition to supporting the students' demands, they called for the resignation of leading political figures.[14]

Even before the General Strike, in the face of massive demonstrations, the regime began to consider concessions, and the armed forces, though mobilised, did not intervene. On 27 November it is estimated that half of Czechoslovakia's labour force took active part in the General Strike, and another quarter (health care workers, elementary school teachers and others who felt that their responsibilities precluded active participation) expressed symbolic solidarity.[15] The regime offered significant concessions as a result, most importantly repealing the constitutional clause guaranteeing the Communist Party a 'leading role' in society. Subsequent weeks followed in the spirit of a quest. While OF in Prague and VPN in Bratislava entered negotiations with federal and republican governments, branches of these associations in provincial centres (together with students in university towns) negotiated with local officials and workplace directors to achieve dramatic changes. Demonstrations and happenings continued in tandem with political events at local, national and international levels. When federal leaders proposed a new government that allotted Communists a majority of ministerial seats, citizens threatened another general strike, compelling OF leaders to press the Communists for a government with a non-Communist majority by 10 December. When Ceaușescu's government massacred peaceful demonstrators in Romania, Czechoslovaks mobilised again, sending trains full of humanitarian aid donated by citizens, businesses and hospitals.

The central theme of romance is transcendence, and reflections on the revolution in 1989 were replete with this idea.[16] Widespread metaphors of cleansing and rebirth expressed a perception of ontological transformation, as did representations of students as knights, Havel as a saint and the people as gods.[17] Many spoke of a 'new society', and one flyer declared that Czechoslovaks were ushering in a new civilisation.[18] Intrinsic to this sense of transcendence was a perceived transformation of human relations. People marvelled that wallets lost in crowds were returned, or that vehicles left unlocked were not stolen.[19] Strangers kissed one another on Wenceslas Square, and happenings throughout the country connected people both physically and emotionally. Recalling one such event in Olomouc, the student Milan Hanuš described 'a feeling of stupendous wholeness and rightness... Around me dozens of unknown and nonetheless intimately familiar faces. And, I believe, even the same feeling within'.[20]

The word 'revolution' was first heard in the student demonstration of 17 November, and began percolating in popular discourse at least as early as 21 November.[21] Many names were given to the revolution in the beginning, including 'Joyful', 'Students'', 'Cleansing' and 'Children's', but 'Gentle Revolution' was the most common.[22] 'Velvet Revolution' (a term coined by a French journalist) later achieved pre-eminence in the Czech lands.[23] These appellations signalled, on one hand, a metaphorical identification of processes unfolding in Czechoslovakia with processes perceived as parallel in other revolutions in European history.[24] On the other hand, they signified a revolt against a revolutionary tradition which was perceived as violent and unclean. By using means that were 'as clean as the goal', Czechoslovaks hoped that their revolution would succeed in preserving the democracy and transcendence that had been ephemeral in other revolutions, avoiding degeneration into violence and dictatorship.[25]

As with all revolutionary rhetoric, the discourse of the Gentle Revolution about itself had political implications. This plot structure trusted people to act in the interests of the common good, and called on them to do so. Indeed, casting the revolution in the romantic mode gave it implications that were, in the strict sense, anarchic, and would quickly generate a more 'sober' reaction.[26]

Revolution as Comedy

> One million seven hundred thousand Communists do not comprise some different biological or moral species than the rest of us.
>
> Václav Havel, December 1989[27]

Comedy is a qualification of romance's quest for transcendence, centring on the theme of reconciliation. It emphasises the common humanity of both protagonist and antagonist, portraying their conflict more as a clash of interests than a struggle between good and evil. The archetypal comedy tells the story of a rising new society struggling against an old; the old eventually accommodates the new and a fresh harmony is created. 'The tendency of comedy is to include as many characters as possible in its final society; the blocking characters are more often reconciled or converted than simply repudiated'.[28] Comedy was the second generic plot chosen to frame the revolution's history, and it was chosen primarily by new elites for the purpose of ending the revolution. On four occasions Havel and those around him tried to present a comic resolution as having occurred, but only the last two attempts achieved widespread, if transitory, acceptance.

Following an informational meeting on 21 November, Prime Minister Ladislav Adamec agreed to negotiations with OF on 25 November. OF invited Adamec to address demonstrators the next day as a sign of good will, and he agreed. At the gathering of half a million, Havel proclaimed that 'the dialogue of power with the public has begun… From this moment we shall *all* take part in the government of this land and *all* of us therefore bear responsibility for its fate.' Havel's words clearly suggested an inclusive, comic strategy for interpreting the present as part of history, and Adamec initially played along by saying he favoured a common solution. Then he proposed that the General Strike be shortened to just a few minutes and that strike committees disband, and noted that he must consult the Party about OF's demands.[29] Applause turned to whistles, and OF leaders reluctantly called for Adamec's resignation if he did not agree to further concessions.[30] Nevertheless, OF leaders tried to demobilise the populace after the General Strike, calling for an end to mass demonstrations and encouraging strike committees to metamorphose into Civic Fora for the purpose of negotiating with local leaders.

Civic Forum's next attempt to present the public with a comic resolution culminated on 3 December, when Adamec was supposed to name a new government. In anticipation, OF leaders encouraged students to discontinue their strike, arguing that the new government would need a chance to work in peace. The most radical students resisted, and it was just hours before Adamec's announcement that all student leaders empowered to make such a decision finally agreed. When the announcement came, featuring a government in which Communists occupied fifteen of twenty ministerial chairs, OF leaders were inclined to welcome it.[31] Again, however, the public reacted antagonistically. The ratio of 15:5 was not

what people envisioned by the end of the Party's leading role, and in protest they took to the streets once more. Students resumed their strike and in some cases intensified it; OF and VPN demanded that Adamec form yet another government by 10 December.[32]

Adamec resigned on 7 December, to be replaced by the vice-premier Marián Čalfa. Civic Forum, having refused the Communists' invitation to Round Table talks based on Polish and Hungarian models, consented nonetheless to a meeting of 'decisive political forces' across an 'Oblong Table'. OF and VPN were to sit on one side, the communists opposite, and lesser parties – hitherto vassals of the Communists – were to choose which side to support.[33] Together these forces agreed on the composition of a new federal government, which Havel dubbed 'the Government of National Understanding'. In subsequent speeches Havel emphasised that Communists were to be included in the new society as equal partners. 'The Communist Party guaranteed the totalitarian system and therefore all Communists without exception carry heightened responsibility for the marasmus in which our country finds itself. This obliges them', he continued, 'to work harder than others today for a free future for us all.' Havel noted that OF and VPN had themselves nominated two Communists to the government, and praised Adamec and Čalfa for their willingness to cooperate.[34] A comic reconciliation seemed to be at hand.

Bowing to popular demands, President Gustáv Husák resigned after swearing in the new government on 10 December. Later that day, OF proposed that his replacement be none other than Václav Havel. To complicate matters, however, five other candidates declared themselves, including Alexander Dubček, rightly or wrongly considered a hero of 1968. OF, confident from its victories thus far, assumed it would be able to convince its partners at the Oblong Table to accept Havel and see to it that the Federal Assembly elect him. The Communists, however, acted as if they had fully adapted to the principles of the new society, and proposed a referendum as the most democratic means of electing the president. The OF leadership was taken aback; it did not want a popular vote, for the simple reason that Havel might lose. Opinion polls suggested that Dubček was the favourite candidate both in Slovakia and the Czech lands, and a further survey showed a majority of the population in favour of direct elections. Unwilling to abandon the idea of making Havel president, OF leaders mustered several reasons why direct elections were not appropriate 'at this moment', including their cost, the time campaigns would take, and tradition dating back to the First Republic that parliament should choose the president. Students, who had rejected OF's renewed appeal to end their strike on 10 December, nonetheless supported Havel and employed their nationwide network of 'agitators' to turn public opinion around. The problem of parliament, however, was solved only when Čalfa, in a private conversation with Havel, offered behind the scenes to rig Dubček's election to the office of Federal Assembly chairman, and to cajole or blackmail deputies into electing Havel president according to existing constitutional provisions.[35]

Of course, these arrangements were not revealed until years later. All the public knew at the time was that students descended on Prague from across the country to demonstrate daily before parliament on Havel's behalf, and that Communist representatives at what had by now become a Round Table agreed ultimately to OF's demands.[36] Thus it seemed, when parliament unanimously elected Havel president on 29 December, that leading figures of the old society had once again acquiesced to the legitimate demands of the new, and the event could be celebrated as a further sign of reconciliation. OF's communiqué praised the Communists' willingness to participate in 'the further development of democracy, humanity, and national understanding'.[37] On the evening of 29 December, a crowning festival typical for the conclusion of a comedy was held on Prague's Old Town Square, attended by Havel, popular actors and musicians, and tens of thousands of people from all over Czechoslovakia, who had come to Prague to witness the election: the 'Ball of National Understanding'.[38] Students, at last, ended their strike.

The attempt to emplot the revolution comically can be seen as a revolt against the continuation of revolution. As in classic revolutions, leaders newly empowered in Czechoslovakia sought to abate the potentially uncontrollable enthusiasm of the mobilised population and turn it to more routine forms of political engagement.[39] It is not surprising, then, that some leaders questioned whether the term 'revolution' should even be used. In a 10 December speech, Havel suggested that while many were calling 'this excited and dramatic period' a 'peaceful revolution', only historians would be able to tell at some future date what it 'really' was.[40] Distancing himself from the concept of revolution was a rhetorical tool for helping to bring about the revolution's end. It was part of a comic emplotment that incorporated both the mobilised populace and all but the most compromised functionaries of the old regime in what was supposed to be a new consensus. The leaders' insistence on legal continuity was likewise part of this emplotment, accepting as it did change only when it resulted in an orderly fashion from negotiations among recognised social actors. The political implications of the comic plot were therefore liberal, potentially even conservative.

Romance and Comedy in Conflict

> Friends, a second revolution has begun, no less exhausting and painful than the first… Let us be wary before the rise of new *apparatchiks* and toadies of power. Let us patrol who speaks for us and where. Let us be uncompromising in the exposition of injustice. Power can quickly turn against us once again.
>
> Martin Mejstřík, January 1990[41]

From the comic perspective, Havel's election marked the revolution's end; for romantics, however, it was merely a brilliant episode in an ongoing quest. In early

1990 many loci emerged where popular desire to continue the revolution clashed with elites' insistence that it was over, but two of the most important were the question of workplace administration and national or regional political representation.

Logically, the end of the party's 'leading role' meant that Communists should cease to dominate decision-making structures, not only at the level of federal and republican governments, but at the level of school, workplace and local administration as well. People began democratising these institutions in December 1989, and continued with increased confidence in January 1990. Students, well organised and enjoying tremendous prestige, managed to achieve representation in academic senates and changes of university personnel without much trouble. Democratisation of local administration proved more difficult, with enormous geographic diversity in the willingness of old *apparatchiks* to bow to popular pressure, but was generally facilitated by federal and republican laws on local government reconstruction in the first quarter of 1990. Democratisation of workplaces proved the most problematic task. Workers everywhere voted confidence or lack thereof in their directors, nominating replacements in the latter case. However, not always did discredited directors agree to leave, nor did local government organs (to which workplace directors in the command economy were answerable) always make the necessary arrangements.[42] Strikes thus broke out in numerous places. In some cases, members of the old *nomenklatura* founded their own VPN or OF within a workplace, challenging the legitimacy of the original association.[43] While perhaps most changes took place in an orderly fashion, the media naturally highlighted sensational examples, and given the hectic conditions prevailing in the Prague and Bratislava coordinating centres, these were the cases OF and VPN leaders learned most about.[44]

OF and VPN leaders feared economic crisis and loss of political credit as a result of unrest in the workplaces, and took dramatic steps to try to eliminate irregularities. Petr Pithart, OF's chief spokesman after Havel became president, went on federal television appealing to workplace OFs to eschew all 'pseudo-revolutionary' methods. 'Continue to call what is happening a revolution if you want. It is after all a question of taste. But let us act decently – decently and reasonably'.[45] Milan Kňažko, a central figure in VPN and one of Havel's advisers, issued a statement that proclaimed the revolution over, and called on workers to stop 'the cadre war'.[46] The response of workplace collectives to these appeals was mixed. Some moderated their methods, some continued as before, and some became internally divided and incapable of collective action.[47] The VPN leadership ultimately decided to disband workplace branches in the spring of 1990.[48]

Slovaks and Moravians sought to continue the revolution by securing their rights to national and regional self-government. Demands for 'a rigorously democratic federation' and the reinstatement of Moravia's political integrity emerged in the first days of the revolution, but assumed ever greater intensity in the spring of 1990.[49] It is generally agreed that the Slovak deputies who began the 'hyphen war' in the Federal Assembly did so for career reasons rather than conviction, but nonetheless the issue of national equality symbolised in the name (Czechoslovakia versus Czecho-Slovakia) stirred popular passions.[50] 'Our gentle revolution ... has not halted, but marches forward!' exclaimed a VPN journalist in Prievidza. 'Recently it has tested its methods of struggle in the contest over the new name of our state ... Even in a gentle revolution we must fight for the identity of our nation, whether other people like it or not'.[51] While those Slovaks demanding outright independence at this time were a minority, they were a loud and flamboyant one; on 1 March Slovak nationalists even invaded the Slovak National Council building in Bratislava.[52] Moravians in Brno also demonstrated (in less insurrectionary fashion) for Moravian territorial integrity. Regarding the Moravian question, OF leaders acknowledged the democratic merits of demands for self-government and thus gave moderate regionalists hope, but insisted that reforms wait until 'questions of federal importance' had been resolved.[53] VPN leaders condemned the radical nationalists as emotional demagogues standing outside the tradition of November, and emphasised that VPN stood for the 'completion' of Slovak sovereignty via legitimate political channels and negotiation with federal partners.[54]

These popular impulses perpetuated a romantic emplotment of the revolution against elite attempts to adhere to the comic storyline. A more complicated rhetorical situation emerged when rank-and-file supporters of OF and VPN sought to democratise these movements themselves. The founders of these civic associations in Prague, Bratislava and other cities were essentially self-chosen; when it became clear that OF and VPN would continue into 1990, the question arose as to whether the coordinating councils really represented all those in whose names they claimed to speak. In some localities votes were held to decide this question, but elsewhere – particularly in Prague and Bratislava – the established leaders resisted opening council membership to district representatives. Justifying such a stance in movements that claimed to champion democracy was obviously a challenge, which leaders surmounted in this case by invoking the revolutionary principle. 'Are we a democratic or a revolutionary institution?' asked OF Council member Václav Benda, arguing against regional representation. 'I am for the revolutionary'.[55] Even as OF and VPN leaders tried to set the terms of debate in other modes, they could not help falling back on the language of revolution.

As elections approached, a variety of circumstances pushed new elites to adopt even more overtly romantic rhetoric. First was the inability to resolve the question of Communist property in a timely manner, and the resulting fear that the party's extensive assets would give it an electoral advantage.[56] Both OF and VPN took to portraying Communists as devils and emphasising the Party's responsibility for all the problems that Czechoslovakia faced. To foster a sense of an all-or-nothing struggle against 'dark forces', they highlighted examples of provincial Communists who vowed retribution against OF and VPN supporters should the Party win.[57] While in a consolidated democracy such representations might seem primarily satirical, in a society where daily citizens were demonstrating and signing petitions for the Communist Party to be outlawed, the romantic element cannot be ignored.[58] Inability to push reforms through parliament or the government was a second romanticising catalyst. The public loudly demanded a definitive solution to the *nomenklatura* problem in workplaces, a transparent dismantling of the secret police apparatus, and concrete proposals for economic reform; OF and VPN accordingly petitioned parliament and the government for action, but with minimal success.[59] The civic movements could retain their credibility only by blaming the Communists. A final factor was what might be called a 'great fear' of the secret police, intensified when the parliamentary commission investigating 17 November suggested that the secret police had partially prepared the massacre. The people demanded lustration of candidates for political office as a means of stamping out the possibility of such conspiracy in the future, and, reluctantly, OF and VPN agreed. Far away now was the idea of 'national understanding' that would include all Czechoslovaks; to the extent that people still adhered to 'the tradition of November', they saw it as a quest.[60]

By the time of the federal and republican elections in June 1990, all attempts at a comic resolution of the revolutionary narrative had been abandoned. In the face of what was increasingly being called 'gentle stagnation', popular antipathy towards the blocking characters mounted, whether these characters were identified with Communists, the secret police or Pragocentrists. Despite the acuteness of social, political, economic and ecological problems, however, people remained largely optimistic that now they would finally be solved – that a freely elected government would be able to accomplish what the 'Government of National Understanding', with its only partially reconstituted parliament, had been unable to do.[61] Alexander Dubček therefore compared the resounding electoral victory of OF, VPN and non-Communist parties to the dismantling of the Bastille.[62] It was a decidedly romantic interpretation of unfolding history.

Revolution as Tragedy

> People still believe in the effectiveness of politics rather than trusting themselves to the impersonal mechanism of the market. To correct this, we need a much deeper revolution than that which occurred after 17 November, a revolution that won't be visible on squares and mass demonstrations, but which will take place inside all of us, which will take much longer, the results of which will long be binding.
>
> Václav Klaus, September 1990[63]

The tragic frame is prompted by failure to achieve transcendence. Belief in the possibility of transcendence is a characteristic that romance and tragedy share, but while romance can attribute failure only to a diabolical antagonist, tragedy is more introspective, asking what flaw of the protagonist's may have contributed to his fall.[64] Given its concern with identifying the *causes* of failure, together with its implicit faith in the possibility of transcendence, tragedy lends itself to radical political programmes.[65] By determining what caused catastrophe in the first instance, witnesses stand a better chance of avoiding it in the second. Tragedy was therefore the emplotment of choice for Czechoslovaks who revolted against the revolution's prevailing course in order to promote a more radical one.

Parliament's post-election decision to go on a two-month vacation precipitated a sharp decline in OF's and VPN's popularity. Everywhere citizens complained of continuing uncertainty about what economic reforms the government would introduce, together with growing doubts about the future of the federation. More loudly, they protested that the 'red aristocracy' remaining in local leadership positions was taking advantage of the uncertainty to steal public property, and that employees who protested were being fired or otherwise persecuted.[66] No one responsible for the November massacre had yet been punished. People began to suggest that nothing had changed since November, or even that matters were worse. Responding to public pressure, district OFs and VPNs issued a string of appeals for radical action, all of which met with the indifference or antagonism of the centres.[67] When, amidst this crisis, parliament went on vacation, people asked how OF and VPN could allow it. Who had won the elections, after all?[68]

The mood at Civic Forum's August convention was imbued with this sense of crisis. 'How dare the government and National Council take vacations when so much urgently needs to be done!' inflamed Bohumil Kubát, the Czech Republic's agriculture minister. 'Let us ask ourselves the basic question, is the outcome of our revolution reversible? I believe that it is, very easily ... We can't continue to use the same methods, when our opponent uses illegal ones. We've lost much time and must stop fighting amongst ourselves. We can't let our movement be debilitated – it would be our absolute end.' The delegates agreed that disunity within their own ranks was a tragic flaw. Some more specifically criticised 'humanitarian' and 'legalistic' policies advocated by Dagmar Burešová (Chairwoman of the Czech National Council) and Petr Pithart (now Czech Premier), which had blocked the punishment of 17 November culprits. A delegate from Chrudim lashed out against Pithart for condemning OF Hodonín's initiative to compile a list of all *nomenklatura* occupying directorships in that district. 'Our mafians walk the street and laugh in our faces, [asking] "what do you want? After all, your premier protects us!"' While Pithart and other leading figures defended their positions, the delegates generally agreed that the revolution had been too 'velvety', and that some kind of radicalisation was in order.[69]

District representatives, having daily contact with problems at the grass-roots level, came ever more acutely to believe that OF's Prague-based leaders were out of touch; already maddened by the centre's resistance to internal democratisation, these representatives grew ever more radical. Václav Klaus – who, unlike his colleagues, did not go on vacation, but travelled throughout the districts, establishing rapport with local leaders – portrayed the difference between Prague and the districts as one between an incompetent, intellectual and moderate 'Left' and a pragmatic, radical

'Right'.[70] Most district representatives, desperate for a solution to their increasing powerlessness and isolation, found this interpretation of OF's tragic flaw inspiring. They therefore voted decisively at the October republican convention to make Klaus their chairman.[71] Klaus proceeded to expel from OF political sub-groupings that had 'departed from OF's political line', and began the process of transforming OF into a 'right-wing' party.[72] While some lamented the passing of OF's original identity as a forum for all citizens, casting the event in a tragic light, others found in Klaus's election an escape from tragedy and embarked on a new romance.[73] 'The Left, with its vague humanism, led society to demoralising and stagnant scepticism,' wrote one student journalist. Klaus's election, however, marked 'the second revolution', the 'real revolution', from which could be expected 'the definitive completion of systemic changes begun almost a year ago'.[74] In February 1991 OF would split officially into a Civic Democratic Party (ODS), led by Klaus and enjoying great popularity among Czech voters, and a Civic Movement (OH), destined for oblivion.

A sense that the revolution had taken a tragic turn similarly rocked VPN. At its September 1990 convention, the outgoing chairman, Ján Budaj, observed that 'people are returning to the apathy and cynicism that served them so well in previous decades. With respect to the people, we face the same atmosphere that existed before 17 November'.[75] The Slovak premier, Vladimír Mečiar, opined that 'No one in Slovakia but VPN has a realistic economic programme, but we don't know how to sell it. We don't know how to impart our perspective to the public and present ourselves as a movement that realises the national interest'.[76] Delegates pointed out specific problems which they claimed contributed to the public's loss of faith – notably lustration scandals and the *nomenklatura*'s growing power – and complained that formation of VPN policy was excessively concentrated among Bratislava elites. VPN leaders dismissed these criticisms as 'natural' and 'emotional', leaving discontent to simmer in the coming weeks.[77] 'Is it good or bad that "we are not like them"?' district leaders began to ask, referring to a distinction made in 1989 between 'the people' and the Communists.[78] 'Today we can be embarrassed only by the fact that we haven't sufficiently taken up the Jacobin movement as a great, optimistic revolutionary tradition of our past'.[79]

A step in this direction was taken when the Trnava district committee called a working meeting of district representatives without informing central VPN organs. This meeting, held on 20 October, sharply criticised the centre for: its lack of anti-Communism, allowing for the survival of 'old structures'; a defensive posture with regard to VPN's national dimension; lack of attention to the social consequences of economic reform; and resistance to internal democracy. Delegates demanded reconstruction of central VPN organs and expressed full support for Mečiar and his government, which they saw as a counterweight to VPN's coordinating committee.[80] Juraj Flamik, chairman of that body, condemned the Trnava Initiative as 'conspiratorial'.[81] Following another convention in February 1991, where motions to make VPN chairmanship elective did not carry, district representatives again acted independently to establish 'VPN-For a Democratic Slovakia' (VPN-ZDS), claiming to defend the movement's 'original platform' and condemning the policies and practices of 'certain leading figures' in VPN.[82] At a VPN-ZDS meeting in March, Mečiar claimed that 'the central leadership ... has betrayed part of the sense of the revolution.' He criticised the centre for closing workplace branches and for being out of touch with the people on social and national policy, and proposed a new type of organisation, where districts would 'transmit the will of the people, not follow orders from a centre'.[83] In April ZDS would officially split from VPN, becoming the Movement for a Democratic Slovakia (HZDS) and Slovakia's most popular political formation. In VPN, as in OF, tragic perception provided the necessary basis for a new romantic endeavour.

Tragic interpretations also came to dominate among the group that had started the revolution: the students. In Bratislava, students greeted the first anniversary of 17 November with an appeal to 'defend democracy', warning that 'the Nation' was becoming 'a manipulated mass in the hands of new Leaders'.[84] Students and other civic groups organised a public commemoration of 17 November under the banner 'humanity, decency, tolerance', but symptomatically nationalists usurped it, turning Bratislava's central square into a site of conflict. In Prague, students observed the anniversary by officially refusing to celebrate it, arguing that basic demands from the previous year remained unfulfilled. 'There is no longer reason to call our revolution "velvet"', they proclaimed. 'Rather, it is a *stolen* revolution!' The tragic flaw responsible for this was, first, 'our lack of follow-through and that of our leaders, who are for the most part sinking in self-satisfaction, complacency, and dangerous softness', and second, the politics of compromise and 'sad experience with left-wing ideas, which take society to be an irresponsible, nameless herd'. The students presented the President and government with thirteen demands, ranging from purges of state institutions to a rigorous transition to a market economy, and repeated their call from the previous year for a thorough investigation of the events of 17 November and punishment of the massacre's perpetrators. The students appealed to the public to abandon flaws that had brought a state of universal disappointment, mistrust, unease and tension, calling on citizens to 'Join us, and we will create a common strength... [T]he voice of the majority will become the genuine expression of the will of the people.' 'We want to become an inspired society,' they entreated, which would live in synergy with 'that force or thought, which exists like a mysterious order over all our earthly life'.[85] Nothing came of the appeal.[86]

Revolution as Satire

There was no revolution in Czechoslovakia in November 1989, because a revolution would have brought new institutions and new ideas to power. But if we want to call it a revolution, then we have to add that that revolution, from inexperience, committed suicide.

Jan Urban, November 1992[87]

Irony is a name given to both a trope (which can be used for effect in any of the generic plots) and a distinct plot structure. Satire is the militant form of ironic emplotment.[88] The central theme here is the disappearance of the heroic. While tragedy is still concerned with the hero's failings, the ironic plot allots virtually no freedom to the hero, and seeks explanations (if any) only in social structures. '*Sparagmos*, or the sense that heroism and effective action are absent, disorganized, and foredoomed to defeat and that confusion and anarchy reign over the world, is the archetypal theme of irony and satire'.[89] Irony destroys all faith in both the ideal good of man and any quest for transcendence; extreme irony raises fatalism to the level of metaphysical belief.

We have already encountered irony as a trope in such formulations as 'gentle stagnation', or when students drew attention to the fact that their 1990 demands repeated those of 1989. None of these expressions, as yet, were components of ironic emplotments because their authors still attributed agency to the people, suggesting that it was possible to learn from errors and correct them. The growing use of irony was natural, however, because the tragic hero's 'fall is involved both with a sense of his relation to society and with a sense of the supremacy of natural law, both of which are ironic in reference'.[90]

In satirical emplotments, human agency is an illusion and political action is therefore pointless, a view which tends to support a conservative, even reactionary stance. The quintessential satires of the Gentle Revolution are those that interpret it as a conspiracy, drawing attention not only to the thesis that the secret police orchestrated the revolution, but to the folly of ordinary people for thinking their engagement in the revolution could possibly have been meaningful. Such interpretations began to appear in the spring of 1990, following the 17 November commission's reports on secret police involvement, and they grew to a flood with the emergence of a tabloid press in October 1990.[91] More poignant than satirical interpretations in the gutter press, however, was militant irony among individuals who had previously identified themselves as protagonists of the revolution. While some students on the first anniversary desperately attempted to recapture lost transcendence, others insisted that there had been no revolution, and mocked people who naively thought otherwise. One student journalist condemned Charles University's plan to erect a monument to the students at the spot where their 17 November demonstration had begun, arguing that 'it is clear today that the "hegemon" of our "revolution" was already on 16 November the highest bosses of the Interior Ministry and State Security'.[92] Following the demise of OF and VPN in 1991, former activists in these associations also began to articulate satirical versions of the 'revolution', invoking ostensibly objective definitions of the term rather than the metaphors that had dominated in 1989. 'We're lying to ourselves,' said one former member of OF's executive council. 'Revolution, as every little child knows, is an upheaval, often violent – something that interrupts continuity and liquidates the old system. This, however, played no role in what happened in November and in what we took particular pride in thereafter: velvetiness and legal continuity'.[93] Jan Urban, who had been OF's chief spokesman from March to June 1990, not only denied in 1992 that any revolution had occurred, but questioned whether what had happened possessed any meaning at all.[94]

If the transition to a emplotment marked a revolt against romantic conceptions of revolution, the transition to satire marked a revolt against the idea of revolution itself. In Czech discourse the events of 1989 are now widely referred to as a *převrat* (upheaval), or 'the so-called revolution'. Even the Civic Forum Foundation, established in 1989 as an institution that continues to support Czech culture, speaks of the revolution in its brochures as 'the November events'; and *Lidové noviny*, an originally *samizdat* newspaper that the revolution made one of the Czech Republic's best-selling dailies, commemorated the fifteenth anniversary of 17 November with a cartoon depicting the revolution as nothing but a conspiracy between Havel and the Communists.[95] Slovak discourse is perceptibly less ironic, with 'Gentle Revolution' remaining the standard name for the events of 1989 both in the media and in popular discourse, but militant irony is a powerful undercurrent there as well.

Conclusion

At various junctures in their revolution, Czechoslovaks revolted either against particular aspects of revolution or against the course they saw the revolution taking. Proponents of the romantic interpretation, with their concern for transcendence, revolted against a revolutionary tradition they saw as bloody and self-destructive. Advocates of the comic interpretation revolted against the revolutionary enthusiasm of the romantics, fearing its latent anarchy and seeking as quickly as possible to end the revolution. Bards of the tragic interpretation revolted against directions in which they saw the revolution heading – directions which they perceived to be leading to disastrous, or at least undesirable, results. Sages of the ironic interpretation, finally, revolted against the idea that there had ever been a revolution. Each new emplotment served as a blueprint for its appurtenant revolt, a map of action or inaction that ultimately served political or moral purposes.

Was there a revolution in Czechoslovakia in 1989? The answer to this question depends largely on how the 'facts' of history are narrated. Narrations, by their very structure, carry political implications, such that they not only reflect reality, but also create it. There are no objective reasons for choosing one plot structure over another; the choice is fundamentally moral. Consequently, it is less interesting that 'the events of 1989' fit or break any particular definition of revolution, as that Czechoslovaks – to an extent and for a time – experienced these events as revolution. They were neither more nor less justified in doing so than the seventeenth-century Europeans who first compared complex sociopolitical upheavals in their countries to the circular motions of the heavens.[96]

Notes

1. Lynn Hunt, *Politics, Culture, and Class in the French Revolution* (Berkeley, CA, 1984), pp. 34–8; Northrop Frye, *The Anatomy of Criticism: Four Essays* (Princeton, NJ, 1957).
2. Quoted in Tomáš Drábek, 'Amerika pláče', *Přetlak*, no. 26 (27 December 1989), p. 3.
3. Some Slovak students later dated the revolution from 16 November 1989, when Bratislava students had demonstrated for higher education reform. This demonstration had neither been suppressed nor had it engendered mass mobilisation, and this interpretation of the revolution's beginnings was very much *ex post facto*. In the beginning, all Slovak students cited the events of 17 November as the reason for their strikes.
4. 'Byla jsem 17. listopadu na Albertově, Vyšehradě a na Národní třídě', Prague, 19 November 1989 (Štátny archív v Bytči, pobočka Považská Bystrica (hereafter PX), súčasná dokumentácia, folder 'Nežná revolúcia – 1989').
5. Radim and Jakub Kalivoda, 'Svědectví' (Státní okresní archiv Louny (hereafter LN), fond 569 'Sbírka dokumentů k 17.11.1989-30.11.1990 v Lounech', box 1, folder 11 '17.11.1989 – svědectví přímých účastníků událostí v Praze').
6. 'Svědectví účastníků' (Archiv města Ostravy, soudobá dokumentace, box 'Revolution [*sic*] 1989. Materiály 1989–90').
7. 'Svědectví' (Státní okresní archiv Kolín, sbírka 1989), p. 2.
8. Frye, *The Anatomy*, p. 33.
9. '17. listopad' (PX, súčasná dokumentácia, folder 'Nežná revolúcia – 1989').
10. Jiří Ceral in Milan Otáhal and Miroslav Vaněk, *Sto studentských revolucí: Studenti v období pádu komunismu* (Prague, 1999), p. 245.
11. Marek Benda et al., *Studenti psali revoluce* (Prague, 1990), p. 31.
12. 'Prohlášení studentů pražských VŠ', Prague, 18 November 1989, in Milan Otáhal and Zdeněk Sládek (eds), *Deset pražských dnů (17.-27. listopad 1989): Dokumentace* (Prague, 1990), p. 32.
13. The English-language literature often mistakenly presents VPN's founding as dependent on and subsequent to OF's. For accurate accounts, see Ingrid Antalová (ed.), *Verejnosť proti násiliu 1989–1991: Svedectvá a dokumenty* (Bratislava, 1998), pp. 22–34; and Jiří Suk, *Občanské fórum: Listopad-prosinec 1989*, vol. 1: *Události* (Brno, 1997), pp. 47–8.
14. 'Na setkání v hledišti … ', Prague, 19 November 1989, in Otáhal and Sládek (eds), *Deset pražských dnů*, pp. 47–8; and 'Stanovisko združenia Verejnosť proti násiliu … ', Bratislava, 21 November 1989, in Ľubomír Feldek (ed.), *Keď sme brali do rúk budúcnosť* (Bratislava, 1990), pp. 14–15.
15. Petr Holubec (ed.), *Kronika sametové revoluce* (Prague, 1990), p. 18.
16. Hayden White, *Metahistory: The Historical Imagination in Nineteenth-Century Europe* (Baltimore, MD, 1973), p. 8.

17. See, for example, 'Pane premiére, žasneme!' and Boris Pentějelev, 'Občané, my všichni jsme se narodili 17. listopadu 1989' (private collection of Lenka Wünschová, Olomouc); 'Svatý Václav drží koně' (Státní okresní archiv Trutnov, fond 'Občanské fórum v Trutnově', box 2); 'Jede se do Prahy', *Přetlak*, no. 18 (15 December 1989), p. 1; Milan Hanuš, 'Ples národního porozumění', *Přetlak*, no. 28 (2 January 1990), p. 3; *Jiskra* (Český Krumlov), 22 December 1989, p. 2; and posters in the Historical Museum of Slovakia's National Museum in Bratislava. The seal of the Professional Union of Students, as printed in the header of every issue of *Informační bulletin celostátního koordinačního výboru vysokých škol*, represented students as knights.

18. Bohuslav Blažek, 'Výraz nové civilizace', Prague, 29 November 1989 (LN, fond 569, box 2).

19. See, for example, Verejnosť proti násiliu and Študentské hnutie, *Nežná revolúcia* (Bratislava, 1990), sound recording.

20. Milan Hanuš, 'Happening', *Přetlak*, no. 9 (5 December 1989), p. 8.

21. Holubec (ed.), *Kronika*, p. 2; and 'Pracující ŠS Stupice!', Stupice, 22 November 1989 (Ústav pro soudobé dějiny, Prague (hereafter ÚSD), archiv KC OF, box '22.11.').

22. 'Nežná revolúcia', or 'něžná revoluce', has also been translated into English as 'Tender Revolution'.

23. Jan Měchýř, *Velký převrat či snad revoluce sametová? Několik informací, poznámek a komentářů o naší takřečené něžné revoluci a jejich osudech (1989– 1992)* (Prague, 1999), p. 13. Though the term 'Velvet Revolution' entered Slovak discourse, it never supplanted 'Gentle Revolution'.

24. 1789 (France) was by far the most common reference in the romantic interpretation of the revolution. Advocates of the comic interpretation cited 1787 (America) as an example to emulate, and 1792 (France) or 1948 (Czechoslovakia) as examples to avoid.

25. Josef Jařab, 'Nedělní zamyšlení', *Přetlak*, no. 21 (18 December 1989), p. 3.

26. White, *Metahistory*, p. 29.

27. Jiří Suk (ed.), *Občanské fórum: Listopad-prosinec 1989*, vol. 2: *Dokumenty* (Brno, 1998), p. 245.

28. Frye, *The Anatomy*, p. 165.

29. *Svobodné slovo*, 27 November 1989, p. 1. Emphasis added.

30. Jiří Suk, *Labyrintem revoluce: Aktéři, zápletky a křížovatky jedné politické krize (od listopadu 1989 do června 1990)* (Prague, 2003), p. 46.

31. Ibid., pp. 57–8.

32. 'Nepřehlédněte!', *Přetlak*, no. 8 (4 December 1989), p. 10.

33. Suk, *Labyrintem*, pp. 155–6.

34. Suk (ed.), *Občanské fórum*, vol. 2, p. 245.

35. We still do not know exactly what Čalfa said to deputies; thus far he has only confessed to being 'really very brutal'. Suk, *Labyrintem*, pp. 200–1, 216–7, 225–7.

36. The formerly puppet parties had lobbied from the beginning for a genuine round table where each party would have the same weight. OF consented to this on 11 December, three days after the 'Oblong Table' meeting. Ibid., pp. 214–15.

37. 'Komuniké k volbě prezidenta', *InForum*, no. 5 (29 December 1989), p. 1.

38. Hanuš, 'Ples'. Similar celebrations took place outside Prague; see, for example, 'Prehľad činnosti VPN v Púchove' (PX, súčasná dokumentácia, folder 'Nežná revolúcia – 1989').

39. See Mona Ozouf, *Festivals and the French Revolution*, trans. by Alan Sheridan (Cambridge, MA, 1988), p. 42.

40. He later reiterated this ambivalence. See Suk (ed.), *Občanské fórum*, vol. 2, pp. 202, 244.

41. 'Vážení přátelé', *Informační bulletin celostátního koordinačního výboru vysokých škol*, no. 0 (15 January 1990), p. 1.

42. See, for example, *Hornonitrianska verejnosť* (Prievidza), 15 March 1990, p. 1, and 22 March 1990, p. 1.

43. Antalová (ed.), *Verejnosť proti násiliu*, p. 42; Petr Pithart, 'Projev P. Pitharta v čs. tevizi [*sic*]', *InForum*, no. 11 (23 January 1990), p. 2; and Suk, *Labyrintem*, p. 298.

44. *Hornonitrianska verejnosť*, 8 March 1990, p. 4; and Pithart, 'Projev', pp. 1–2.

45. Pithart, 'Projev', pp. 2–3. For the Slovak translation, see 'Je to revolúcia?', *Telefax VPN*, no. 1 (2 March 1990), pp. 1–3.

46. Milan Kňažko, 'Vážení priatelia, čas revolúcie na uliciach … ', January 1990 (PX, súčasná dokumentácia, folder 'Nežná revolúcia – 1989').

47. Bohumil Pečinka, 'Skutečná revoluce', *Studentské listy*, vol. 1, no. 20 (November 1990), p. 2.

48. Antalová (ed.), *Verejnosť proti násiliu*, p. 108.

49. 'Programové vyhlásenie občianskej iniciatívy Verejnosť proti násiliu a Koordinačného výboru slovenských vysokoškolákov', Bratislava, 25 November 1989, in Feldek (ed.), *Keď sme brali*, p. 35; and Miroslav Richter, 'Provolání Moravského občanského hnutí ze dne 20.11.1989', Brno (Státní okresní archiv Uherské Hradiště, sbírka nezpracovaných materiálů, box 7, folder 'Letáky a plakáty všeobecné').

50. For more on the hyphen war, see Milan Šútovec, *Semióza ako politikum alebo 'Pomlčková vojna': Niektoré historické, politické a iné súvislosti jedného sporu, ktorý bol na začiatku zániku česko-slovenského štátu* (Bratislava, 1999).

51. *Hornonitrianska verejnosť*, 12 April 1990, p. 1.

52. Suk, *Labyrintem*, p. 186.

53. Minutes of the '0th' republic-wide OF convention (ÚSD, archiv KC OF, 'OF – interní písemnosti: Sněmy OF', box 1, folder 'Nultý sněm OF (16.12.1989): Setkání zástupců krajských a okresních OF'); and 'Rozhovor s panem Pithartem, tiskovým mluvčím OF a panem Kotrlým, členem koordinačního centra OF', *Přetlak*, no. 28 (2 January 1990), p. 4.

54. 'Komuniké', *Telefax VPN*, no. 5 (3 April 1990), p. 1.

55. Suk, *Labyrintem*, p. 306.

56. 'Zápis ze sněmu OF dne 31.3.1990' (ÚSD, archiv KC OF, 'OF – interní písemnosti: Sněmy OF', box 1, folder 'Sněmy OF: 31.3.1990', p. 4).

57. See, for example, *Občanský deník*, 26 May 1990, p. 2; *Občanský deník*, 1 June 1990, p. 2; and *Telefax VPN*, no. 8 (25 April 1990), p. 8.

58. See Suk, *Labyrintem*, pp. 397–8.

59. 'Zápis ze sněmu OF dne 31.3.1990', p. 11.

60. *Občanský deník*, 24 May 1990, p. 3.

61. *Fórum*, 11 July 1990, p. 6.

62. Alexander Dubček, 'Dobyli sme Bastilu', *Telefax VPN*, nos 16/17 (20 June 1990), p. 5.

63. *Akcia* (Košice), 1 October 1990, p. 3.

64. Frye, *The Anatomy*, pp. 210–2.

65. White, *Metahistory*, p. 29.

66. For examples, see *Nitrianska verejnosť*, 6 September 1990, pp. 1–3.

67. *Respekt*, 22 August 1990, p. 2.

68. *Fórum*, 29 August 1990, p. 12.

69. 'Zápis ze Sněmu OF dne 18.8.1990' (ÚSD, archiv KC OF, 'OF – interní písemnosti: Sněmy OF', box 2, folder 'Sněmy OF: 18.8.1990'), pp. 5–6, 8–9; and Vladimír Šuman, 'Postupovat radikálněji', *InForum*, no. 36 (21 August 1990), pp. 7–8.

70. See Suk, *Labyrintem*, p. 459.

71. The other candidate, Martin Palouš, received only 31 per cent of the votes. 'Sněm OF', *InForum*, no. 44 (17 October 1990), p. 1.

72. Měchýř, *Velký převrat*, p. 212; see also *Fórum*, 14 November 1990, p. 2.

73. *Fórum*, 17 October 1990, p. 2.

74. Pečinka, 'Skutečná revoluce', p. 2.

75. *Akcia*, 1 October 1990, p. 1.

76 Vladimír Mečiar, 'Prispôsobiť sa novým požiadavkám', *Telefax VPN*, no. 20 (19 September 1990), p. 6.

77. 'Stretnutia s médiami', *Telefax VPN*, no. 21 (21 September 1990), p. 3.

78. *Akcia*, 20 October 1990, p. 6.

79. *Akcia*, 15 October 1990, p. 8.

80. 'Závery', *Telefax VPN*, no. 24 (24 October 1990), p. 3.

81. Juraj Flamik, 'Stanovisko k stretnutiu v Trnave', ibid., p. 3. VPN had one chairman for its coordinating committee and another for the organisation as a whole. It is worth noting that neither was elected by republic-wide assemblies, as was the case with OF after October.

82. 'Vyhlásenie zástupcov OR VPN pri konštituovaní pôvodnej platformy VPN zo dňa 5.3.1991 v Bratislave' (Štátny archív v Bratislave, pobočka Trenčín, box 'ODS-Slovensko 1992 / VPN okr. TN 1990, 1991', folder 'VPN').

83. Vladimír Mečiar, 'Aby ľudia mali komu veriť (Vystúpenie Vladimíra Mečiara na stretnutí PZDS v Martine dňa 23.3.1991)', *Telefax VPN*, no. 4 (26 March 1991), p. 6.

84. 'Iniciatíva na obranu demokracie: Vyhlásenie členov novembrového Koordinačného výboru vysokých škôl Slovenska', Bratislava, 28 October 1990, in *Echo*, vol. 1, no. 10, p. 1.

85. 'Provolání VŠ studentů k vyročí 17. listopadu', *Studentské listy*, vol. 1, special issue (Autumn 1990), pp. 1–2. Emphasis added.

86. Bohuslav Fic, 'Ke druhému výročí 17. listopadu', *Studentské listy*, vol. 2, no. 23 (November 1991), p. 5; and Jan Kavan and Libor Konvička, 'Youth Movements and the Velvet Revolution', *Communist and Post-Communist Studies*, vol. 27, no. 2 (1994), p. 168.

87. Jan Urban, 'Bezmocnost mocných', *Listy*, vol. 23, no. 5 (1993), p. 7.

88. Frye, *The Anatomy*, p. 223.

89. Ibid., p. 192.

90. Ibid., p. 37.

91. See *Fórum*, 12 December 1990, p. 3; and Měchýř, *Velký převrat*, p. 213.

92. Martin Bartůněk, 'Mládí vpřed!', *Studentské listy*, vol. 1, special issue (Autumn 1990), p. 2.

93. Pavla Grünthalová, 'Requiem za 17. listopad: Rozhovor s Pavlem Naumannem', *Ty rudá krávo*, no. 27 (1992), p. 5.

94. Urban, 'Bezmocnost', p. 3.

95. *Lidové noviny*, 15 November 2004, p. 12.

96. See Ilan Rachum, 'The Meaning of "Revolution" in the English Revolution (1648–1660)', *Journal of the History of Ideas*, vol. 56, no. 2 (1973), pp. 30–8.

–11–

Afterword: East or West?
Tony Kemp-Welch

The editors may have hoped for a concluding taxonomy of revolution in Eastern Europe. But I cannot improve on their typology of national communism, intellectual dissent, armed rural resistance and popular protest. Moreover, the chapters that follow their introduction tell the stories for differing countries with too much skill and admirable archival scholarship for a neater overview. So, accepting the broad categorisation on which the book is based, I will take up the question underlying most contributions: What was the changing role of the Soviet Union? and add one of my own: Did Western policy have any real impact on it?

Stalin's policy towards post-war Eastern Europe was simple. He sought secure borders in the West, through which Russia had been invaded twice in a generation. The military imperative for a protective glacis between itself and a resurgent Germany was provided by the territories held under Red Army occupation from 1944. A second objective of Soviet policy in Eastern Europe was less forced. In Moscow's view, Germany had caused the war and should pay for it. Its zone of occupation should be used to speed Soviet economic recovery. Thus East Germany was stripped of industrial assets, which were transported and reassembled in the Urals. A similar attitude was taken to all new allies: Polish coal was compulsorily delivered to the Soviet Union at a tenth of the price paid by Denmark, and Czechoslovak uranium sent east at a fraction of world prices. It did not require great sophistication to understand such exploitation. Beneath the soothing parlance of 'People's Democracies', Eastern European states were being used as colonies by the Soviet Empire. I agree with Peter Grieder's description of the eventual retreat as 'decolonisation' and will argue later that it took place as part of a general rethink during the 1980s.

To the United States, the post-war goal was European economic recovery in the shortest possible period. Since this was impossible without Germany, the American approach entailed a readiness to forgive (or overlook) past culpabilities, and the speedy involvement of all 'rational' parties in a reconstruction programme. This process would require supervision, which meant putting the United States into the balance of power in Europe permanently, and backing it by the threat of nuclear war. At the same time, the USSR was excluded from any role in post-war Western Europe. By the early 1950s, however, the Soviet Union had achieved comparable nuclear status, changing the rules of the game.

The rhetoric of 'roll-back' was obsolete and dangerous once the Soviet Union had the capacity to retaliate. It was quietly dropped. A cultural Cold War continued with the loud – and to the Soviet Union inflammatory – broadcasts of Radio Liberty and Radio Free Europe, but finding wider political alternatives proved problematic. Scholars started to recognise that notions of security 'depend as much on a state of mind as on physical evidence, in any situation where there is no actual aggression'.[1] So far as they relate to the social and psychological imbalances that military deployment seeks to redress, this suggested a fresh look at Soviet intentions. Was the Soviet Union driven by 'Riga Axioms', a messianic drive for world mastery, or by 'Yalta Axioms', jockeying for position within a traditional Great Power system?[2]

The Stalinist pattern of development, strictly enforced from 1948, insisted that the allies must all follow the Soviet 'model'. This did bring some to the first stages of industrialisation. Yet there were rigidities: Hungary, devoid of iron ore and coal, had to have a steel mill (at Sztálinváros). Such absurdities did nothing to reduce anti-Soviet sentiments. Social protests in Eastern Europe were endemic after the demise of Stalin. Matthew Stibbe documents those in East Germany in 1953, and Johanna Granville those in Poland and Hungary in 1956. While government officials always sought to portray such outbursts as exceptional upsets to the status quo, the contrary can be suggested. As Jan Gross puts it, crises are the moments of normality when the false façade of 'unanimity' is torn off, exposing the contesting parties as they really are.[3] Even when not suppressed by force, they necessitated regular emergency supplies or credits from Moscow.

The Warsaw Pact, founded in 1955, did not necessarily pose a threat to countries not under its hegemony. This 'dovish' argument was given support by the Soviet Communist Party's Twentieth Congress in February 1956. Lenin's theory of imperialism was dropped. The final victory of communism, though still assured, would not now be reached as the successful outcome of a world war, since that would result only in mutual destruction. But where did this leave the 'great contest' between rival systems? Would this doctrinal revision usher in a long duration of peaceful competition, a contest that each side, assured of the superiority of its own system, expected to win? Or might the East revert to the military option? Under the guise of coexistence, the Soviet side might continue to arm for a final conflict. This possibility required the West to remain both patient and vigilant. It was a very long wait.

The delay was compounded by the Soviet-led invasion of Czechoslovakia in August 1968. NATO had accepted Moscow's reassurances that the invasion posed no threat to them. There was not even a general alert. US forces in Europe were pulled back some 200 kilometres. All those Dubček met in Washington much later praised his calmness in face of the invasion, and mentioned that any other response 'would have posed a danger, and a danger not only for you, but one that could have meant a catastrophe for all of Europe and ultimately, perhaps, for the whole world'.[4] Yet for home consumption, the Soviet Union had argued the opposite: that the invasion was to forestall Western 'revanchism', even informing incredulous Czechs that West German divisions were massing on their borders. The lessons of US passivity were not lost on Johnson's successors. Zbigniew Brzezinski, National Security Adviser under President Jimmy Carter, was determined that weakness in the White House should not be repeated in the crisis over Solidarity.

The invasion of Czechoslovakia did not cause a major international crisis, and at no point was there any likelihood that war would result. And yet it was a major crisis in the development of European society. For the first time, the Soviet Union, 'in collusion with other powers, acted as a deliberate aggressor without even the pretence of legality behind it'.[5] Unlike Hungarians in 1956, Czechs and Slovaks had remained loyal to the Warsaw Pact. A joint document, signed in Bratislava on 4 August 1968, affirmed the sovereignty of Czechoslovakia and the inviolability of its borders. Since this had been torn up three weeks later, the question arose whether the Soviet government could be trusted in international relations again.

Brezhnev's speech to the Polish Party's Fifth Congress in Warsaw in November 1968 elaborated alibis for the invasion. Though acknowledging that it had been 'an extraordinary step, dictated by necessity', he offered no justification for the use of military power and no basis either in international law. Instead, he clothed the unprovoked attack – which the recipients had said in advance they would not resist with force – within the broadest ideological framework. There was an inevitable struggle between the forces of socialism and imperialism, Brezhnev taught, which had reached a new stage. Having been held at bay by the threat of nuclear retaliation – which Khrushchev had recognised in 1956 would mean mutual annihilation – imperialism was up to new tricks. Czechoslovak state sovereignty, while still intact, had to take second place to the 'sacred duty' of acting on behalf of the socialist solidarity of the 'socialist commonwealth'.[6]

This argument was self-defining. The Warsaw Pact would invade (itself) wherever socialism was in danger: but the defining of danger, and of socialism, was done in Moscow. In 1956 the Hungarians had experienced the collapse of their Communist Party and had left the Warsaw Pact. It is argued that their neutrality was only declared after reports showed that a second Soviet invasion was in hand: it was a failed attempt to avert such intervention.[7] The Czechs and Slovaks had done neither, yet the outcome was just the same. It was thus difficult to see what conclusions could be drawn from 1968 about the limits, or otherwise, of Soviet military and political behaviour. The 'Brezhnev Doctrine' seemed a carte blanche for interventionism.

One answer was to offset the 'Brezhnev Doctrine' by addressing the Soviet Union's wider security needs. The Soviet leadership sought recognition as a global superpower. It hoped for rapid expansion of East–West trade to remedy the growing lag of Soviet technology in many spheres, though not rocketry. This prospect raised a host of other issues. Could Moscow be trusted as a partner in any deal? If the Soviet Union did settle down as a global superpower with the United States' active assistance, where did this leave Europe? Was it to be a permanent victim of bipolarity? Unexpectedly, there turned out to be more positive implications. While the Prague Spring had indicated the limits to internal change, it had also shown that the Eastern European societies were permeable. Despite realist international theory, they were not 'billiard balls', but consisted of real people, making genuine demands. How then could Western intentions and Eastern European aspirations be conjoined without giving the Soviet Union a pretext for further intervention?

The chosen instrument was détente. At the primary level, this meant arms control. In May 1971 Moscow agreed to Mutual Balanced Force Reduction (MBFR) talks on the military side; in December 1971 NATO accepted that a European Security Conference should be convened. Although MBFR discussions soon became embroiled in political controversies – from which they were not extricated until the late 1980s – talks about a conference proceeded more smoothly. Nixon's first administration sought an 'era of negotiations' to replace the previous policy of confrontation towards the Soviet Union. This meant, first, recognising that the Soviet Union had vital security interests in Eastern Europe, which the United States had no intention of undermining. Second, the countries of Eastern Europe were seen 'as sovereign, not as parts of a monolith'. Hence no doctrine was acceptable that sought to abridge their rights to seek 'reciprocal improvement of relations with us or others'.[8]

While this was primarily directed towards the Soviet Union's most recalcitrant satellite, Romania, and the already polycentric Yugoslavia – the new President visited both – there were wider implications. Proponents of second-level détente – in Europe – now saw an opportunity to mitigate one of its most unacceptable consequences: permanent division of the continent. Their hopes included an eventual reunification of Germany and a gradual reorientation of Poland away from the Soviet sphere. Of course, Poland could not (as wits suggested) change places with Spain or Portugal; long-standing boundaries between the blocs were not going to change overnight; nor were more recently constructed walls going to come tumbling down. However, there could be a policy shift from the strident rhetoric of anti-Sovietism to a subtler approach, drawing the Soviet Union into more constructive international relations, above all the maintenance of peace in Europe's volatile and highly militarised arena.

The Soviet Union, meanwhile, had dropped its objection to the USA and Canada attending the long-heralded Conference on Security and Cooperation in Europe (CSCE). Its implicit agenda, of excluding and eventually dissolving NATO, disappeared. And there was also a new openness in economic relations with the capitalist world. Brezhnev told business leaders in Washington in June 1973, that 'we have been a prisoner of old trends and to this day have not been able fully to break those fetters'.[9] Now, he assured them, the Soviet Union sought a new era, based on stability and permanence. It was marked by the signing of a mutually advantageous grain deal, to compensate for fluctuating Soviet harvests and the failures of its agriculture. The super-powers declared that international relations were to move from 'from confrontation to negotiation'.[10]

This charm offensive, which offered rich pickings for the West, convinced many of the sceptics. Even if this were a temporary manoeuvre by the Soviets, a cunning ruse to be reversed later, it was worth a try. As Brezhnev put it, 'To live in peace, we must trust each other, we must know each other better'.[11] It was quite widely believed that mutual self-interest, through bilateral trade, credits and even shared technology, would eventually lead to a convergence of the two systems. Revival of the 'end of ideology' thesis gave renewed impetus to détente. Foreign Ministers engaged in extensive final discussions from 1973, leading to a signing ceremony in July 1975. At Helsinki, the high representatives of the thirty-five participating states adopted a new set of principles on security in Europe. They started with sovereignty.

Signatories would refrain from the threat or use of force, except where allowed under the Charter of the United Nations. They would respect each other's 'sovereign equality' – leaving this tautology unexplained – and territorial integrity. There would be confidence-building measures, such as prior notification of military manoeuvres 'exceeding a total of 25,000 troops', and efforts would be made 'to complement political détente in Europe' with disarmament. Signatories would also allow free scope for others to choose their own 'political, social, economic and cultural systems'. Second, there should be cooperation in the field of economics, science and technology, and the environment (oceanography and glaciology were mentioned); and tourism should be promoted in a positive spirit, including 'the formalities required for such travel' (i.e. the issuance of passports and exit visas). Finally, in Basket Three, there was to be cooperation in 'Humanitarian and Other Fields'. This provided for meetings between and reunifications of families; marriages between citizens of different states; travel for personal or professional reasons; and 'Meetings among Young People'.[12]

Helsinki provided an unexpected argument for the nascent Eastern European opposition. It enabled citizens to address their authorities on principles to which they had adhered voluntarily: 'We are merely asking you to keep your international agreements'. Helsinki Monitoring Groups were founded by independently minded citizens in Moscow, Kiev, Tbilisi, Erevan and Vilnius. The Moscow Helsinki Committee prepared 26 documents for the Belgrade Review Conference in 1977, and dispatched 138 reports to the Madrid Review Conference two years later. However, all such groups were much persecuted by the authorities.

These initiatives found a counterpart in Romania, as Dennis Deletant shows, but drew inspiration from Prague, where the Czech Chartist, Jiří Hájek, wrote of the 'international of human rights' which had emerged through conventions since 1945. In particular, the advancement of human rights by the Helsinki process offered 'a conception of a pluralistic society of sovereign European states, differing in size and strength, but equal in rights, and acting in accord with agreed rules of behaviour'. He called for pressure from below, located in peace movements, to give Helsinki momentum, lest it degenerate into a routine diplomatic exercise, endangered by a renewed Cold War and 'the growing influence of the military-industrial complexes'.[13]

The election of 1976 brought to the White House a President, Carter, who sought a moral dimension to foreign policy. Republicans distanced themselves from what they saw as Carter's overzealous and counterproductive espousal of human rights. Their criticism has been reiterated in subsequent historiography. Yet normative foreign policy had much external resonance at the time. In the USSR, dissidents such as Andrei Sakharov considered resolute and sustained pressure from the West necessary. It was the only way to make communist governments respect their Helsinki undertakings on human rights.

In the summer of 1980 Poland erupted for the third time in a decade, this time through peaceful mass strikes and demonstrations. In its first public statement on the Gdańsk events, the US State Department considered current difficulties ones for 'the Polish people and the Polish authorities' to work out by themselves. A clarifying comment added that past US statements on behalf of 'rebel workers' had been counterproductive. Nothing should be done to show a 'red flag – or a trigger – to the Soviets'.[14] On 25 August, National Security Adviser Brzezinski urged the President to underline American interests in these developments through letters to Western European leaders. Their purpose was to initiate an exchange of views on Poland, 'so that a common Western policy would emerge'. They might also express American concern about possible Soviet intervention, though not to Moscow directly. Brzezinski included the Pope in this purview. At a private meeting in June 1980, he had found 'a man of extraordinary vision and political intelligence. In a sense, I think it is fair to say that today he is the outstanding Western leader'.[15]

US policy towards Poland was evolving rapidly. As usual, Washington was speaking in several voices. There was an intention to 'calm the Poles down' in order to stabilise the internal situation. In particular, the policy was to deter false hopes that an armed uprising in Poland would receive Western military assistance (on the lines of that given to Afghanistan). The Poles were to be given support to strengthen their resistance to 'Marxist-Leninist totalitarianism' and to help emancipate the region from Soviet hegemony. In the latter view, the Polish crisis which began in 1980 proved to be the 'last major, protracted Cold War battle in Europe, involving competition between the two super-powers over the international orientation and domestic system of one of the major nations of Europe'.[16] A corollary of this Washington analysis was that the Western European states, 'perceiving the Polish events as destabilizing and hopeless', distanced themselves from attempts to influence Soviet policy, thereby weakening the American ability to do so.[17]

Behind closed doors in Washington, the predominant view in September 1980 was 'the likelihood, [as] most people saw it, of Soviet military intervention, sooner or later, to crush the Polish reform movement'.[18] East European and Soviet specialists were mindful of the 1956 and 1968 precedents. While Poland (which had not been invaded since the war) was regarded as a more complex military target, from which resistance could be anticipated, so also was its strategic position more vital for the Soviet Union. 'The widely-held view was that the USSR would not hesitate for long before stamping out a threat to Polish Communist rule and its own hegemonic position'.[19]

Brzezinski personally thought that Moscow would give the Polish leaders time to attempt an internal resolution of their political crisis. But he had already called for a CIA report on the likelihood of, and possible preparations for, a Soviet invasion. A year earlier, President Carter had been widely criticized for not making public the accumulating evidence of the Soviet military action in Afghanistan. It was not a mistake his administration wished to repeat. While the US military made its estimates, Brzezinski was trying to put together a package to deter a Soviet invasion. Diplomatic deterrents were considered to include strong pressure from Western Europe, with the French President and German Chancellor seen as the significant figures. In the event, reliance on Chancellor Schmidt proved unfounded. He told a meeting of the four-power (QUAD) conference (with Britain, France and the United States) that détente should not become the victim of such a Soviet intervention. Should it take place, German relations with the USSR and its allies would be unimpaired. It would be business as usual. A dismayed Brzezinski remarks: 'This is the best proof yet of the increasing Finlandisation of the Germans'.[20] There was also reliance on Soviet fears of a Chinese reaction, especially if it led to closer US–Chinese military collaboration, which would enhance Moscow's phobia of 'encirclement'.

A third deterrent was 'strong Polish resistance to any invasion'. There was a CIA consensus that the Poles would fight, though it was not clear how organised such resistance would be. Tacit encouragement of Polish resistance might seem a risky strategy, leading to a war in central Europe, but the dangers of passivity were considered to be greater. The example of 1968 was considered minatory. The Johnson Administration had treated the potential Soviet invasion of Czechoslovakia as more or less a domestic affair. The effectiveness, or otherwise, of his subsequent rebuke to Moscow was to be reviewed, 'to see if it had any applicability to the current crisis'.[21]

However, by the early 1980s, a body of expert Soviet opinion began to think of ways to end the new Cold War. Domestically, they took the view that economic reform, though imperative, was not possible without a more far-reaching programme, known for short as *perestroika*. That, in turn, required a new form of international relations. Iurii Andropov, Brezhnev's successor, encouraged his East European analysts to speak off the record at weekly briefings. The intention was to promote blue-skies thinking unencumbered by written protocols which might later be held against them. Unfortunately, the position papers which they brought to the meetings remain deeply hidden in KGB archives.

Leonid Abalkin, head of the Institute of Economics in Moscow, assailed the 'mental inertia' which had sabotaged earlier reforms. Reform was risky and could 'change human conduct in an unpredictable way'. Hence 'people in the corridors of power started to lose their customary duties, while retaining their administrative mentality, [and] developed a phobia of becoming unwanted'.[22] The party rank-and-file endorsed these fears. Under the unreformed system they were protected by helping hands from above; radical change would be a voyage into the unknown. It would bring greater rights, but also greater responsibilities. The impact on Gorbachev of such sophisticated thinking resulted in the impact of Gorbachev on Eastern Europe.

Rational Soviet analysis suggested that the three main reasons for being in Eastern Europe had turned into their opposites. A sought-for security zone was chronically unstable. The areas of economic exploitation had become the reverse. It became apparent, especially after the Western energy crisis from 1973, that this was empire of a novel sort: the centre was subsidising the periphery. Finally, instead of endorsing and following the 'Soviet model', most East European states were incurably revisionist. The first split with Tito, ably analysed by Leonid Gibianskii, was followed by the Soviet-Yugoslav rapprochement after Stalin's death. National communism seemed thereby to be sanctioned.

Gorbachev buried the Brezhnev Doctrine at the autumn 1987 session of the UN General Assembly. Soviet troops were brought home from Afghanistan, a process completed by February 1989. The concomitant message to East European communist leaders was clear: make what compromises with your local populations that you need to stay in power; there will be no ultimate sanction of force to sustain your rule. It is an irony of history that the Eastern European leaders, even the few who were relatively young (with the possible exception of General Jaruzelski in Poland), missed the message. Given the golden opportunity to present themselves as national leaders, differentiated and freed from Moscow, they missed out and disappeared altogether. Their hesitation may have been through lack of imagination. It was also the product of experience: Gorbachev was a reformist leader, promising to underwrite dramatic changes. But would he last? If he did not, his Eastern European adherents would look vulnerable and probably be disposed of by Gorbachev's more orthodox successors.

We did not blow the planet up during the Cold War, though we came close, but neither did we live at peace. Cold War peculiarities were anticipated by Hobbes: 'as the nature of Foule weather lyeth not in a showre or two of rain; but in the inclination thereto of many dayes together: So that the nature of War, consisteth not in actuall fighting; but in the known disposition thereto, during all the time there is no assurance to the contrary. All other time is PEACE'.[23]

Notes

1. Robert Hunter, *Security in Europe* (London, 1969), p. 3.
2. Daniel Yergin, *Shattered Peace. The Origins of the Cold War and the National Security State* (London, 1980), pp. 10–11.

3. Jan Gross, 'Thirty Years of Crisis-Management', in Theresa Rakowska-Harmstone (ed.), *Perspectives for Change in Communist Societies* (Boulder, CO, 1979), pp. 150–1.

4. Cited in Jaromír Navrátil (ed.), *The Prague Spring 1968. A National Security Archive Documents Reader* (Budapest, 1998), p. 307 (interview from August 1990).

5. Philip Windsor and Adam Roberts, *Czechoslovakia 1968. Reform, Repression and Resistance* (London, 1969), p. 3.

6. Brezhnev, as cited in *Documents on British Foreign Policy*, Series III, vol. 1 (London, 1992), pp. 100–10 (Sir D. Wilson to Mr M. Stewart, 9 December 1968).

7. György Litván (ed.), *The Hungarian Revolution of 1956. Reform, Revolt and Repression 1953–1963* (London, 1996), pp. 87–90.

8. *U.S. Foreign Policy for the 1970s. A New Strategy for Peace. A Report to Congress by Richard Nixon, 18 February 1970* (Washington, DC, 1970).

9. Cited in Walter Laqueur, *A Continent Astray. Europe, 1970–1978* (Oxford, 1979), pp. 180–4.

10. Ibid.

11. Ibid.

12. *Conference on Security and Cooperation in Europe. Final Act* (London, 1975), pp. 1–5.

13. Cited in H. Gordon Skilling, Samizdat *and an Independent Society in Central and Eastern Europe* (London, 1989), pp. 143–4.

14. Thomas Cynkin, *Soviet and American Signalling in the Polish Crisis* (London, 1988), p. 42.

15. Zbigniew Brzezinski, *Power and Principle. Memoirs of the National Security Adviser, 1977–1981* (London, 1983), p. 464.

16. Arthur Rachwald, *In Search of Poland. The Superpowers' Response to Solidarity, 1980–1989* (Stanford, CA, 1990), p. xii.

17. Ibid.

18. Francis J. Meehan, 'Reflections on the Polish Crisis', *Cold War International History Project Bulletin*, no. 11 (1998), pp. 43–7.

19. Ibid.

20. Zbigniew Brzezinski, 'White House Diary, 1980', *Orbis* (Winter 1988), p. 34.

21. Ibid., pp. 32–3.

22. A. Kemp-Welch, 'Change in Eastern Europe: The Polish Paradigm', in D.W. Spring (ed.), *The Impact of Gorbachev: The First Phase, 1985–90* (London, 1991), pp. 150–1.

23. Thomas Hobbes, *Leviathan*, chapter XIII, 'Of the Natural Condition of Mankind, as concerning their Felicity, and Misery' (Cambridge, 1991), pp. 88–9.

Index